The
Pioneer Picnics

Santa Maria Valley Pioneer Association

The Story of the
PIONEER
PICNICS

held annually by the
Santa Maria Valley Pioneer Association

Pioneer Park

BY R.H. TESENE, JIM MAY
AND PAULINE LOWNES NOVO

THE STORY *of the* PIONEER PICNICS

ISBN 0-933380-20-8

Copyright © 2002 by R.H. Tesene
Santa Maria, California
Printed in the United States of America

Written and prepared by

R.H. TESENE, author of the books *Santa Maria Style Barbecue* and *The Beacon Story;*

JIM MAY, author of the book *Fifty Fabulous Years, 1945-1995;*

and **PAULINE LOWNES NOVO,** historian for the Santa Maria Valley Pioneer Association, who wrote or collected the family histories of many of the local Pioneer families.

ACKNOWLEDGEMENTS

Edited, designed and typeset by Richard Cole, Graphics LTD, Santa Maria, California

Many thanks to all who contributed stories, photographs, and other material for this history. Special acknowledgement is made to the Santa Maria Public Library, the *Santa Maria Times,* the *Santa Maria Free Advertiser,* the Santa Maria Valley Historical Society Museum, Pauline Lownes Novo, Vicki Anderson Wilson, D.L. Cole, Carolyn Conrad McCall, Clarence Donati, and Jim May.

THE OLIVE PRESS PUBLICATIONS
P.O. Box 99 • Los Olivos, CA 93441
(805) 688-2445

THE SANTA MARIA VALLEY PIONEER ASSOCIATION

Membership in the Pioneer Association (1) requires a residency in the Santa Maria Valley and surrounding areas prior to and through 1940. All descendants of such a person are eligible for membership. Anyone who marries a Pioneer is automatically a member. (2) Once the children marry and leave home, they must apply for their own membership to be included on the mailing list of the Pioneer Association. (3) An individual qualifies for an Associate membership if he or she has lived in the valley or surrounding areas for 30 years. Lifetime membership fee: $10.00 per family. Associate membership fee: $20.00 per family.

THIS BOOK IS DEDICATED

to all the Santa Maria Valley Pioneers, who had a part in the planning and putting on of the first Pioneer Picnic held in an area along the Cuyama Road 11 miles east of Santa Maria in San Luis Obispo County in 1925, and in their own Pioneer Park, 13 miles east of Santa Maria in Santa Barbara County in 1926, and for the thousands of Pioneers who have planned for, served as officers or board members, and attended and supported the annual Santa Maria Valley Pioneer Picnics for the past 77 years, and for all the Pioneer volunteers who spent many hours and days building their own Pioneer Park on West Foster Road, in Santa Maria, California, for its grand opening on July 13, 1996.

To all the members and associate members of the Santa Maria Valley Pioneer Association and their relatives and friends

We hope you enjoy reading this book as much as we enjoyed writing it and putting it together. We regret any omissions, errors, or misspellings—this book was a real challenge!

R.H. TESENE, *age 90, author,* also wrote *Santa Maria Style Barbecue* in 1997 and *The Beacon Story* in 2000. Tesene has also produced videos on Santa Maria Style Barbecue and Santa Maria Tri-Tip Barbecue, as well as a historical "Color Me" layout, showing the changes in Santa Maria from 1800 to 2000, and various postcards.

R.H. TESENE, AUTHOR

JIM MAY, *researcher,* checked every source of information available about Pioneer Picnics, events, and presidents—not an easy job. This book could not have been written without his continuing efforts. May is the author of the book *Fifty Fabulous Years, 1945–1995,* and was a key figure in the efforts to negotiate the 25-year lease on Pioneer Park between the Santa Maria Airport Board and the City of Santa Maria.

JIM MAY, RESEARCHER

PAULINE NOVO, *"Mrs. Pioneer Park,"* pushed for a Pioneer Park in Santa Maria for many years. She is also the ***historian*** of the Pioneer Association and has compiled many large scrapbooks of photos and clippings which provided material for this book. She also collected many of the Pioneer family histories that appear in this book.

PAULINE NOVO, HISTORIAN

RICHARD COLE, *designer,* has also worked on R.H. Tesene's books *Santa Maria Style Barbecue* and *The Beacon Story,* as well as *The Real Stuff* by Ed Horkey and *The Good Years* by Shirley Contreras.

RICHARD COLE, DESIGNER

A Decision Was Made

by R.H. Tesene

Many times I thought about the Pioneers of the Santa Maria Valley, who for over 75 years had enjoyed their annual Pioneer Picnics—yet, as far as I know, no one had ever written a book covering these annual Pioneer Picnics that started in 1925.

I contacted several active Pioneers and volunteered to help write a book. Their reply was that they did not know how to *start* writing a book, to say nothing about actually writing it. That was the way I felt, too before writing my first book, *Santa Maria Style Barbecue.*

I decided to write the book myself. So I jotted down a possible title and wrote *Part 1, Page 1* on a blank sheet of paper. Looking at that, I had the feeling that I was off to a great start—something like taking the first step when going for a walk.

Since I had no way to contact the early Pioneers, I had to seek the information elsewhere—namely, write-ups in the *Santa Maria Times,* found at the Santa Maria Public Library, where they have all the old editions of the newspaper stored on rolls of microfilm.

Jim May, son of an old Pioneer family, graciously volunteered to have printouts made of the articles on each Pioneer Picnic. He found it easy to find the right roll of microfilm, once he knew the exact date of the picnic, but getting a printout of it turned out to be quite frustrating. You have to center the article you want on the machine and press the right buttons to enlarge or reduce it, and perhaps make other adjustments as well. Sometimes the story is continued to another page. The *Times* usually ran a story announcing the Pioneer Picnic a day or two beforehand, announcing who would probably be elected president for the following year; then, another article would appear a day or two after the picnic where the current president presided. Sometimes the reporter would cover the program and picnic in detail; other reports gave very few details. We are very grateful to the *Santa Maria Times* and the Santa Maria Public Library for having these articles available for us volunteers to reproduce.

Some of the stories were also available in the *Santa Maria Free Advertiser* in the Santa Maria Historical Society Museum.

I have written about each Pioneer Picnic that has been held since the first one in 1925. For a long time the picnics were held on or near May 1st, but the dates varied when the location was changed, first to Waller Park, then to the Union Oil Picnic Grounds, and finally to their own new Pioneer Park in Santa Maria on West Foster Road.

Many years ago people did not have fancy cameras like they have today, and they did not take many pictures. In fact, many could not afford to buy a camera. This gave me a problem, since I always like to have many pictures scattered throughout the entire book as I tell a story. I was able to secure pictures of the majority of the presidents who served each year, and these have been included in the write-ups. I like stories about comical things that happen at the picnics, but these were not available either.

During the last few years, when the Pioneer Picnic was held at Union Oil Picnic Grounds and Pioneer Park, many pictures were taken and placed in large scrapbooks for everyone to enjoy. Many of these pictures will appear in this book.

I also decided to include a few pages excerpted from my book *Santa Maria Style Barbecue,* which was published in 1995. These included many pictures and write-ups showing many volunteer Pioneers building the barbecue pit, the restrooms, picnic tables, and other facilities necessary to have the first Pioneer Picnic at their own Pioneer Park in Santa Maria, California, on July 13th, 1996.

I also decided to include the history of many Pioneer families that had been collected over a period of time by Pauline Lownes Novo, the Pioneer Association historian. The histories of other Pioneer families have been added as well.

I hope you enjoy this book as much as Jim May, Pauline Novo and I enjoyed writing it.

Table of Contents

The Story of How a Rancher's Barbecue in 1923 Eventually Turned Into the First "Santa Maria Valley Pioneer Picnic"

BY ELIZABETH OAKLEY MAY

In the spring of 1923, two brothers, W.C. "Will" Oakley and J.A. "Ace" Oakley, and their nephew B.W. "Ben" Stowell, all ranchers, killed a beef and invited their friends to a barbecue to celebrate the completion of a bridge over Huasna Creek on the road to Cuyama. The picnic was held along the Alamo Creek just above the Porter Ranch on the newly completed Cuyama Road, which they had leased that year. Most of the guests were pioneer friends and their families who enjoyed the affair so much that an idea for a repeat was voiced.

On July 23 of that same year, a dinner meeting was held at Hotel Bradley, at which time the "Old Timers of Santa Maria Valley" was organized. The following people were present at this organizational dinner. Also shown is the year when each of them came to the valley.

W.H. Tunnell	1868
W.C. Oakley	1869
W.C. Adam	1869
C.W. Smith	1871
W.H. Rice	1873
W.J. Brown	1873
S.T. Coiner	1873
Harry Saulsbury	1877
W.L. Smith	1876
S.J. Jones	1871
F.C. Twitchell	1878
Judge Crow	1878
Dr. W.T. Lucas	1879
James Letora	1880
A.L. Ames	1883

Dr. W.T. Lucas was temporary chairman and C.W. Smith temporary secretary. Regular officers were elected that night, with F.C. Twitchell as president and Harry Saulsbury as secretary.

The "Old Timers" included all who had come to the valley up to and including 1890. The "valley" was defined as including the Garey, Sisquoc, Orcutt, Casmalia, Guadalupe, Nipomo and Santa Maria areas. Later, a 30-year qualification was made for Associated Members.

W.H. Rice suggested May first for the date and W.C. Oakley suggested a basket picnic. It was to be held on the Alamo Creek just beyond the bridge, on the road to Cuyama.

In 1924 committees were appointed, and $8.00 was collected to pay for sending out cards and like expenses. The name of the organization was changed to "Santa Maria Valley Pioneer Association."

However, due to the hoof-and-mouth disease that spring, and on request of the then Mayor E.D. Rubel, these conscientious ranchers called off the picnic for 1924. The officers continued until the first Pioneer Picnic on May 1, 1925.

While listening to arguments at a preliminary organizational meeting of the Pioneer Association in 1924, Justice L.J. Morris idly drew two coins from his pocket, a dollar and a half dollar, and threw them on the table, where they formed an overlapping circle. From this he fashioned a design which was accepted as the official emblem of the Pioneer Association at their first meeting on the Alamo in 1925.

Fashioned in bronze, the emblem contained the wording, "Pioneer, Santa Maria prior to 1890." The decorative touches were provided by a picture of a log cabin and a farmer with a plow.

Five hundred of the emblems were ordered. The men's emblem was designed for the coat lapel, and the women's to pin on her dress. As far as is known, no other emblems were ever ordered.

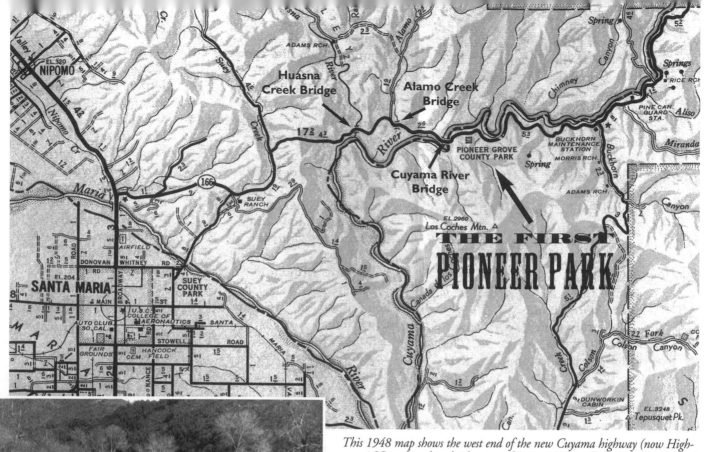

THE FIRST PIONEER PARK

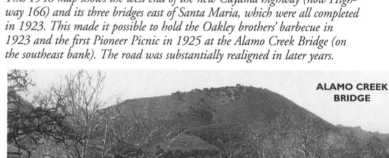

This 1948 map shows the west end of the new Cuyama highway (now Highway 166) and its three bridges east of Santa Maria, which were all completed in 1923. This made it possible to hold the Oakley brothers' barbecue in 1923 and the first Pioneer Picnic in 1925 at the Alamo Creek Bridge (on the southeast bank). The road was substantially realigned in later years.

ALAMO CREEK BRIDGE

The Huasna Creek bridge (above, looking east) as seen en route to the Pioneer Picnic site. Since Twitchell Dam and Reservoir were completed, this bridge is underwater whenever the reservoir is partly filled. A realigned Highway 166 and its bridges are routed above the reservoir level. The Alamo Creek bridge (right, looking west) today is covered by water only when Twitchell Reservoir is nearly full, a rare event. The 1925 picnic was on the riverbank at left in this photo.

HUASNA CREEK BRIDGE

CUYAMA RIVER BRIDGE

The Cuyama River bridge (left, looking west) enabled the traveler to cross the river south from San Luis Obispo County to Santa Barbara County and on to Pioneer Park. This bridge is no longer a part of Highway 166, but is entirely on private Suey Ranch property. Bridge photos courtesy of CalTrans.

THE FIRST
PIONEER PARK

PICNIC AREA

The approach to Pioneer Park from the west finds it just around the bend from the Cuyama River bridge. This photo, taken around 1926, shows Pioneer Park virtually hidden under a thick canopy of ancient oaks. The arrow points to the area where cars parked, the picnic barbecue was prepared and eaten, and the outdoor dance pavilion was located. Traffic was practically non-existent back in those days; it took many more years before the Cuyama highway reached the Cuyama Valley, and even more years before it was extended to Maricopa and the Central Valley. The Cuyama River, usually a small, slow-moving creek, is hidden at the left, on the north side of the highway. It was a great place for kids to wade and catch frogs, polliwogs and minnows. This County Pioneer Park was abandoned during World War II.

The History of the
Annual Santa Maria Valley Pioneer Picnics

1925

On Friday, May 1, 1925, practically all business houses in Santa Maria, California, closed all day in order to give their employees an opportunity to attend the first Pioneer Picnic, eleven miles east of Santa Maria on the Alamo Creek at the second bridge on the road to Cuyama. The Santa Maria Valley Pioneer Association included all who lived in the Santa Maria Valley or vicinity in 1890 or earlier. Relatives of the pioneers were also invited to attend. Each family brought their picnic lunch, and free coffee was available. Fremont (F.C.) Twitchell, president of the Santa Maria Valley Pioneer Association, started the program at 10:30 a.m. Brief talks were given by prominent pioneers; Chester and Ruby Cox and Arthur Haslam performed songs, and Susan Lincoln reviewed information on Pioneer Days. At the business meeting, it was decided to make the May 1st Pioneer Picnic an annual affair, with a barbecue to be served each year. The picnic lunch was at 12 o'clock, followed by games and good old socializing.

FREMONT TWITCHELL
President, 1925

In the evening, a dance was held at the Princess Hall, where old-time music was played from 8:00

1925

May 1, 1925: Santa Maria Valley residents commemorate the first Pioneer Picnic by posing for their photograph. Pioneer Association officers are seated at left.

p.m. to 9:30 p.m. A six-piece orchestra furnished modern music for the remainder of the evening.

1926

Most business firms in Santa Maria closed on Saturday, May 1, 1926, for the second Pioneer Day Picnic. Approximately 1000 persons attended. A lease was arranged with the Newhall Land and Farm Company for use of a plot of land for the Pioneer Picnics and a platform for dancing. The dedication of the new County Pioneer Park on the Cuyama Highway, about a quarter of a mile east of the third Cuyama River bridge, was by C.L. (Leo) Preisker, Chairman of the Santa Barbara County Board of Supervisors. Speakers included W.H. Rice, president of the Santa Maria Valley Pioneer Association, and other prominent valley citi-

WM. HICKMAN RICE
President, 1926

C.L. (LEO) PREISKER
Dedication Speaker

zens. The program started promptly at 10:00 a.m., and T.R. Finley made the main speech of the day. Those attending brought their basket lunch, cups, knives, forks, spoons, and a pitcher for coffee. A barbecue was served at 12:30 p.m., including beef, chili sauce, coffee and milk. A long permanent pit had been built of bricks for the barbecuing fire. The pit was covered with grates which were not adjustable up and down over the hot oak coals, so the heat had to be controlled by sprinkling water on the hot coals. Other equipment for cooking meat had been installed at the park for the year-round use of the general public. Judge L.J. Morris was in charge of the Boy Scouts who were in charge of the parking of automobiles. A public dance was held at 8:00 p.m. in the Princess Hall. The old-timers and the Campbell's orchestra furnished the music at the park for the old-

SANTA MARIA VAL
1890

time dancing that was about the only type of dance that could be done, as the weather did things to the floor of the dance platform that were not conducive to modern ballroom steps. The old-timers orchestra included T.B. Rice, Fred Fowlers, and Mr. and Mrs. Horace Campbell. G.M. Root played old-time fiddle tunes, assisted by Louis Sibilio. The general public were invited to join the Pioneers for the 1927 picnic.

1927

Most of the businesses in Santa Maria closed on Monday, May 2, 1927, in honor of the third Pioneer Picnic at Pioneer Park. Hundreds of pioneer residents of the Santa Maria Valley and others attended the Pioneer Picnic. W.C. Oakley, the president of the Pioneer

WILLIAM C. OAKLEY
President, 1927

Association, delivered the welcome address at 10:00 a.m. A barbecue to supplement the picnic basket was served at noon. A business meeting was held at 2:00 p.m., followed by dancing in the afternoon and that evening in Princess Hall. Bob Bryson's orchestra furnished the music.

1928

Most businesses closed in Santa Maria in honor of the fourth Pioneer Picnic held at Pioneer Park on May 2, 1928. More than 400 attended a program at 10:00 a.m. W.H. Tunnell, president of the Santa Maria Valley Pioneer Association, presided. Speakers included W.H. Rice, who spoke about the Pioneer Days, and Fred Schauer of Santa Barbara, originally

WILLIAM H. TUNNELL
President, 1928

LLEY PIONEER'S PICNIC
90 — 1925

STONEHART STUDIO

of Santa Maria, who briefly reviewed the history of the valley from 1867 to 1928. A beef barbecue and picnic lunch was enjoyed, followed by election of officers and dancing and games, which took up the daylight hours. A grand ball at Princess Hall climaxed the festivities for the day. Justice of the Peace L.J. Morris was elected the new president of the Pioneer Association.

1929

Most businesses in Santa Maria closed on Wednesday, May 1, 1929, in honor of the fifth Pioneer Picnic at Pioneer Park. Over 1,000 members, families and friends attended. Judge L.J. Morris, president of the Pioneer Association, presided. Speaking, barbecue, picnic lunch-

JUDGE LOUIS J. MORRIS
President, 1929

es, dancing, and games were the features of the day, with dancing in the evening at Princess Hall. Radio station KSMR (Santa Maria Railroad) had been announcing the picnic all over the state. Members brought their picnic baskets and were furnished barbecued meat, coffee and cream. There was a charge for each head of the family to help defray the expense. An article in commemoration of Pioneer Mothers was read by George Washington (G.W.) Battles.

1930

Merchants in Santa Maria again declared a holiday on May 1, 1930, in honor of the sixth annual Pioneer Day, held at Pioneer Park, which is thirteen miles upstream in an oak grove on the south side of the road, across from the Cuyama

JUDGE SAMUEL E. CROW
President, 1930

River. Judge S.E. Crow, president of the Santa Maria Valley Pioneer Association, presided. More than 1,000 pioneers and their friends enjoyed the program, which commenced at 10:00 a.m. It included community singing, instrumental music, and addresses by several pioneers at this largest get-together. Attorney T.A. "Cap" Twitchell spoke on "The Spirit of the Pioneers." At noon, a barbecue with cream and coffee was provided by the Pioneer Association to supplement the other goodies each family had in their picnic basket. Games for youngsters and adults with "get together" conversation with old friends were enjoyed in the afternoon. The celebration continued in Santa Maria at 8 o'clock in the high school gymnasium, where the Pioneer Ball was held to enjoy old-fashioned music and dance.

HARRY R. SAULSBURY
President, 1932

to hold their eighth annual reunion in Pioneer Park. Harry R. Saulsbury, president of the Pioneer Association, presided. The day's activities started at 11 o'clock. At noon a barbecue was served, with the Pioneer Association furnishing the meat, coffee and cream. Dancing commenced at 2 o'clock in the open-air park pavilion under a high oak canopy until 4:00 p.m. It was resumed at the high school gymnasium at 8:30 o'clock. On Saturday night, all the alumni of Santa Maria Union High School in the classes up to 1906 gathered in the Santa Maria Inn for dinner. All merchants, public offices, banks, and schools were closed on Monday in commemoration of Pioneers Day.

1931

On Monday, May 1, 1931, a crowd of 500 pioneers and their families assembled for the seventh Pioneer Picnic at Pioneer Park, in spite of the inclement weather. Major P. Baker, president of the Pioneer Association, presided. The program started at 10 o'clock, followed by barbecue and picnic basket lunch at noon. Games and dancing were part of the entertainment, while many renewed old friendships with those who came from all parts of the state for the annual get-together. There was old-time dancing at the high school gymnasium in the evening, providing a festive climax for the day.

MAJOR P. BAKER
President, 1931

1932

With picnic baskets brimming and fair weather guaranteed by the governmental forecasters, pioneers of the Santa Maria Valley awaited the arrival of Monday morning on May 2, 1932,

1933

Pioneers of the Santa Maria Valley and vicinity and their friends and guests held the ninth annual Pioneer Picnic at Pioneer Park on Monday, May 1, 1933.

About 1,000 attended and enjoyed the fun and frolic and the renewing of old acquaintances.

The invocation was delivered by Rev. A.L. Nagel at 10:00 a.m., and a few old songs were sung prior to President H.C. Tunnell's opening of the business session. He introduced W.H. Rice and W.C. Oakley, both past presidents, who gave talks. Other past presidents attending included Judge L.J. Morris, S.E. Crow, Major P. Baker, and Harry R. Saulsbury.

A huge barbecue was held at 12:00 noon, lasting until 1:30 p.m. James Morin, a graduate of a local school, gave the address of the day, entitled, "Pioneers, Old and New." Among the highlights of the day was the grand march at the park, led by Judge L.J. Morris and Mrs. S.B. Niverth.

Old-time dances were held at the high school gymnasium in the

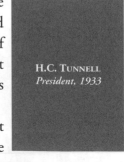

H.C. TUNNELL
President, 1933

evening, when Judge Morris again chose his daughter to lead the grand march.

1934

JOHN FESLER
President, 1934

Most stores in Santa Maria were closed on May 1, 1934, in honor of the tenth annual Pioneer Day at Pioneer Park, with John Fesler, president of the Pioneer Association, presiding. Attorney T.A. "Cap" Twitchell, himself a descendant of a Pioneer family, was the speaker of the day. The 11 o'clock program was followed at noon by a beef barbecue, furnished by the Pioneer Association to supplement each family's own basket lunches. About 650 attended. The price was $1.00 per couple and $0.25 for unescorted ladies. The annual Pioneer Picnic dance was held at the pavilion in the park from 2:00 to 4:30 o'clock following the program and picnic. A chorus of twenty voices, made up entirely of pioneers, was enjoyed by all. Also enjoyed was a quartet selected from the ranks of the pioneers. At 8 o'clock the annual Pioneer dance was held in the high school gymnasium. It took a good constitution to dance all afternoon and evening, but some of the older pioneers never missed a dance.

1935

ALYCE LEWIS
President, 1935

The eleventh annual Pioneer Picnic was held in Pioneer Park on May 1, 1935, with about 700 persons in attendance.

Alyce Lewis, president of the Pioneer Association, presided. Attorney Clarence Ward of Santa Barbara, a former Santa Maria resident, delivered the address of the day. Rev. Samuel Kennedy offered the invocation.

A former district attorney was the speaker of the day. The program also consisted of a violin solo, a colonial dance, a piano duet, a piano selection, another violin solo, and songs by various members and their families. Other entertainment included a Spanish dance to the music of "Adios, Amores."

Past presidents who were introduced included Judge S.E. Crow, Judge L.J. Morris, William Rice, W.C. Oakley, Harry Saulsbury, John Fesler, and M.P. Baker.

At the outdoor dance in the afternoon, nieces danced with their great-uncles, and grandsons danced with their grandmothers. Many wore costumes that had become family heirlooms.

About 700 pounds of young beef, specially selected by George Read, was barbecued and served by "Bud" Boyd, Joe Calderon, Lawrence Mendoza, Jack Roberts and Frank May.

A dance at night ended the program.

Among the many family reunions at the picnic tables was that of the Bradley family. The eight sisters who were together for the day were Mary Tunnell, Annie Long, Agnes Forbes, Sadie Kelley, Alyce Lewis and Rachel Niverth of Santa Maria Valley, as well as Mrs. Elliott of Los Angeles and Elizabeth Howerton of Santa Barbara.

1936

A.F. ("POP") BLACK
President, 1936

During the 12th annual celebration of the Santa Maria Valley Pioneer Association, Friday, May 1, 1936, the citizens of Santa Maria found local businesses closed, except the banks, and everyone headed to the Pioneer Picnic or for the nearest fishing hole.

May 1st marked the opening of the trout fishing season, as well as Pioneer Day, and from time immemorial this has been a day for fathers and sons. To make the day interesting, the State Fish and Game

Commission stocked the Santa Ynez River from Paradise to Gibraltar Dam with 20,000 catchable-sized trout that week—and did the fishermen go after them!

Banks could not close that day because May 1, 1936, was not a legal holiday regardless of the fact that it was as official as any holiday in the calendar for the citizens of Santa Maria.

A.F. ("Bert") ("Pop") Black, president of the association, presided. Frank L. Shuman, San Francisco attorney and son of J.L. Shuman, the pioneer homesteader in the Santa Maria Valley who sank the first water well in the present city, delivered the principal address. Other numbers included Spanish dances by twins Harry and Edward Goodchild with Marie and Charity Goodchild, a piano solo by Patty Boyd, and a vocal duet by Madge Horn and Mrs. C.W. Hatch, accompanied by Mrs. Ray Baker.

The program was followed by a barbecue.

The annual Pioneer ball was held in the evening in the high school gymnasium.

1937

About 800 attended the 13th annual Pioneer Association picnic at Pioneer Park on May 1, 1937. The Pioneers, relatives and guests started gathering at 9:30 a.m. Many who had moved away from Santa Maria "came home" for family reunions held in conjunction with the picnic.

Joe S. Calderon, president of the Association, presided. He introduced the past presidents in attendance, William H. Rice, Judge L.J. Morris, Judge S.E. Crow, Harry R. Saulsbury, John Fesler, Alyce Lewis, and A.F. Black.

Rev. R. Banes Anderson invoked the blessing of God at the opening of the program, and Joseph Tolick led the crowd in the singing of "America."

Judge Morris introduced the speaker of the day, Jack Glines, local attorney and member of two prominent Pioneer families, Glines and Holloway. Mr. Glines's father came to this valley when he was three years old.

JOE S. CALDERON
President, 1937

The Santa Maria High School double quartet, accompanied by Dorothy Crandall, delighted the audience with their numbers. Joseph Tolick sang three songs, and Mabel Soares and Arthur George danced a Mexican folk dance; Joseph Quijada, accompanied by Dorothy Schenck, pleased the audience with three early California songs. Emilio Sutti won long applause with three fine accordion solos, and Essie McMichael gave a reading of "Out Where the West Begins."

The entertainment concluded with dancing of the lancers by members of the Young Pioneer Club, who were taught the dances by Rachel Niverth. They were all dressed in costumes of the 1880's.

Frank May served as chairman of the barbecue committee and was assisted by a large number on his committee. Boy Scouts of the Kiwanis Troop 2, of which Otto Kramer is chairman, helped with traffic and parking, under the direction of Ray Ow.

The Simas Orchestra played for dancing at both the afternoon dance and the evening dance at the high school gymnasium. The evening dance drew the largest such crowd to date. Dances included square dancing, the varsouvienne, the schottische, the Paul Jones, the polka and the rye waltz, with a few modern dances for variety.

1938

On April 29, 1938, about 800 Santa Maria Valley Pioneers from all parts of California assembled in Pioneer Park for the fourteenth annual Pioneer Picnic. The program started at 10 o'clock with President Lou S. Drumm presiding. Carrie Boyd arranged for the program.

LOU S. DRUMM
President, 1938

The placing of the flag was by the Boy Scouts of Rotary Club Troop 1, of which Dr. Harley B. Towsley was Scoutmaster. Gerald Keyser, who led the salute, presided. Elton Triplett was the color bearer, with Bruce Alexander and Edwin Wallace serving as color guards.

The speaker of the day was Leon Libeu, a Santa Maria attorney and former County Fish and Game Warden. The attendant physician was Dr. Albert Missal. All out-of-town pioneers and their guests were invited. The barbecued beef and coffee were served at 12 o'clock. The Pioneers brought their own bread and other food.

During the afternoon there were Danish dances by Mr. and Mrs. Carl Jensen, Mr. and Mrs. Hans Carstensen, Mr. and Mrs. Pete Mortensen, Mr. and Mrs. Vilhelm Heideman, and Viggo Henricksen. The accompanist was Mrs. Bruce.

The old timers enjoyed dancing by the Junior Pioneers, songs, guitar and accordion selections, interpretive dancing, and music and singing by Bobby Garcin, a strolling troubadour.

In the evening, the annual dance was held at the high school gymnasium from 8 o'clock until 12 o'clock midnight. Johnny Simas' orchestra played for both the dancing in the afternoon at the park as well as in the evening at the high school gymnasium.

1939

The fifteenth annual Santa Maria Valley Pioneer Association picnic was held in Pioneer Park on May 6, 1939. About 700 Pioneers and their relatives and friends attended.

Frank May, president of the Association, presided.

The principal speaker of the

FRANK C. MAY
President, 1939

day, Leon J. Libeu, was introduced by Judge L.J. Morris. Libeu declared that the Pioneers who settled this valley remained to build it and that they still remain today to continue the building. The morning program included local numbers by Bradley Burns, violin solos by Wesley Foxen, accordion numbers by De Ette Baxter, and a series of songs and dances arranged by Ida Davis Hall and Glendon Lawson.

Joe Calderon presided over the barbecue pits, and Dave Boyd's corps of waiters served a delicious barbecue steak dinner at noon.

At 2:00 p.m., heads of the Pioneer Association led a grand march to the park dancing platform, where the afternoon was spent in old-time dancing. In the evening, 200 pioneers attended the annual Pioneer Dance, held in the Veterans' Memorial Hall.

1940

JACK H. GLINES
President, 1940

Pioneers and their families flocked to the Pioneer picnic grounds on Cuyama Road early on the morning of May 4, 1940, for the sixteenth annual picnic. The previous night, the barbecue and other committees were busy getting things in readiness so that the sizzling barbecued steaks would be ready by 12 o'clock. President Jack Glines presided at the mid-morning program, which opened with the singing of "America," led by Robert Garioto, who also sang a group of solos and led community singing at another point in the program. President Glines introduced all the past presidents in attendance.

Other music was by a male quartet made up of Bradley Burns, Glendon Lawson, Gordon Gillian and William Tyler, accompanied by Mrs. Bradley Burns on the piano. Teresa Burns was program chairman.

Judge C. Douglas Smith was the speaker of the day. In the afternoon there was a program of music and dancing. The annual ball was held at the Veterans Memorial Building beginning at 8 o'clock. The public was admitted to the dance, which featured both old-time and modern music.

1941

Pioneer families began their annual trek to Pioneer Park early on the morning of May 3, 1941, for the seventeenth annual picnic which had become a May tradition in Santa Maria.

At 10 o'clock, President Manuel Bello called the meeting to order. The program began with the singing of "America." Bill Elliott played a violin solo, Julia Smith sang, Billie Jean Garlick played an accordion solo, and C.W. Hatch sang a solo before leading group singing. President

Manuel Bello
President, 1941

Bello introduced all the past presidents who were present, and Gaylord Jones introduced Ed Coblentz from San Francisco, the publisher of the *Call & Bulletin*. Coblentz, a member of one of Santa Maria's oldest pioneer families, was the principal speaker for the day, although he had never attended a Santa Maria Pioneer Picnic before.

A barbecue was served at noon beneath the shade of the ancient oaks. Families gathered in customary groups. During the afternoon there was old-time dancing on a platform in the park.

The annual Pioneer dance was held in the evening in the Veterans Memorial Hall. Campbell's orchestra played both modern and old-time music.

1942

Apparently because of America's involvement in World War II and gasoline and tire rationing, the thinning ranks of the Santa Maria Pioneers held their eighteenth annual Pioneer Day picnic in May of 1942 nearer home in Waller Park. Only about 250 attended, instead of the hundreds who had gathered at Pioneer Park on the Cuyama Road in former years. Very few came from other regions. Younger men were being encouraged to become officers of the Association.

Gaylord Jones, president of the Pioneer Association, presided. He introduced Harry Nuss, speaker of the day, who was a member of the Pioneer set owing to having mar-

Gaylord Jones
President, 1942

ried a daughter of the W.H. Rices, one of the valley's best known pioneer families who came to Santa Maria in the 1860's. Members of the Rice family were absent from the 1942 picnic because of the serious illness of 85-year-old W.H. Rice.

After the election of officers and a program, there was a basket lunch at noon. Because of wartime meat rationing, the usual barbecue was not held. The afternoon was spent visiting and resting up for the dance at night, while the children played games. The annual dance was held in the evening at the high school gymnasium. Both old-time and modern music were played.

1943

The Santa Maria Valley Pioneer Association held their second war-time reunion on May 1, 1943, in Waller Grove. It was also the 19th annual meeting of the group. The president, Dr. Leland Smith, presided at the annual business meeting and program, at which, for the

Dr. W. Leland Smith
President, 1943

first time since its organization in 1924, the Association heard a woman as principal speaker: Mrs. Edna Laurel Calhan of San Francisco, youngest daughter of Charles Haskell Clark and Eliza Clayton Clark, pioneers of Point Sal.

Quoting from the annals of her family, Mrs. Calhan said her parents came to Point Sal in 1868 after Mrs. Clark's father had given her the ranch there as a birthday gift. They settled on the bleak, undeveloped, unfenced land, built a home and a business, and reared eight children.

Point Sal, Mrs. Calhan recalled, was the only outlet for the Santa Maria Valley for many years. Mule and ox teams hauled grain there for shipment by sea, and lumber was brought in for the return haul to the valley. After the building of a wharf, a thriving village grew up. The wharf was destroyed in a storm, and in the ensuing years even the ground where many of the houses stood has been washed into the sea.

The program opened with the pledge of allegiance to the flag. Rev. Banes Anderson delivered the prayer, after which Mrs. Ray Baker presented a program of songs by children of the Pioneers. There was a roll call of past presidents.

The annual old-time dance started at 8:30 p.m. at the high school gymnasium. The Grand March started at ten o'clock. Music was by William Elliott and a group of Pioneers.

1944

The Pioneers of Santa Maria Valley held their 20th annual Pioneer Picnic at Waller Park on May 6, 1944. President Leonald Adam presided.

LEONALD ADAM
President, 1944

The program opened with the pledge to the flag and "The Star-Spangled Banner." Rev. Roy O. Youtz gave the invocation.

President Adam introduced County Supervisor T.A. ("Cap") Twitchell, a native and graduate of the local high school, as the speaker of the day. Cap noted the hard life and sacrifices that the early pioneers endured in order to develop their dream community. He stressed the importance of water for the farming industry of our valley. He warned that we must be vigilant to "preserve at all costs the democratic form of government, the freedom and liberty and the system of private enterprise" that we enjoy.

Maria Baker presented songs, dances, and instrumental numbers, after which the group adjourned for a basket picnic.

1945

The Santa Maria Valley Pioneer Association held its 21st annual picnic reunion in the bowl at Waller Grove on Saturday, May 3, 1945. Walter W. Stokes, president of the Association, presided. The program opened with the pledge of allegiance, the singing of the national anthem, and the invocation by Rev. A.C. Bussingham. President Stokes introduced the past presidents who were in attendance.

WALTER W. STOKES
President, 1945

Vice President Audel Davis introduced Judge Marion Smith, son of pioneer C.W. Smith, as the speaker of the day. His mother, Myrtle Hudson Smith, was born in Guadalupe. His subject was "The Pioneer Spirit." In defining the spirit of the pioneers, Judge Smith said it was that spirit possessed by all pioneers, which gave them strength, endurance and the ability to succeed.

The meeting was then turned over to Mrs. M.F. Turnage, who presented her program of songs, dances, and readings. C.W. Hatch sang several vocal numbers, accompanied on the piano by Mrs. Hatch. He also gave a blackface skit. Clara Stearns gave a reading of "Out Where the West Begins," followed by a tap routine by Norma Ann Johnson and a tap duet in company with little Susan Coy Gregory, granddaughter of Essie Turnage. Mrs. R.E. Hawkins read a history of the valley compiled from excerpts of the *Santa Maria Times* of fifty years ago.

The meeting closed with the singing of "God Bless America." The Pioneers then seated themselves for the basket lunch picnic.

In the evening, a traditional Pioneer dance was held at the high school gymnasium to the music of William F. "Bill" Elliott, Mrs. Hatch and their old-time orchestra. The grand march at ten o'clock was led by Mr. and Mrs. Audel Davis, Walter W. Stokes and daughter and other past presidents. There were square dances, a Paul Jones, and others.

1946

Pioneers gathered at Waller Park on Saturday, May 4, 1946, for the 22nd annual Pioneer Picnic. Audel "Bub" Davis, president of the Pioneer Association, presided.

Audel Davis
President, 1946

Morris Stephan, a prominent local attorney who recently returned from several years of Naval duty, was the speaker of the day. He pointed out that pioneering is not limited to a period of the past, and that it is in the quality in the person of the pioneer which is more important than the time in which he lives. "Pioneer, as defined in the dictionary," he said, "means one who prepares the way for others. Seventy years from now, those living will look back on those of the present day as pioneers, and will expect the way to have been prepared somewhat for them."

After the program, the pioneers attending dispersed into groups for a barbecue luncheon and visiting from group to group, for reminiscing of times gone by.

In the evening, the Pioneers kicked up their heels and swung their partners at the dance as usual in the Santa Maria High School gymnasium.

1947

Raymond Strong
President, 1947

Waller Grove was the scene of merriment on Saturday, May 8, 1947, as members of the Santa Maria Valley Pioneer Association and their families gathered there to celebrate the twenty-third annual Pioneer Day picnic.

President Raymond Strong called the meeting to order at 11 o'clock. This was followed by singing led by Helen Hatch and accompanied by her mother, Mrs. C. Wesley Hatch, playing the piano. Katie Peterson Fickert introduced the past presidents in attendance as well as the program chairmen, and welcomed new members of the Santa Maria Valley Pioneer Association. The program included "Marimba," by Charmian Turner. The second act of the program featured Freddie Sherrill in a tap dance,

accompanied by Mrs. Hatch on the piano. The third act was three Spanish dances by Mary Lou Rivas; the fourth number was a reading by Edna Callion, and the fifth was a piano selection by Johnny Bowles, followed by a dance given by Barbara Sumner and her escort team of the Native Daughters of the Golden West.

Ralph Dyer, a former Santa Marian now living in Los Angeles, was the main speaker. Born in Iowa, he lived on a farm until 1906, when his family moved to Santa Maria, where he went to Santa Maria Union High School. He was the guest of honor at the dinner given at the Ranch House dining room by his class of 1907.

A barbecue for the pioneers was held at noon, with the meat, coffee and cream furnished to complement the other food that the picnickers had brought along in their own picnic baskets. Many of the ninety-three pioneers, relatives, and friends who attended the 40th reunion of the class of 1907 at the Santa Maria Club on Friday attended the barbecue and other ceremonies at the Pioneer Picnic and dance. The annual dance was held in the evening at the high school gymnasium.

1948

Clear skies after unsettled weather made it possible to hold the 24th annual Pioneer Picnic in Waller Park, as planned, and many of the early families were represented at the gathering. **Ida Hawkins,** president of the Pioneer Association, presided. Catherine Fickert was the program chairperson.

At nine o'clock in the evening, the annual old-time dance was held at the Santa Maria High School gymnasium, where the dancers stepped off to measures of the quadrilles and varsouvienne as well as the more modern dances.

1949

Santa Maria Valley paused to honor its founders at the 25th annual Pioneer Day picnic celebration in Waller Park. Valley pioneer families from all parts of the state and nation attended.

Ernest Righetti, president of the association,

presided at the 11:00 a.m. meeting. The meeting was opened with a salute to the flag, after which Miss Beverley Strong, great-great-granddaughter of the late pioneer Charles H. Clark, who settled at Point Sal, conducted the musical program. Included was a girls' chorus composed of

ERNEST RIGHETTI
President, 1949

Verona and Jo Ann Adams, Patsey and Peggy Maughan, Jeanette Johnson, and Carol Novo. Verona Adams accompanied on the piano. Dick Atnip played a trumpet solo.

Committee members in charge of the celebration included Mrs. Elmer Elliott, W.H. Rice, Gertrude France, Gaylord Jones and W.H. "Bill" Saladin.

Frank Shuman, San Francisco attorney and member of one of the Valley's earliest families, was the principal speaker. He spoke about "Old Times and Old Timers."

The program was followed by the traditional barbecue dinner at 12:30 p.m., enjoyed by the over 250 attending. The meat was barbecued by Paul Fox, C.L. "Larry" Kyle, L.T. "Lou" Thompson, Sr., Charles "Charlie" Buck and Gene Brown. During the barbecuing, the heat from the fire caused the expansion of a pipe, which blew out a clog of dirt and rust into the face of Philip Smith, son of Dr. and Mrs. Leland Smith, but without serious injury to the lad.

The Pioneer dance was held in the evening at the high school gymnasium. The Pioneers and guests got all of the kinks out of their muscles after the all-day picnic. Dancing included hoedowns, square dances, schottisches, and waltzes.

1950

The Pioneer Association annual Pioneer Picnic was held in the Waller Park bowl on Saturday, May 6, 1950. **President Catherine Fickert** presided over the program and welcomed everyone at 11:00 a.m. "The Star-Spangled Banner," led by

Rosalee Cutler, was sung by the audience with Alfa Mason accompanying. The pledge of allegiance to the flag followed.

The Rev. Oscar F. Newby of First Methodist Church offered the invocation, followed by the introduction of past presidents.

Program numbers included selections of old-time music by Tommy Rice, pioneer dance fiddler, and Ramona Jenkins, balladist and guitarist; accordion numbers by Audrey Moore and Danny Johnson; "sister" tap dances by Phyllis, Thelma, and Carla Jean Kauffman; a vocal number by Mrs. Cutler with Alfa Mason accompanying; and violin and guitar old-time tunes by Mrs. Jenkins and Rice.

A beef barbecue was served at 12:30 p.m. Picnickers furnished their own side dishes, utensils, etc.

Dancing in the high school gymnasium began at 9 o'clock, with the Grand March at 10 p.m. Music was played by Matt Rojas and his orchestra, with quadrilles, lancers, and other square dances called by Joe S. Calderon.

1951

The Santa Maria Valley Pioneer Association held their 26th annual picnic on May 5, 1951, in the bowl at Waller Park. Marion B. Rice, Association president, presided at the program. It opened at 11 o'clock with the invocation by the Rev. Roy O. Youtz of the First

MARION B. RICE
President, 1951

Christian Church. Principal speaker of the day was former president Walter W. Stokes.

After the singing of "The Star-Spangled Banner," followed by a roll call of past presidents, Charlotte Radke, program chairman, arranged for a group of musical numbers. The eighth grade girls' chorus from El Camino Junior High School sang, followed by community singing led by Flora Wilman and accompanied by Mildred Andrews. Tommy Rice, old-time fiddler, offered some violin selections and Ramona Jenkins played her guitar. At 12 o'clock the crowd enjoyed a basket lunch.

The Pioneer Dance was held at 8:30 in the high school gym. Roy Stanley and his orchestra furnished the music. Old-time numbers predominated.

1952

FRED L. MAY
President, 1952

Pioneers came from far and near for the 28th annual Pioneer Day Picnic at Waller Park among the lovely trees. Fred L. May, president of the Santa Maria Valley Pioneer Association, presided.

It didn't take the children long to get acquainted and enter into games while their elders spent the time reminiscing. Following the formal program of the day, a barbecue was enjoyed by an especially large turnout, and talk turned to "Do you remember when . . ."

The head barbecuer was Joe Calderon, who proved the importance of his job at the picnic by the company he kept. He was referring to Barbara Summer, the new vice president of the Pioneer Association, and Essie Turnage, the new secretary, who were standing by him at the barbecue pit.

Members of Pioneer families from Santa Maria and from out of town were justly proud that their ancestors had a part in developing this area from a stretch of sand and sagebrush into a "valley of gardens." The few frame houses and shops were added one by one, and as more people chose to locate here, a thriving community developed.

The annual Pioneer dance was held in the evening at the high school gymnasium.

1953

The 29th annual Pioneer Picnic was held on May 4, 1953, at Waller Park, with association president Dave Boyd presiding. He introduced Winston Wickenden, who was the speaker for the day. Wickenden enthralled the large audience of pioneers, their descendants and guests with his account of the first settling of the Tinaquaic land grant by his great-grandfather, Benjamin Foxen, in 1837. The land grant was made to Foxen, a former sea captain, by the newly independent Mexico.

DAVE BOYD
President, 1953

Following the program, a barbecue was served. The annual ball of the association was held that night at the high school gymnasium.

1954

The 30th annual Pioneer Picnic was held at Waller Park. Barbara Niverth Sumner, president of the association, presided at the meeting. Mrs. Sumner introduced Mrs. Alfa Mason, who was in

BARBARA SUMNER
President, 1954

charge of the presentation of the gift of an American flag and California bear flag from the Santa Maria Parlor, Native Daughters of the Golden West, to the Pioneer Association. The Native Daughters escort team assisted with the presentation.

William Fisher, a retired exporter of India and a resident here some 45 years ago, was speaker of the day at the barbecue. He was introduced by Fred L. May, a former president of the association.

A program of dances by pupils of Lorraine Goble Loomis provided colorful and enjoyable entertainment.

A vote of thanks was given to the barbecue crew for an excellent job of cooking the meat to perfection in the valley's best traditional style.

The annual dance was held that night at the Santa Maria High School gymnasium, where all Pioneer families of the community and their friends were invited.

1955

The 31st annual Pioneer celebration began on an evening at the Santa Maria Inn, where more than 70 Santa Maria High School alumni met for dinner.

JAMES G. BATTLES
President, 1955

The next day, pushed inside by threatening weather, Pioneers and members of their families enjoyed a barbecue dinner in the Veterans Memorial Hall. Jim Battles, president of the Association, presided. Clifton Pettit, a 1914 graduate of Santa Maria High School, was the speaker of the day. He spoke on the theme, "Connotation of a Pioneer."

The annual Pioneer dance, previously scheduled to be held in the afternoon at Waller Park, was rescheduled for 8:30 p.m. at the high school girls' gymnasium due to an unanticipated rainstorm with thunder and lightning. This shows that sometimes plans have to be changed without too much advance notice!

1956

The 32nd annual Pioneer Picnic, to be held in Waller Park Bowl, weather permitting, had to be changed to the Veterans Memorial Building the night before because of rain.

Ellis Fesler, president of the Association, presided. Fred May introduced the speaker of the day, Mayor Curtis Tunnell,

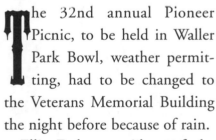

ELLIS FESLER
President, 1956

grandson of Martin Luther Tunnell, who settled in the Santa Maria Valley in 1868. He spoke on "Past, Present, and Future of the Valley."

A barbecue was served at 1:00 p.m., followed by dancing.

1957

Pioneers of the Santa Maria Valley gathered in sun-swept Waller Park on May 4, 1957, for the 33rd gathering of early-day settlers and their descendants.

Monica Bradley Touchstone, president of the Association, presided.

George C. Smith, Jr., a native of Santa Maria and the son of the late Mr. and Mrs. George C. Smith, who pioneered in real estate and insurance in the Santa Maria Valley, was the speaker of the day. He had been active in public community life and was familiar with past history, as well as with plans for Santa Maria's future development.

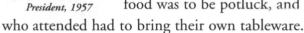

A Santa Maria style barbecue was one of the highlights of the meeting. Porfirio Ontiveros and his crew barbecued 400 pounds of the best beef that was purchased by Joe Calderon. Only meat and coffee were furnished. All other

MONICA TOUCHSTONE
President, 1957

food was to be potluck, and those who attended had to bring their own tableware.

Dancing was held in the afternoon in Square Cove to the music of a country style orchestra.

1958

The 34th annual Pioneer Picnic was held in Waller Park on Saturday, May 3. George Radke, president of the Association, presided.

The 1908 Santa Maria High School Alumni held their 50th reunion at the Santa Maria Inn on Friday night, and many of them came to the picnic.

GEORGE RADKE
President, 1958

The Rev. Paul H. Elliot, assistant pastor of the First Presbyterian Church, said the prayer.

The speaker of the day was Maurice Twitchell,

attorney with the law firm of Twitchell and Rice. He is the son of the late T.A. "Cap" Twitchell and Edwina Quaresma Twitchell of Santa Maria. His grandfather, Fremont Twitchell, who settled in Santa Maria in the last century and engaged in farming south of town, was the first president of the Santa Maria Valley Pioneers Association.

A Santa Maria style barbecue and a dance topped off the day's celebration at Waller Park.

1959

Many old-timers of Santa Maria and their families met on Saturday, May 2, 1959, at the 35th annual Pioneer Association barbecue in Waller Park. Approximately 400 attended. **Opal Frye,** president, presided. She welcomed all those attending at the 11:00 a.m. meeting and called upon Boy Scout Charles E. Lancaster to lead a pledge to the flag.

The Reverend Charles Gibbs of the First Christian Church offered the invocation. Julia Beeson Smith (Mrs. W. Leland Smith) led the singing of "The Star-Spangled Banner." Local attorney Jack Glines introduced Fred H. Schauer, from Santa Barbara, the speaker of the day. A native of Kansas, he was the son of the late Samuel Benjamin and Eva Hayes Schauer, who came to Santa Maria near the turn of the century when Fred was six years old. Fred went to local schools, and then to several colleges; he passed the bar examination in 1907.

Monica Touchstone arranged entertainment on the program to include songs on guitar accompanied by Ralph Thomas and by Frances Plummer Ontiveros, who sang songs from the days of the Dons.

Porfirio Ontiveros headed the barbecue crew and served barbecued beef and coffee. The rest of the picnic was pot luck, with the families furnishing their own silverware.

1960

The Santa Maria Valley Pioneer Association held the 34th annual picnic at Waller Park.

Lesley Holland, president of the Association, presided. The business meeting was held out of doors in the bright sunshine that warmed the many old timers on hand for the event and brought forth many tales of days gone by. The pioneers were entertained by square dances.

A barbecue prepared by Joe Calderon and Porfirio Ontiveros was served at noon. One hundred members of the Santa Maria High School class of 1910 held a reunion the night before at the Santa Maria Inn, and

1959

many of them were in attendance at the picnic.

1961

The Pioneer Association held its 37th annual Pioneer Picnic at Waller Park on Saturday, May 6, 1961. Gertrude Rice France, Association president, presided at the meeting. She extended a welcome to the crowd of about 300, and introduced the new officers and past presidents in attendance. After the pledge of allegiance to the flag, Kenneth Hibbard sang "The Star-Spangled Banner." The invocation was by Rev. J. Stanley Parke of St. Peter's Episcopal Church.

GERTRUDE RICE FRANCE
President, 1961

The speaker of the day was Santa Maria native Judge C. Douglas Smith, who was introduced by local attorney Maurice Twitchell. Mrs. Ida Hawkins introduced the entertainment numbers, provided in dances and sketches by a beautifully costumed group from the Lorraine Loomis School of Dance.

Porfirio Ontiveros and ranchers from Tepusquet Canyon did the barbecuing; Marinus Nielsen arranged for serving by the Junior Park Rangers as well as for accordion and trumpet music by the strolling musicians Aage Porsborg and L. Christensen.

1962

The annual Pioneer Picnic was held for the first time at the Union Oil picnic grounds, where it would be held annually for the next 34 years. Chester A. Davis, president of the Pioneer Association, presided. The meeting

CHESTER A. DAVIS
President, 1962

drew a large representative group from the valley's early day families. President Davis welcomed the ones attending.

Robert E. Easton, pioneer cattleman, banker, businessman and civic leader, was the speaker of the day. His speech was a tribute to the families who lived in the upper Sisquoc area some 60 years ago. Men in the cattle business claim him as their friend and associate through his work as secretary-manager and as superintendent of Sisquoc Ranch from 1899 to 1950.

Ida Wylie Jones (Mrs. Gaylord

ROBERT E. EASTON
Speaker of the Day

Jones) arranged for the program to begin at 11:00 a.m. Rev. Wallace Williams of the First Presbyterian Church offered the invocation. There was a pledge of allegiance to the flag, after which Julia Beeson Smith led the audience in the singing of "America," accompanied by Mrs. Leonald Adam, who also played for the community singing of several old-time songs.

A beef barbecue was served at noon. Many of the 150 or so who attended the Santa Maria High School alumni dinner the night before attended the picnic.

1963

The annual Pioneer Picnic was held on Saturday, May 4, 1963, at the Union Oil picnic grounds on Newlove Hill. President Gertrude McIntosh Clemons presided, welcoming the old-timers and their families, many in the group having traveled some distance to Santa Maria for this homecoming event.

GERTRUDE M. CLEMONS
President, 1963

Judge Morris Stephan, who was introduced by Walter Stokes, was the guest speaker; he entitled his discourse "Remember When." The speech was interesting enough to be included below in its entirety for the enjoyment of the reader.

Porfirio Ontiveros and his experienced crew did the barbecuing, which was served by the Tepusquet Canyon Future Farmers of America under the supervision of Jim Battles.

There was community singing of old-time songs led by Mrs. Leland Smith and accompanied by Mrs. Leonald Adam, as well as broadcast music of the old favorites. The past presidents were introduced.

"Remember When"
Address by Morris Stephan, 1963

When people who have been separated for awhile get together, they enjoy a pastime which we will call "Remember When." At such meetings the conversation soon gets to the point of "remember when" so-and-so did "such-and-such," which then will be followed by someone else remembering when somebody else did "such-and-such." It is fun to "remember when." We enjoy reliving that occasion. Sometimes the occasion involves physical danger, or an accomplishment; sometimes it is a prank; sometimes it is recalling an incident of lasting importance and value. Today, when we gather as Pioneers, we also engage in this game of "Remember When"—only instead of remembering incidents which happened to us individually and personally, we can now remember incidents which occurred to our predecessors in this area.

Each person here represents a particular segment of our community. Each person's predecessors played an important role in the development of our valley.

It is impossible in a few moments to discuss and give credit to all families, all predecessors and all pioneers. Hence, the most we can do is try to discuss a few of the incidents, not with the idea of glorifying them to the exclusion of others, but to show a pattern in the development of this wonderful valley. While we are speaking of giving credit, much of the information contained herein was obtained from, and should be credited to, the book *This Is Our Valley,* by Vada Carlson.

At the outset, let us consider: What is a Pioneer? Our association by-laws provide that a Pioneer is a person who has lived here for 30 years or who was born and raised here, or whose spouse so qualifies. According to the dictionary, a "pioneer" is a forerunner, or "a person who prepares the way for those who follow." Thus, a pioneer is a person of vision who can see what advantages and advancement can be made from a crude beginning. There are pioneers of all kinds. We hear of modern pioneers now planning wonderful things for the future: pioneers in chemistry, space, metallurgy, electronics, oceanography, and other matters which will play important roles in our future. Today, however, we are thinking of the pioneers of our valley. Who were they? How important were they and their vision?

If you will pardon a personal experience, I may tell what I observed in watching a pioneer in action—my father. It is true that he was not born here, nor did he move here in the very early days of settlement, but he did exactly what the early pioneers did. Fifty years ago, in 1913, my father and mother moved from a comfortable home in Los Angeles to 60 acres of barren, sandy soil about four miles south of Santa Maria on the road to Orcutt. At that time it was not paved, but it was a partially surfaced road. Occasionally automobiles used it, but more frequently horses, buggies and wagons. Because I had been ill in Los Angeles, the doctor advised that they take me to the open air. Hence, in 1913 they brought me to an area where there was nothing but open air. The city of Santa Maria was a very small village at that time; the means of access to the railroad at Guadalupe was an electric car. The 60 acres of bare land which my father then acquired had no improvements of any kind, so the first thing he did was to build a shed to afford temporary shelter. He and his father, by horse and wagon, hauled the lumber to the bare land, and, by working long and hard, soon had a shed built of pine and redwood. Then we moved into the shed and lived there for several months while my dad and his father built a small living house. While we were living in the shed, our floor was the earth. My mother tried to protect us by putting canvas and empty sacks on the ground to try to keep us warm. She used a wood stove to cook on. Coal oil lamps and lanterns were our lights. When the house was built, my father then turned to the water problem, because we were living on water hauled in barrels. Some of you have had to go through the ordeal of living on water so hauled. Every drop is precious, every drop is important. The water in the barrel gets stale; danger of contamination may require that the water be boiled. So my father drilled a water well. He found good water, so he installed a pump run by a gasoline engine. From that time we could share our water with other people who were moving into the area but as yet had no water. Then, as a protection from the heavy westerly winds, my father planted some Blugum trees west of the

MORRIS J. STEPHAN
Guest Speaker

house so it would be sheltered from such wind. Then he planted fruit trees so we could enjoy and market fresh fruit; ultimately berries were planted. I can remember my mother swallowing her natural pride, but in order to pay for the necessities of life, she took butter, eggs, fruit and vegetables to sell to people in Santa Maria. Some of you were her customers. Twice a week she would harness the horse and buggy and drive to town with such products. It was necessary, because with the little money she obtained we were able to buy things for the farm, as well as food and clothing. The people she sold the produce to were pleased, because it was good quality and farm fresh. When I read the history of our valley, I find that what my parents did is exactly what most of the people did who prepared the way for the rest of us here today. They were pioneers in that they prepared our way, they were willing to undergo hardship, they had the vision of what could be done by improving the barren area which they then saw.

Let us look back further to see what early conditions were. At first only Indians lived here. The Spanish priests established their missions in about the 1770s. In 1775 a Spanish expedition under Col. De Anza visited this area. With him were four soldiers who liked what they saw and later returned to this valley to settle it and from whom there are descendants here today. May I mention their names, because to the people involved they can point back and say "thank you" to these men of vision. They were Ignacio DeSoto, Manuel Ramírez Arellanes, Joaquín Isidro DeCastro, and Santiago DeLaCruz Pico. Ignacio DeSoto's daughter, María Josepha, later married James Stokes and was the great-grandmother of our Program Chairman today—Mr. Walter W. Stokes. Rudolph Bagdons is a descendant of both the Castros and the Picos; his maternal grandmother was a Pico before marrying Rafael Castro. Of course we know that the Arellaneses remaining in this area point back to Manuel Ramírez Arellanes. At the time when these men first visited this area, it was undeveloped. They could see, from the lagoon which took a great part of the lower valley, and from the other springs and streams around which were growing willows and undergrowth, that the soil was fertile. The climate and terrain were good. Hence, these men wanted to acquire rights in the area. So, when the land grant ranchos were created, these men with others were lucky enough to acquire some of the land. In order for us to remember the times involved, may we mention that the Suey Rancho was created in 1837; Tepusquet Rancho in 1838; Los Alamos Rancho in 1839; Guadalupe Rancho in 1840; Todos Santos y San Antonio Rancho in 1841; Tinaquaic Rancho in 1842; Cuyama #1 Rancho in 1843; Punta de la Laguna Rancho in 1844, and Sisquoc Rancho in 1845.

Captain Benjamin Foxen was reportedly the first white man who actually built and settled in this area in 1837; at that time other white men were running cattle, but had not yet built their buildings. As you know, Capt. Foxen located in the Foxen Canyon. Bears and wild Indians roamed the Valley. He built iron bars across inside his fireplace chimney to keep Indians out. There is a fascinating story of what he did toward improving this area. When Fremont and his Americans were going down this coast to take the area for the United States, the southern Californians planned to resist them and ambush them at Gaviota Pass. Capt. Foxen so advised Fremont and guided the Americans through the San Marcos Pass to avoid the ambush, and they were able to capture the city of Santa Barbara without bloodshed. However, in retaliation Foxen had his home burned, possessions ruined by the natives, and he and his family had to live in hiding for several years before the turmoil passed.

Don Juan Pacífico Ontiveros built his home at the head of the valley and is credited with having named the river, his rancho and the nearby mesa after Mary, the mother of Jesus, thus calling it "Santa Maria." This man of vision could see the value of this area as one of God's greatest gifts and had that thought in mind when he named it after the mother of Jesus.

Diego Olivera built the first dwelling, an adobe, in the western part of the valley on Guadalupe Rancho. Guadalupe for a while appeared to be the center of growth because of the rich soil there. There was a Frenchman named Theodore LeRoy who loaned money on the Guadalupe Rancho, but due to exces-

sive dry years, many cattle died, and the early rancheros were in desperate financial straits—thus, when the owners of the Guadalupe Rancho were unable to pay the mortgage, they turned the property over to Mr. LeRoy. In 1870, he sold portions of it to farmers and dairymen. He also laid out the town of Guadalupe and established LeRoy Park in perpetuity. In the meantime, word of this wonderful area was spreading. It was reported to be a vast land in which the soil was good, water available, and the land procurable. It seems that in the 1860s some of the land was made available for homestead purposes. It was in that period of time that most of our early people moved here. For instance, in 1868 Charles Bradley and family landed in San Francisco on a steamer from England. They made up their own caravan. They had their usual covered wagon to carry Mrs. Bradley and the newborn child; they also had a spring wagon loaded with household equipment, followed by a wheelbarrow loaded with an iron cook stove. This family group slowly made its way down from San Francisco and settled here. They flourished in many ways. When they held their first family reunion in 1939, there were 69 members of the family present.

Mr. C. C. Oakley arrived in 1869 and homesteaded a quarter section of land at what is now Blosser Road and Main Street. Later, in 1880, he bought 3,000 acres on the Alamo Creek and moved there. His son, Will Oakley, was a farmer and moved back to Santa Maria in 1902 so that his children could be educated in Santa Maria. Will Oakley ran a steam power threshing machine, threshing beans and grain; he served as the Mayor of our early City, was County Supervisor and thence our State Assemblyman. Just this week the Oakley family had its big family reunion. I am sure they remembered when.

William Smith and wife Sarah arrived from England, but the ship carrying them and their household goods foundered and sank near San Francisco's Golden Gate, so they lost all their belongings. They were thankful to save their lives, and moved to Virginia City, where Charles William Smith was born in 1868. When he was three years old, in 1871, the

Smith family moved to and settled in this valley, settling southeast of Santa Maria. Mr. Smith appreciated the value of schools, so he donated one acre of land, on which the Pleasant Valley Schoolhouse was built. His son, Charles W. Smith, was the father of C. Douglas Smith, Judge of the Superior Court; Dr. Leland Smith; and former Supervisor Attorney Marion A. Smith.

William Laird Adam, his wife and five children arrived in 1869, brought their own herd of cattle, settled on 160 acres near the river, built a small house, and dug a well, thus eliminating the carrying of water in barrels from their neighbor.

The Battles family arrived at about this time and likewise settled southeast of Santa Maria. Their descendant, Jim Battles, is usually in charge of serving the meat at these annual barbecues. Other people who arrived about this time, which again indicates how the word had spread, were Lorenzo Blosser and wife, Anna Van Volkenberg, who arrived in 1869, the same year that William Alexander Haslam arrived, as did Francis Marian Bryant.

The city of Santa Maria started from nothing; people began to build small houses in this part of the valley because they found the soil was rich, although more sandy than the soil in the Guadalupe area. At first the town was called Grangeville, but the name was changed to Central City because it was centrally located. The town itself was started by four men who had great vision for the future of this area. Many of you are descendants of these four men, so let us name them and give a brief description of their contribution.

Rudolph D. Cook came to homestead in this area and first lived in the Guadalupe adobe. He acquired land which is now in the southeast quarter of the city of Santa Maria. He built a two-story house which was the mansion of that age. Even before he moved into the house, he gave a party and a public dance in his home in order to raise funds for a schoolhouse. Those people well recognized the value of schools. The Pleasant Valley School was built with some of those funds, and the school building itself cost the fantastic sum of $510.00. It convened in February of 1870. Many of you here and your parents attended that school.

John Thornburg acquired the land which became the southwest quarter of our city. He donated a lot for the First Methodist Church, to be built on what we now call South Lincoln Street. Those men recognized the value of churches, too.

Isaac Fesler, Sr., acquired property in the northwest segment of our city. In order to encourage town development, he donated a lot where Kaiser Bros. built a store, and thus accelerated the growth of the town. He also donated land for the Pacific Coast Railway right-of-way, which was the narrow gauge railroad from San Luis Obispo, which later extended to Los Olivos.

Isaac Miller acquired property in the northeast portion of our city; he planted large acreage in fruit trees and sold fresh and dried fruits. These four men could see the need and value of developing a planned community, so they met and platted the townsite; each man platted a quarter section of land in the areas above noted. Likewise, in order to assure the proper growth of the town, they each donated strips of land for streets to be 120 feet wide in the center of town. The map was recorded in Santa Barbara in 1875.

Samuel Jefferson Jones, then age 18, and his father, T.A. Jones, arrived in 1871. T.A. Jones married Sophie Thornburg, daughter of John Thornburg. T.A. Jones was a carpenter, so he opened a business under the name of T.A. Jones and Son, making furniture, cabinets and coffins. Ultimately Albert A. Dudley came, and a mortuary was established. T.A. Jones and Son built a two-story wooden business building, but when fire destroyed it in 1883, they rebuilt the first brick business building in this area.

Time does not permit details, but about this time other men arrived, such as Ruben Hart in 1872, John H. Rice in 1873, whose family included William Hickman Rice, then age 17. Martin Luther Tunnell arrived in 1868, and his son, George, married Ellen Kortner, who are the parents of Curtis Tunnell, our present Supervisor. Cassius Glines arrived about 1874, settled in the Pine Grove area about seven miles south of Central City, and his son John married Dora Holloway. Alvis H. Davis was residing in this area in 1883. The Glines and Davis families have remained active in civic matters ever since.

In thinking of these early pioneers and their contributions, we must think of Charles Haskell Clark, who arrived in 1868. He owned 1000 acres in the Point Sal area. We who now enjoy our wonderful roads can hardly visualize the problems of early transportation. Our early settlers had to depend only on what could be hauled by carrying on their backs or horses, in wagons, or by ocean. The wagon roads were trails in which the earth would get packed by natural use; however, in rainy weather, muddy mire would develop, and in dry seasons, the light sand would cause the tire wheels to sink and make it difficult to haul heavy loads. Where possible, early settlers would spread straw over the sandy areas to keep their wheels from sinking too deep in the sand. Most commerce was then on the ocean. The nearest seaport was at Port Harford and at Cave Landing in the Avila Beach area. Our settlers had to take their big wagons to that area to pick up lumber, food and other necessities. It entailed four to six days to make the round trip. Hence, when Charles Clark saw the Point Sal area, he envisioned ways and means of having the ships load and unload at that point, thereby saving local settlers many miles of hauling. Accordingly, in 1871, he built a wharf at Point Sal so that ships could unload merchandise and haul away our products. However, a fierce storm in 1876 smashed the wharf, and also wrecked the schooner known as *Anna Lyle*. His wife, Mrs. Eliza Clark, envisioned the need of a schoolhouse, so she traded her gold watch to the ship's owner in exchange for whatever the Clarks could salvage from the schooner. The ship's cabin became the Point Sal schoolhouse, while the ship's timbers provided portions of the building. The ship's bell, being too large for the little schoolhouse, was sold to the Methodist Church of Central City.

The need for the ship landing was urgent, so the wharf was rebuilt. The steep road up Point Sal hill was a problem. It took two days for local farmers to haul grain to the landing. However, the road was very well used by the slow plodding wagons. An additional wharf in that area was built a little south of Point Sal by a group of Santa Maria men and was incorporated as Chute Landing in 1880. Instead of having a long wharf for the ships to pull into, this project had a short wharf with a long wire cable anchored to huge iron rings embedded in the side of the cliff with the

other end fastened to a buoy 600 feet to sea. A traveling cage on wheels rode up and down on the cable carrying the ship's cargo. Ships would bring in lumber, food, and dry goods, and haul out grain, butter, potatoes, and beans. The power for pulling the cage up the cable was furnished by a donkey engine built on top of the bluff. In two years' time, the wharf paid for itself. They had a busy but dangerous port.

We who sometimes have difficulty getting to church services should take heart from the fact that Mrs. Clark traveled 20 miles one way on bad roads to Santa Maria to attend her church. This was done by horse and buggy. I can appreciate that, because I can remember as a boy how my father and mother used to take their family on fishing trips. We had a two-seat spring wagon in which my dad would load hay and water for the horses; then my mother would pack food and blankets for our family. We would leave our ranch about three o'clock in the morning, drive to Casmalia Beach, and arrive at about 9:30 a.m. Then we would start home at 2:00 in the afternoon and arrive home long after dark. On other occasions, we would leave on Saturday, drive to Oceano or Oso Flaco, camp out all night on the beach, enjoy clamming and fishing, start back Sunday morning, and arrive home after dark Sunday night.

Since the only means of travel was by horse and wagon, it was mighty important when railroads began to develop in this area. In 1882, the narrow gauge Pacific Coast Railway was completed from San Luis Obispo, through Port Harford to Central City. Following that, the wharves at Pt. Sal were no longer needed. The railroads could carry the loads cheaper and easier.

In 1878, Dr. J. R. Shaw and Thomas Bell bought land from owners of Rancho La Laguna and Rancho Los Alamos, and created the town of Los Alamos, each setting aside one half square mile for the town. In 1884, the Pacific Coast Railroad extended its line to the town of Los Alamos, thereby giving a link of transportation between Central City and Los Alamos. It was truly a great day.

The name of the town Central City was changed to Santa Maria, as was noted in the first issue of the *Santa Maria Times,* published way back on April 22,

1882. At that time, H.J. Laughlin was proprietor and S. Clevenger was the Editor and Manager. The reasons? Postmasters were having trouble, confusing mail addressed to Central City, California, with mail addressed to Central City, Colorado. Hence the city became Santa Maria, because that was the name of the mesa on which it was located. The name reminds us of God's great gift—really significant.

Water is always a problem in any growing community. Ruben Hart established the town's water works in 1879. He dug an 85-foot-deep well, laid pipes, pumping water by steam power into an overhead tank which then furnished water to nearby residents. The water was sold at a small flat charge per month.

When the roads required improving, it was found that asphalt from this area made excellent road surfaces when mixed with sand. Hence, many roads were surfaced with that mixture. In the 1890s, our asphalt became in demand for roads in other areas, and was exported from this vicinity.

In 1891, many of the residents felt the need of a secondary educational system, so 22 educational districts were united and formed the Santa Maria Union District; a high school was thus organized. The Union District bought 10 acres on South Broadway from Ezra Morrison, Sr. They built a new building there in 1894 at a cost of $12,000.00, and by 1896 the high school had been so improved that it was accredited by the State University. By 1902, there were four teachers teaching high school. Many of you here today were students under those teachers. When I started high school in 1920, I remember that large two-story building. Since I had attended a small country school in which all eight grades were taught in one classroom by one teacher, when I first went to the huge two-story high school, it was magnificent. Many of you can remember the study hall on the second floor. Sometimes, in order to let off steam, students would shake their feet up and down in unison while sitting at their desks. The rhythm would cause the floor to shake up and down until the study hall teacher would order the commotion stopped.

When automobiles made their appearance about 1900, they created a demand for better roads, and likewise a demand for petroleum products. In 1904, Union Oil Company drilled its Hartnell #1 well, which blew in as a gusher; it also blew in a new industry. It produced 10,000 barrels a day, and started an oil rush boom to this area.

In 1905, Santa Maria was incorporated as a city. The total votes cast at the election were 368, with 202 voting for incorporating while 139 voted against it. Thomas Preisker, father of Leo, was the first City Attorney.

In 1907, a group of men piped natural gas to Santa Maria, and when the lines were first opened, they only had 30 customers. Bob Easton came here as a surveyor in 1899 to survey the Sisquoc Ranch, and in 1909, he became the secretary of the Gas and Power Company, which in 1911 reorganized as the Santa Maria Gas Company. By 1932 it had expanded to serve 8,000 customers and had 335 miles of pipe lines.

Near the turn of the century, men began wondering about how to control the water being wasted by running down the Santa Maria River to the ocean, causing damage as it flowed. In 1924, a Chamber of Commerce committee was formed to study the problem. This Committee, of which Mr. Walter W. Stokes was a member, made its survey and recommendation. Later, another survey was made, known as the Lippincott Survey. Leo Preisker was County Supervisor at the time of the water surveys and was anxious to have water protection, as well as water reclamation.

Following World War II, Cap Twitchell, as Supervisor, exerted a great deal of effort in having a dam planned and built at Vaquero Flats at the head of our Valley. It is now known as Twitchell Dam, and was created to control the floods and furnish an orderly replacement of underground water. The value of this project is tremendous. It should be observed that last year, we had a fairly heavy rain over a short period. The streams all flooded; however, the Cuyama River was held in check by the Twitchell Dam. A huge lake formed, then the water was permitted to dissipate in an orderly fashion after the rains ceased. Such water percolated underground. If a dam had not been completed, the Santa Maria River undoubtedly would have flooded many homes in the lower sections of the city. Hence the vision of these pioneers in giving water protection.

In 1898 some men conceived the idea that our soil was good for more than merely growing grain and beans. A sugar factory was conceived at what is now Betteravia. It furnished much employment, not only in the processing of sugar beets, but in growing them.

Our area has become a true melting pot of many nationalities. Peoples from many nations have been accepted on the basis of what they can do, what improvements they can bring. Hence the finer traits of other countries have enriched our region.

In 1908, L.D. Waller came to this area to raise flower seeds. He found the conditions, soil and climate so favorable that in 1912 he and Dr. Franklin formed the Waller-Franklin Flower Seed Company. It has furnished a great deal of employment for local people, distributing flower seeds throughout the world.

In 1925, Capt. G. Allan Hancock purchased the Santa Maria Ice and Cold Storage Company in Santa Maria. He also bought 400 acres east of Santa Maria, and created vegetable commercial farming, as well as poultry farms in that portion of our valley. In order to provide Santa Maria with a connection to the Southern Pacific Railroad, which was completed in Guadalupe about 1902, Capt. Hancock purchased the Santa Maria Short Line Railway and enlarged it. It is now the Santa Maria Valley Railroad, which ties into the Southern Pacific line so that oil cars and produce cars can be loaded in Santa Maria, taken to the Guadalupe freight yard, and thence throughout the United States. In addition to being a pioneer in furnishing railway and vegetable packing accommodations to this portion of the valley, Capt. Hancock also pioneered air travel. In approximately 1926, he created Hancock Field, and then Hancock College of Aeronautics. In 1939, his was one of nine air schools in the United States who contracted to train Army Air Corps pilots then so desperately needed by the United States.

As truck transportation became more prevalent, the truck industry in Santa Maria began to flourish, and now is doing tremendous business. When it used to take days for Santa Maria products to reach Los Angeles or San Francisco, it can now be done in a few hours.

These early pioneers were eagerly interested in schools. They did a great deal to improve education. For that reason, our present-day pioneers in education have wisely named many present schools after some of these pioneers. For instance, Blochman School, Cary Calvin Oakley School, William Hickman Rice School, William L. Adam School, Isaac Fesler Junior High School, and even present educational pioneers are honored with names such as Ernest Righetti High School, Joe Nightingale School, Robert Bruce School, and May Grisham School.

Most of you here remember 1957, when our local papers announced that Camp Cooke was to be revived as a Missile Training Base for the Air Force. This announcement presaged a completely new industry and a new way of life. Instead of the Base being merely a training base, it has also become operational in that missiles are there which can be fired in anger if necessary; also there is now underway a new development in space travel. It is found that Vandenberg Air Force Base and Point Arguello are ideally located for orbital polar space launchings, plus rockets are able to launch to the west or south over water, making ideal conditions for future space exploration.

Today we have been remembering when over 100 years ago this was a barren country, but rich in promise, which through the vision and planning of our pioneers has developed into a rich thriving community. It is a community of which we are proud and equally proud to share with others who desire the best of living conditions.

Now we are at the threshold of these new developments. Pioneers in science, metallurgy and electronics which have developed in the missile age are now planning wonderful new things for our use. New metals, plastics, and electrical developments now planned for space exploration will be used in our domestic living. Many of the fine people who have moved here recently want to remain; they are pioneers in their science fields; they want to be eligible to be members of our Pioneer Association, by living here more than 30 years. If we could gather here 30 years from now, I am sure we will look back at 1963 and say that was the beginning of a new golden era for this area. Let us do our utmost to afford the best accommodations, churches, schools, culture and opportunities to these people now moving here and who will remain. Let us invite them to help us plan and work for a better Santa Maria area of the future, just as our predecessors planned so well for those who followed—us. We know that we have one of God's greatest gifts in climate, soil and location, so it is up to us to plan for the best use of these gifts. It is a challenge given to us so that the pioneers of tomorrow may look back and say "thank you" for what is now being planned.

I hope each of you may return to next year's Pioneer Anniversary and can look with pride on accomplishments of this next year.

1964

The Pioneer Association held their annual Pioneer Picnic at the Newlove Hill Union Oil Company picnic grounds on Saturday, May 2, 1964. Marinus Nielsen presided over the program. The barbecue was prepared under the direction of Porfirio Ontiveros and served by the Future Farmers of America under the supervision of James

MARINUS NIELSEN
President, 1964

Battles. The speaker at the picnic was Mrs. Fred Carlson, the former Martha Hanson, whose talk dealt with reminiscences of early Santa Maria. Featured on the program were songs led by Kenneth Hibbard and accordion selections by Emilio Sutti. Sutti also entertained during the barbecue and led the audience in some old, well-known songs.

Rev. J. Stanley Parke gave the invocation; Gene Tognazzini, a Boy Scout, led the pledge of allegiance, followed by a roll call of departed Pioneers read by secretary Marie Murray.

The Pioneer Dance was held on Saturday, April 25, at the Sisquoc Grange Hall, with both old-time and modern dancing. The Martinaires began playing at 8:30 p.m., featuring such old-time favorites as the varsouvienne, the rye-waltz, and the schottische.

1965

Approximately 200 persons gathered at the Union Oil picnic grounds, on Orcutt Hill between Mount Solomon and the Newlove School, to take part in the 41st annual picnic

and program for Pioneers and guests, some coming from as far north as Oroville, California, and as far south as Texas to meet with relatives and friends. The Pioneer Picnic had been moved to Orcutt Hill in 1962 and would continue to be held there annually for over thirty years.

IDA WYLIE JONES
President, 1965

The president of the association, Ida Wylie Jones, presided. The program opened with the national anthem, led by Kenneth Hibbard, accompanied by Mrs. Leonald Adam. The pledge of allegiance was led by Michael Murray, followed by words of welcome from Ida Wylie Jones, outgoing Pioneer president, who welcomed the people attending and said that even though the numbers of old Pioneers were dwindling, she hoped that the newer ones would continue the traditions laid down by the older generation. Judge Morris Stephan was elected president.

"Beautiful Dreamer" and "Summertime" were sung by Vicki Anderson, accompanied at the piano by Ann Matlack.

A beef barbecue followed, with Manuel Bello supervising the pit. Jim Battles was in charge of serving, which was done by the Future Farmers of America. Emilio Sutti entertained the diners with his accordion.

The annual dance was held in the evening at the high school gymnasium.

1966

The Santa Maria Valley Pioneers held their 42nd annual picnic on Saturday, May 7th, starting at 11:00 a.m. at the Union Oil Company picnic grounds, about 10 miles south of Santa Maria off Highway 101. A large crowd of Pioneers and their families and guests assembled at the picnic place from all over California to meet their relatives and friends and to enjoy the picnic. The weather was ideal.

Municipal Judge Morris Stephan, Pioneer Associa-

JUDGE MORRIS STEPHAN
President, 1966

tion president, presided. Mrs. George Radke was program chairman, assisted by Mrs. Morris Stephan.

Richard P. Weldon, local attorney and pioneer of Santa Maria Valley, was the featured speaker of the day and spoke about pioneering. He was born in Santa Maria, the elder of two sons born to Thomas P. Weldon and Olga Giacomini Weldon. His grandfather, Paul Giacomini, came to the Central Coast area in 1890 and was in the flower seed and cattle business in Guadalupe. His maternal great-grandfather, Peter Grisinger, came to California in 1870, operated a hotel in San Luis Obispo, and later farmed in Guadalupe. His father is now a municipal court judge in Santa Maria.

Weldon said the present generation faces the challenge of continuing to build on this foundation. He praised the pioneers as hard-working men and women who had vision and self-discipline.

A beef barbecue was served at noon. James "Jimmy" Battles supervised the serving of the meat by members of the Future Farmers of America. Barbecued beef and coffee was furnished by a donation at the gate: $2.00 for adults and $1.00 for children under 12.

Judge Stephan announced that the association was now incorporated as a non-profit organization. Twenty past presidents of the group, which was founded in 1924, were on hand and introduced. Included on the program were songs by Margie Stephan and the presentation of a piano to the organization by Mr. and Mrs. Robert E. Easton.

1967

About 350 persons attended the 43rd Santa Maria Valley Pioneer Picnic at the Union Oil Co. picnic grounds. Association president Elizabeth Oakley May presided over the program. Special entertainment was provided, with old time songs played and sung by professional folk singers Keith and Rusty McNeil. Keith was a grandson of W.C. Oakley, the third president of the Pioneer Association.

ELIZABETH OAKLEY MAY
President, 1967

The invocation was delivered by Judge Morris J. Stephan, a past president of the organization.

Besides the many out-of-town visitors who gathered here, many of the past presidents of the association were present.

A Santa Maria style barbecue was served at noon.

1968

About 300 pioneers gathered for the annual Pioneer Picnic at the Union Oil Company's picnic grounds on Orcutt Hill. William "Bill" Elliott, association president, presided. Hugh Kelley Radke, speaker of the day, reviewed the development of the valley and described what might develop in the future.

WILLIAM F. ELLIOTT
President, 1968

Old-time music was played by Winnie Adam, pianist, Emma Brians Davis, banjo player, and William Elliott, violinist. Julia Beeson Smith sang a group of selections of the early era. Margie Stephan sang "Drink to Me Only with Thine Eyes."

A Santa Maria style beef barbecue was served at noon.

1969

Pioneers and their families gathered on the Orcutt Hill's Union Oil Co. picnic grounds for the 45th annual Santa Maria Valley Pioneer Association picnic, and found that the typical cold spring winds in the valley had also joined the festivities. The 260 persons in attendance were kept warm by coats, quilts, and greetings from long-time friends.

GLENN ROEMER
President, 1969

Association president Glenn Roemer presided. Mayor George Hobbs, a native of Santa Maria, was the speaker of the day. The pioneers gathered around tables stacked with home-made cakes, salads, and other picnic dishes including beans and Santa Maria style barbecue, dining much the same as did those who attended the first gatherings some 45 years before.

1970

The Santa Maria Valley Pioneer Association held their 46th annual Pioneer Picnic on Saturday, July 11th, 1970, at the Union Oil Company camp grounds on Newlove Hill. Dorian Davis, Pioneer Association president, presided at the 12 o'clock program. More than 300 Pioneers

DORIAN DAVIS
President, 1970

and their families and friends attended. The Rev. Robert S. Rickert gave the benediction. Senior Girl Scouts of Troop 187 presented the flags while the audience was led in singing "The Star-Spangled Banner" by Julia Smith.

After the program there was music by Bill Elliot and the Serenaders and by Johnny Battistella and His Boys, featuring old-time songs and dance tunes.

Class reunions of Santa Maria High School are held each year on the eve of the picnic, bringing many people back to the two-day homecoming event.

Extra plates and tableware were provided for the out-of-town guests. Local residents brought their own salads and table settings.

1971

The Santa Maria Valley Pioneers held their 47th annual picnic at the Union Oil picnic grounds on Newlove Hill on Saturday, July 10, 1971. President Emilio Sutti presided. The day's events

began with a program presented by Allan Woods, vice president of operations, Union Sugar Company. He spoke about the sugar beet industry, its history, and its part in the development of the Santa Maria Valley as an important agricultural center in California.

The prayer was under the direction of the St. Mary

EMILIO SUTTI
President, 1971

of the Assumption Catholic Church. Senior Girl Scouts of Troop 187 performed the flag drill. Mrs. Leland Smith led the audience in singing "The Star-Spangled Banner." Following the program, informal entertainment was provided by John Battistella and his dance band.

At 1 o'clock, barbecued beef, beans, French bread and coffee were served. Members brought their own dishes, salads and desserts. Nick Ardantz and Milo Ferini barbecued, and the Future Farmers of America, under the supervision of Jim Battles, did the serving. Over 300 Pioneers and their families attended.

1972

The Santa Maria Valley Pioneer Association held their 48th annual picnic on Saturday, July 8, 1972, at 12 o'clock, on the Union Oil picnic grounds on Newlove Hill. President William ("Bill") Ruiz presided.

Information is not available about the program, held at 12

WILLIAM RUIZ
President, 1972

o'clock, beyond the fact that Tom Weldon spoke on Santa Maria's redevelopment project. A barbecued luncheon was served at 1:00 p.m.

New officers installed were Butch Simas, president; Bull Saunders, vice president; and Betty McDonald, secretary-treasurer.

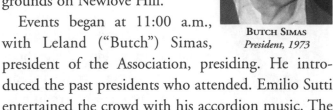

1973

"Ready to go" was the word from the Committee for the Santa Maria Valley Pioneer Association's 49th annual Pioneer Picnic, held at the Union Oil Company picnic grounds on Newlove Hill.

BUTCH SIMAS
President, 1973

Events began at 11:00 a.m., with Leland ("Butch") Simas, president of the Association, presiding. He introduced the past presidents who attended. Emilio Sutti entertained the crowd with his accordion music. The speaker of the day was T.A. "Ted" Bianchi, president of the Santa Maria Historical Society, who was introduced by Judge Morris Stephan.

At noon a barbecue was served, with the Simas brothers doing the honors at the pit and served with the assistance of their helpers. Coffee, toasted and buttered french bread and beans were served with the barbecued beef. The donation was $3.00 for adults and $1.25 for children under 12.

Following the barbecue and throughout the afternoon, there was dancing to music by the Senior Citizens Orchestra.

1974

BULL SAUNDERS
President, 1974

The 50th annual Pioneer Picnic was held on Saturday, July 13th, 1974, at the Union Oil Company picnic grounds on Newlove Hill. Wilfred ("Bull") Saunders, president of the Pioneer Association, presided at the program that began at noon. Following the program, Eddie James and his barbecue crew served a Santa Maria style barbecue at 1:00 p.m. Many of the out-of-town persons who attended the Santa Maria High School Alumni Association dinner on Friday night attended the picnic.

1975

The Santa Maria Valley Pioneer Association held its 51st annual picnic on July 12, 1975, at 12 o'clock at the Union Oil Picnic Grounds on Newlove Hill. President Ivan ("Hap") Worsham presided over the program.

Over 400 attended the Santa Maria style barbecue and picnic. Everyone brought their own table service,

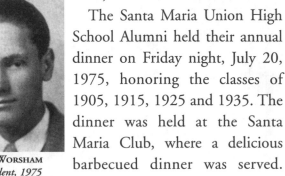

HAP WORSHAM
President, 1975

salad, dessert and cold drinks.

The Santa Maria Union High School Alumni held their annual dinner on Friday night, July 20, 1975, honoring the classes of 1905, 1915, 1925 and 1935. The dinner was held at the Santa Maria Club, where a delicious barbecued dinner was served. Many of the alumni also attended the Pioneer Picnic on Saturday.

An unusual aspect of this picnic was the publication of a two-page announcement of both the picnic and the high school alumni banquet the night before. Included was a large photograph of the Pioneers attending the Pioneer Picnic in 1959 and congratulatory ads by the two dozen Pioneer businesses and farms who sponsored the joint announcement.

1976

The 52nd annual Pioneer Picnic was held on Saturday, July 11th, 1976, at the Union Oil picnic grounds on Newlove Hill. Chester A. Norris, president of the Pioneer Association, presided at the program that started at noon. He introduced the past presidents who attended.

George C. Smith, Jr., a Santa Maria native and the owner and operator of Smith Transportation, was the speaker of the day. Being interested in the economic development of Santa Maria and active

CHESTER A. NORRIS
President, 1976

in many community organizations and public offices since entering business over thirty years before, he chose as his topic "The New Face of Santa Maria."

At 1:00 p.m., Bill Pryor and his barbecue crew served about 300 persons. Many of the out-of-town Pioneers who attended the annual Santa Maria High School Alumni Association dinner on Friday night attended.

1977

BOB RIVERS
President, 1977

The 54th annual Pioneer Picnic was held at the Union Oil Company picnic grounds on Newlove Hill. The president of the Pioneer Association that year was cattleman and former World War II prisoner of war Robert W. Rivers, who presided. The program followed the usual procedure, starting at noon with the flag salute, the benediction, and the introduction of the past presidents attending, with the picnickers feasting on Santa Maria style barbecue afterwards. Beyond that, there is no available record of the particulars of the 1977 picnic.

1978

The 54th annual Pioneer Picnic was held Saturday, July 8, 1978, at the Union Oil Company picnic grounds on Newlove Hill. Edward ("Crow") James, president of the Pioneer Association, presided. The program started at noon with the flag salute, the benediction, and the introduction of the past presidents attending. Bill Delessi was the speaker of the day. The program was followed by a Santa Maria style barbecue served at 1:00 p.m.

EDDIE JAMES
President, 1978

Al Novo, Eddie James, Hap Worsham, and Harry Goodchild were on the cleanup crew. Most everyone comes to the picnic, buys raffle tickets, pays for the barbecue, eats and enjoys the chatter with other Pioneers and friends, not realizing that other Pioneers have volunteered to clean the tables and cover them with paper tacked down with staples. After the barbecue, Pioneers like the ones listed above had volunteered to do the cleanup work. At the next Pioneer Picnic, you might consider volunteering to assist in putting on a better Pioneer Picnic in the future.

1979

The 55th annual Pioneer Picnic was held on Saturday, July 8, 1979, at the Union Oil picnic grounds on Newlove Hill. Alex Ontiveros, president of the Pioneer Association, presided at the program held at noon, which included a salute to the flag and the introduction of the past presidents who attended.

A Santa Maria style barbecue was served at 1:00 p.m. to the more than 500 Pioneers, their families and guests who spent the afternoon feasting, merrymaking, and visiting under the old oak trees. Music by Joe Herrman and

ALEX ONTIVEROS
President, 1979

his group was provided throughout the afternoon.

Many locals and out-of-towners who had attended the annual Santa Maria High School Alumni Dinner at the Vandenberg Inn on Friday night attended the Pioneer Picnic.

1980

ALEX ONTIVEROS
President, 1980

The 56th annual Pioneer Picnic was held on July 12, 1980, at the Union Oil Company picnic grounds on Newlove Hill. Alex Ontiveros, president, presided for the second year in a row. Apparently no written records of the 1980 picnic have survived.

1981

The 57th annual Pioneer Picnic was held on July 25, 1981, at the Union Oil Company picnic grounds on Newlove Hill. Pauline Lownes Novo, president, presided. Presentation of the flag was by Steven and Cheryl Novo and Doug and Melissa Cox, 7th generation Pioneers.

PAULINE LOWNES NOVO
President, 1981

Peggy Sheehy Bogue sang "America the Beautiful," accompanied by Joe Herrman and his orchestra. The flag salute was led by Virginia Erickson Minks, followed by "The Star-Spangled Banner" by Joe Herrman on harmonica.

John Norris introduced the past presidents. Pauline Lownes Novo welcomed the crowd. The benediction was by Father Bede Johnson.

1982

BETTY MCDONALD
President, 1982

The 58th annual Pioneer Picnic was held July 10, 1982, at the Union Oil picnic grounds on Newlove Hill. Pioneer Association president Betty McDonald presided at the program that started at noon. Father Mark Newman gave the invocation, followed by the playing of "The Star-Spangled Banner" on the harmonica by Joe Herrman, a tearful moment for some.

The flag salute was led by former resident and Pioneer Virginia Erickson Minks. Past presidents introduced by Pauline Novo included Ivan Worsham, Chester Norris, Robert Rivers, Edward James, Barbara Sumner, Gaylord Jones, Dr. Leland Smith, and Glenn Roemer.

Joe Herrman and his group provided music throughout the day. Eddie James and his crew served about 500 members and guests a Santa Maria style barbecue with all the trimmings. Dancing started at about 2:00 p.m.

The annual Pioneer Dinner Dance was held at a later date at the Elks Lodge.

1983

Members and guests of pioneer families held the 59th annual Pioneer Picnic on July 9th, 1983, at the Union Oil Newlove Hill picnic grounds. Curtis Tunnell, president of the Pioneer Association, presided. About 500 pioneers and their families and friends attended.

The day began with a brief opening ceremony that included the presentation of the flags, by Zelda Elliott and Elsie Hayes, and the flag salute, led by Melissa Cox, 15, a 4-H member and seventh-generation Santa Maria Valley resident, followed by a rendition of "America the Beautiful" by Peggy Bogue, with accordion music by Roland Lanini and an invocation by Rev. J. Stanley Parke. The Pioneers and their families and

CURTIS TUNNELL
President, 1983

guests were welcomed by President Tunnell. Pauline Lownes Novo, secretary, introduced the past presidents who were in attendance. At 1:00 p.m. the Santa Maria style barbecue was served.

Many of the Pioneers who attended the Santa Maria Union High School class reunion dinner in the D.E.S. Hall on Friday night for the classes of 1923, 1923½, and 1933 and 1933½, also attended the Pioneer Picnic.

The second annual Santa Maria Valley Dinner Dance was held on August 23, 1983, at the Santa Maria Elks Lodge, with a chicken barbecue followed by dancing to the music of the "Swinging Forties."

1984

Pioneer members and their families and friends attended the 60th annual Pioneer Picnic at the Union Oil picnic grounds at noon on July 14, 1984.

PARNELL TILLEY
President, 1984

Parnell Tilley, Pioneer Association president, presided. The program included the presentation of flags by Fred Buzzini and Elmore Litten; the flag salute, led by Melissa Cox; "America the Beautiful," by Peggy Sheehy Bogue, accordion music by Roland Lanini, invocation by Rev. J. Stanley Parke, and welcome by President Parnell Tilley.

A special award was presented to the past presidents, namely, Jack Glines, Dr. Leland Smith, Gaylord Jones, Ernest Righetti, Barbara Niverth Sumner, James Battles, Ellis Fesler, Monica Bradley Touchstone, Gertrude Rice France, Morris Stephan, Glenn Roemer, Emilio Sutti, William Ruiz, Leland ("Butch") Simas, Ivan Worsham, Chester Norris, Robert Rivers, Edward James, Alex Ontiveros, Pauline Lownes Novo, Betty Evans McDonald, and Curtis ("Curt") Tunnell.

After the ceremonies, a Santa Maria style barbecue was prepared and served by Eddie James and his crew. Many of the Santa Maria Union High School alumni who attended the annual dinner at the D.E.S. Hall on Friday night honoring the classes of 1924, 1934, and 1944, attended the picnic on Saturday.

The third annual Santa Maria Valley Pioneer Dinner Dance was held at the Elks Lodge on Saturday, November 17, 1984.

1985

PARNELL TILLEY
President, 1985

The 61st annual Pioneer Picnic was held on Saturday, July 13, 1985, at the Union Oil picnic grounds on Newlove Hill. Parnell Tilley, president of the Pioneer Association, presided. Peggy Sheehy Bogue and the crowd sang "The Star-Spangled Banner," followed by the presentation of the flag by Fred Buzzini and Elmore Litten, after which Melissa Cox led the flag salute. Peggy Sheehy Bogue sang "America the Beautiful." Accordion music was by Roland Lanini, and the invocation was by Rev. J. Stanley Parke. Past presidents were introduced by Vivian Dutton.

A Santa Maria style barbecue prepared by Eddie James and his crew was served at one o'clock. At two o'clock, Omer Meeker's band played for dancing on the 30-foot round dance floor provided through the efforts of Ike Simas. Entertainment was presented by the Ocean Waves square dance group, with Bill Hay doing the calling. The Central Coast Chordsmen, a barbershop group, entertained the crowd with their songs.

Babe Litten and Jim DeRosa conducted a horseshoe tournament, and others played volleyball in the morning. More than 700 attended the Pioneer Picnic. The Pioneer Association 4th annual Dinner Dance was held November 2, 1985, at the Elks Lodge.

1986

SUE STENNER KRAFFT
President, 1986

The Santa Maria Valley Pioneers held their 62nd annual picnic on Saturday, July 12, 1986, at the Union Oil picnic grounds on Newlove Hill, with the program beginning at 12:00 noon.

Sue Stenner Krafft, president of the Pioneer Association, presided. Peggy Sheehy Bogue sang "The Star-Spangled Banner." The presentation of the flag was by Fred Buzzini and Elmore Litten, with the flag salute led by Allison Hallock. Next, Peggy Sheehy Bogue sang "America the Beautiful" and "You're a Grand Old Flag." The invocation was delivered by Rev. J. Stanley Parke, followed by "The Lord's Prayer," sung by Vicki Anderson Wilson.

The president welcomed everyone and introduced all of the past presidents in attendance. She also introduced the new officers: Vivian Dutton, president;

Clarence Donati, vice-president; Jean Denmun, secretary; and Evelyn Muscio, treasurer.

A Santa Maria style barbecue was prepared and served by Eddie James and crew at 1:00 p.m. Dancing started at 2:00 on the round dance floor, with music by the Ponca City Band.

Many of the Santa Maria Alumni Association members who attended the annual dinner on Friday night attended the Pioneer Picnic.

The 5th annual Pioneer Dinner Dance was held on Saturday, November 1, 1986, at the Elks Lodge. Ralph McGray, 96, was crowned King at the dance.

1987

VIVIAN LITTEN DUTTON
President, 1987

More than 800 Pioneers and their descendants attended the 63rd annual Santa Maria Pioneer Association Picnic at the Union Oil campground on Newlove Hill. Vivian Litten Dutton, Association president, presided.

The program started at 12 o'clock noon. Peggy Sheehy Bogue opened the ceremony by singing "God Bless America" and "You're a Grand Old Flag" as the flags were presented by Fred Buzzini and Elmore Litten. Rev. J. Stanley Parke gave the invocation, and Vicki Anderson Wilson sang "The Battle Hymn of the Republic." There was such a crowd at the picnic that Paul Righetti and Carl Novo hauled in a truck loaded with extra tables.

A horseshoe tournament started at 10 o'clock under the direction of Babe Litten. A barbecued beef lunch was prepared and served by Eddie James and his crew at 1:00 p.m. Ike Simas was the coordinator.

The Ole Nelson family had a family reunion in conjunction with the picnic, with 125 members attending.

At 2:00 p.m. the dance floor was crowded. Raffle winners were Bob Eams, Ed Florey, Bill Bright, Barbara Moorhead, Steve Tilley, Shirley Barbezat, and

George Oliver, with Joe Machael winning the afghan donated by Ecelia Enos. The wheelbarrow filled with party supplies was won by Suise Meyers.

1988

CLARENCE DONATI
President, 1988

From old-timers to new children, more than 800 people showed up for sunny skies and good old-fashioned fun at the 64th annual Santa Maria Valley Pioneer Association Picnic at Union Oil picnic grounds on Newlove Hill on July 8, 1988. Association President Clarence Donati presided at the program, which began at 12:00 noon.

The flags were presented by Fred Buzzini and Elmore Litten. Peggy Sheehy Bogue sang "God Bless America" and other patriotic songs, with the audience joining her. The flag salute was led by Allison Hallock, granddaughter of Clarence and Nancy Donati. Rev. J. Stanley Parke delivered the invocation, followed by Vicki Anderson Wilson singing "The Lord's Prayer."

President Clarence Donati welcomed the crowd, and past president Pauline Novo welcomed the new officers. President Donati introduced the past presidents. Assistants for the program were the Police Cadets.

The horseshoe tournament began at 10 o'clock under the direction of Babe Litten. A Santa Maria style barbecue prepared by Eddie James and his crew was served at 1:00 p.m., with dancing at 2:00 p.m. to the music of the Ponca City Band.

The annual Pioneer Dinner Dance was held on November 26 at the Elks Lodge.

1989

The Santa Maria Valley Pioneer Association held its 65th annual picnic at the Union Oil picnic grounds on Saturday, July 8, 1989, with a horseshoe tournament starting at 10:00 a.m. under

CLARENCE DONATI
President, 1989

the direction of Babe Litten.

President Clarence Donati presided at the 12 o'clock noon program. The presentation of the flags was done by Fred Buzzini and Elmore Litten; "The Star-Spangled Banner" was sung by Joe Herrman, with the flag salute by Allison Hallock, granddaughter of Clarence and Nancy Donati. The invocation was delivered by Rev. J. Stanley Parke, after which Vicki Anderson Wilson sang "The Lord's Prayer." Tom Anderson played several numbers on his guitar.

President Donati welcomed the crowd and introduced the new officers and the past presidents. The assistants were the Police Cadets.

A Santa Maria style barbecue was prepared and served by Eddie James and his crew at 1:00 p.m. Ike Simas was the coordinator.

Dancing started at 2:00 p.m. to the music of the Ponca City Band.

Many of the ones attending the Santa Maria Union High School alumni dinner on Friday night at the D.E.S. Hall attended the picnic.

The annual Dinner Dance was held November 25 at the Elks Lodge.

1990

The Santa Maria Pioneer Association held their 66th annual Pioneer Picnic at the Union Oil picnic grounds on Saturday, July 2, 1990. Approximately 600 attended on a picture-perfect day. Eddie James, president of the Association, presided.

EDDIE JAMES
President, 1990

Participants gathered as early as ten o'clock to get a parking space and to attend a day-long game of horseshoes. The program began at noon with the presentation of the flags by the Boy Scouts, followed by patri-

otic songs by Peggy Bogue, "The Star-Spangled Banner" by Joe Herrman on his harmonica, and the flag salute by Jennie Openshaw, daughter of Mr. and Mrs. Dale Openshaw. "The Lord's Prayer" was sung by Vicki Anderson Wilson.

President James welcomed the crowd and introduced the new officers and the past presidents.

The Central Coast Cloggers enlivened the crowd with some fancy dance steps, after which Gene Leis' one-man band played dance music for the audience. The Elks Kadiddlehopper Clowns entertained the crowd; Boo-Boo the Clown enjoyed showing his "invisible dog" to the children.

Many out-of-towners attended the picnic. A Santa Maria style barbecue was served at 1:00 p.m. Those in attendance brought their own tablecloths, plates, utensils, salads, desserts and drinks. Some Pioneers take advantage of the annual picnic as a setting for their own family reunions.

Dancing started at 2:00 p.m. to the music of the Ponca City Band.

The annual Pioneer Dinner Dance was held November 17 at the Elks Lodge.

1991

EARL BURGER
President, 1991

The Santa Maria Valley Pioneer Association held their 67th annual picnic at the Unocal picnic grounds on Newlove Hill on July 13th, 1991. Earl Burger, Association president, welcomed the crowd as the meeting began at 12 o'clock noon, followed by the presentation of the flags and the flag salute. Joe Herrman played "The Star-Spangled Banner" on his harmonica, and Peggy Sheehy Bogue and her Pioneerettes warmed things up with some patriotic songs. The benediction was by Rev. Bernard Carreira, son-in-law of Pioneers J.C. and Mary Conn. President Burger also introduced the new officers and then the past presidents. New officers announced were Jim May, president; Oliver Nelson, vice president; Jean Denmun, secretary; and Ike Simas, treasurer.

The horseshoe tournament started at 10:00 a.m. under the direction of Babe and Charlie Litten.

A beef barbecue was served at 1:00 p.m. along with beans, toasted garlic bread, and coffee. Those attending furnished their own tablecloths, plates, utensils, salads, desserts, and drinks.

Dancing started at 2:00 p.m. and lasted until the last couple fell by the wayside.

The annual Dinner Dance was held on November 30, 1991, at the Elks Lodge, with Jean Hadsell serving as chairperson.

1992

The 68th Annual Pioneer Picnic was held at the Unocal Oil Picnic Grounds on Newlove Hill on Saturday, July 11, 1992. Jim May, president of the Pioneer Association, presided. The program started at 12:00 noon. The presentation of flags was by Justin Dutton and

JIM MAY
President, 1992

Teri Anderson-Buttitta, with the flag salute led by Tommy Wilson and patriotic songs sung by the Pioneerettes. The benediction was by Reverend Bernard Carreira, son-in-law of Pioneers Mary and J.C. Conn. Vicki Anderson Wilson followed with a religious song, "Bring Him Home."

President Jim May welcomed the crowd and introduced the new officers and the past presidents in attendance.

The Police Cadets assisted in many ways, from helping the old folks to directing orderly parking.

Honorary board members named were Chester Norris and Robert Rivers. The program was planned by Vicki Anderson Wilson. Jim Michael, Joe Hadsell and crew were the barbecuers. The horseshoe tournament was held at 10:00 a.m. under the direction of

Babe and Charlie Litten. Dancing began at 1:00 p.m.

The annual Pioneer Dinner Dance took place at the Elks Lodge on November 28. Jean Hadsell was in charge.

1993

OLIVER NELSON
President, 1993

The Santa Maria Valley Pioneer Association held their 69th annual Pioneer Picnic at the Unocal picnic grounds, Newlove Hill. Oliver Nelson, Pioneer Association president, presided over the short program that started at 12 o'clock with the pledge of allegiance to the flag. The Pioneerettes sang many wonderful songs, which everyone enjoyed. It was announced that the Santa Maria Airport Board and the Santa Maria City Council are still negotiating for our planned Pioneer picnic grounds.

A Santa Maria style barbecue was served at 1:00 p.m. along with beans, bread and coffee. Participants brought their own tablecloths, plates, utensils, salads, desserts and drinks.

The annual dinner dance was held at the Santa Maria Elks Lodge on November 3, 1993. Jean Hadsell was chairman for this special occasion.

1994

The Santa Maria Valley Pioneer Association held their 70th annual picnic on Saturday, July 9th, 1994, at the Unocal picnic grounds on Newlove Hill. Betty Haslam Carr, president of the Pioneer Association, presided.

The program began at noon with the presentation of the flags by the Boy Scouts of America Troop 72, with Scoutmaster Mike Velasquez, followed by the flag

BETTY HASLAM CARR
President, 1994

salute by Betty Haslam Carr.

The Pioneerettes—Meleny and Jennifer Gotchal, Katie Novo, Aimee and Kara Marchant, Christina Ploutz, Katlyn Wilson and Darico Hadsell—sang "The Star-Spangled Banner" and a sing-along of memory songs. The invocation was by Rev. Bernard Carreira, son-in-law of Pioneers Mary and J.C. Conn.

President Betty Carr then welcomed the crowd and introduced the past presidents attending. Honorary board members were Chester Norris and Robert Rivers.

A Santa Maria style barbecue was served at 1:00 p.m. by Jim Michaels, Joe Hadsell and crew. Al Novo and his crew toasted and served the buttered French bread, while Eddie James and his crew prepared and served the beans.

The annual Pioneer Dinner Dance was held on November 12th at the Elks Lodge; the chairperson was Jean Hadsell.

1995

JAY OPENSHAW
President, 1995

The Santa Maria Valley Pioneer Association held its 71st annual picnic at Unocal picnic grounds—the last time at this location.

Jay Openshaw, president, presided. The program, under the direction of Vicki Anderson Wilson, began at noon with the Pledge of Allegiance, followed by patriotic songs sung by the Pioneer-ettes. Children were encouraged to participate.

A new American flag was donated to the Pioneers from Andrea Seastrand and presented to President Jay Openshaw by Kathryn Brickey Williams.

At 1:00 p.m. a barbecue was served, consisting of barbecued beef, beans, bread and coffee. Pioneers brought their own tablecloths, plates, utensils, desserts and drinks.

During the afternoon, Pioneers enjoyed a horseshoe tournament, live music, and a raffle.

Boy Scout Troop No. 57 assisted in the day's activities, under the direction of Scoutmaster Craig Beebe.

1996

RICHARD CHENOWETH
President, 1996

The Santa Maria Valley Pioneer Association's 72nd annual picnic and new Pioneer Park dedication was held on Saturday, July 13, 1996, at the new Pioneer Park at the intersection of West Foster Road and South Blosser Road. Association President Richard Chenoweth presided.

The program started at 12:00 noon with the presentation of the flags by Albert Novo and Jim May, followed by the salute by Pauline Lownes Novo. Earl Jennings, vice-president, welcomed the crowd of about 1000 and introduced the new officers.

The Proclamation was by Joe Centeno, mayor pro-tem of Santa Maria, after which Clarence Donati spoke about "The Reality of Pioneer Park." Rev. Bernard Carreira gave the invocation. President Chenoweth introduced the past presidents, followed by patriotic songs by the Pioneerettes, Bret Bennett, Jennifer and Melodie Gotchal, Dariel Hadsell, Katie Novo and Katlyn Wilson.

Following the program, Ike Simas, Jim Michaels, Joe Hadsell and crew prepared and served a Santa Maria style barbecue, accompanied by bread from Albert Novo and crew, and beans and coffee by Ed James and crew. Dinner ticket takers were Yvonne Bilardi and Laverne Hesson. Others on the picnic production staff included the vendors of barbecue tickets and name tags, organizers of the raffle and the raffle gifts, clean-up crew, and assistant Boy Scouts. It takes a lot of volunteers to put on a successful barbecue!

The annual Pioneer Dinner Dance was held on November 13, 1996, at the Elks Lodge. The chairperson was Jean Hadsell.

1997

The Santa Maria Valley Pioneer Association held its 73rd annual picnic in the new Pioneer Park on West Foster Road on Saturday, July 12, 1997. George Hobbs, association president, presided.

GEORGE HOBBS
President, 1997

The presentation of flags was by Al Novo and Clarence Donati; the salute was led by Jud and Marilyn Bell Munger, followed by an invocation by Rev. Bernard Carreira and the welcome and introduction of new officers by President George Hobbs, who also introduced the honorary board member Robert Rivers.

The past presidents attending were Pauline Lownes Novo, Richard Chenoweth, Glenn Roemer, Betty Haslam Carr, Ed "Crow" James, Bob Rivers, George Hobbs and Jay Openshaw.

George Hobbs said the largest crowd in the Association's history attended the 72nd annual picnic in 1996. It was the first at our new picnic grounds on West Foster Road. "This year's picnic should tell us whether people just came out to see the new Pioneer Park last year," he noted, "or whether the close proximity of the new park will result in larger attendance from now on."

Vicki Anderson Wilson was in charge of the program. Ed James and crew did the barbecuing; the sound system was courtesy of the Elks (Ike Simas); the raffle was conducted by Jean Hadsell and Grace Glenn Kyle, with assistance by the Boy Scouts.

Music at the picnic was by Mike Arriola, leader of the volunteer band "Class Action." The Elks Lodge Kadiddlehopper Clowns entertained the children.

The barbecue was served at 1:00 p.m. and included barbecued beef, beans, coffee and garlic bread.

1998

The Santa Maria Valley Pioneer Association held its 74th annual Pioneer Picnic at Pioneer Park on West Foster Road on July 11, 1998.

Vicki Anderson Wilson, president of the Association, presided. Tommy Wilson and Makenzie Novo presented the flags. Clarence and Nancy Donati led the flag salute; Joey Buttitta played the national anthem on the saxophone, Rev. Bernard Carreira gave the invocation, and Vicki Anderson Wilson gave the welcome and introduced all the past presidents attending.

The Junior Pioneers who performed consisted of Christina Ploutz, Kevin McCall, Jennifer Gotchal, Katlyn Wilson, Maggie Evans, Trent Evans, Sam Evans, Whitney Bouquet, Dayna Bouquet, Travis Carr, Delaney Carr, Joseph Reynoso, Scott Chenoweth, Brian Chenoweth, T.J. Chenoweth, Matt Chenoweth, Meghan Olivera, Katie Novo, and Joey Buttitta. Christopher Donati performed "The Orange

VICKI ANDERSON WILSON
President, 1998

Blossom Special"; Christina Ploutz, "I've Got Rhythm"; and Meghan Olivera, "Boogie Woogie Choo Choo Train."

Bob Black conducted the horseshoe tournament.

A Santa Maria style barbecue was served at 1:00 p.m. by Ed James and his crew. Members brought their tablecloths, utensils, plates, salads, desserts and drinks.

Entertainment was provided by the Class Action band, the Kadiddlehopper Clowns, and the Junior Pioneers (grandchildren).

Many of the Pioneers work hard before each Pioneer Picnic to make new improvements or additions so as to have an even better Pioneer Park for the annual Pioneer Picnic and many others who enjoy the park for their parties.

Family and memorial bronze plaques displayed at the park are available for a $300 donation. This money is used for improving the park.

1999

VICKI ANDERSON WILSON
President, 1999

The Santa Maria Valley Pioneer Association held its 75th annual Pioneer Picnic at Pioneer Park on West Foster Road on July 10, 1999.

Past presidents of the Pioneer Association Clarence Donati and Pauline Novo brought in the flags with an honor guard of all past presidents attending the picnic. The American flag which had covered the casket of Carl D. Lownes, Pauline Novo's father, in 1920, was raised on the new flagpole designed by Louie Avila. Secretary Joann Enos Kauffman led the Pledge of Allegiance, and president Vicki Anderson Wilson sang "The Star-Spangled Banner." Vice-president Carolyn Conrad McCall gave the invocation.

Ike Simas was the barbecue coordinator, with Jim Erickson and crew doing the barbecue. These old timers certainly have the know-how to put on a good barbecue.

There was dancing to the music of Sound on Sound; the Kadiddlehopper Clowns were there for the children, and there was entertainment by the grandchildren, the Junior Pioneers.

This year the Junior Pioneers were Meghan Olivera, Blake Ferini, Kara, Terra, and Tori Marchant, Joseph Reynoso, Bailey Graf, Corrie Williams, Kaitlyn Fitz-Gerald, Clairesse Brogoitti, Danielle and Jenna Narron, Alexandra and Keaton Eldridge, Kevin McCall, Christina Ploutz, Jennifer Gotchal, Britney Glenn and Seth Wilkinson.

2000

The 76th Annual Pioneer Picnic was held on July 8, 2000, at beautiful Pioneer Park. From 10:00 a.m. to 1:00 p.m. the Pioneers could buy barbecue tickets from Les Leal, Joann Kauffman, and Ann Openshaw, raffle tickets from Jean Roinestad Hadsell, and 50/50 drawing tickets from Jo Teixeira. The dinner ticket takers were Carolyn McCall and Tricia McCall; Ernie George and George Hobbs served as greeters. Cleanup was done by Frank Marta and his crew, while plaques were provided by Earl and Bobbie Jennings. The Boy Scouts served as assistants. Music for the picnic was provided by the band Sound on Sound. Mailing of the picnic letters had been done by Jean Roinestad Hadsell.

The day's program began at 12:00 noon, with Vicki Anderson Wilson, president of the Pioneer Association, presiding. Past presidents Clarence Donati, Pauline Lownes Novo, and Vivian Litten Dutton brought in the flags, with an honor guard of

VICKI ANDERSON WILSON
President, 2000

past presidents including Oliver Nelson, Edward James, George Hobbs, Betty Haslam Carr, Robert Rivers, and Jay Openshaw. Tommy Wilson led the Pledge of Allegiance. The invocation and presentation of the president's plaque were done by Carolyn Conrad McCall, president-elect for the year 2000-2001.

Next on the program were songs and dances by the Junior Pioneers, which were enjoyed by everyone. Participants included Meghan Olivera, Kevin McCall, Kevin and Kayla Brown, Bailey Graf, Joseph and Jacob Reynoso, Alexandra Eldridge, Jenna and Danielle Narron, Amy Stowe, Corrie Williams, Chelsey and Katie Harper, Onjolee McGill, and Christina Ploutz.

A Santa Maria style barbecue was served by Joe Hadsell and his crew at 1:00 p.m. Ike Simas, the barbecue coordinator, joined Don and Kirk McCall and Norman Burke in preparing the toasted garlic french bread. The beans were cooked by Eddie James and his crew. They all pitched in to serve and keep the lines rolling for the 900 who attended.

We've mentioned the names of the above participants to show that these Pioneer Picnics don't just happen all by themselves. Many of the Pioneers and their families may have the impression that the picnic experience amounts to being there, buying your tickets for various things, listening to the program, enjoying the companionship of old friends, eating a delicious barbecue, and then wandering home without too much thought about the many volunteers who made it possible.

The annual Dinner Dance was held later in the year, on November 18, at the Santa Maria Elks Lodge. The chairperson was Jean Hadsell.

2001

The Santa Maria Valley Pioneer Association held their 77th annual Pioneer Picnic at Pioneer Park on July 14, 2001.

Carolyn Conrad McCall, Pioneer Association president, presided. The program started at noon with the presentation of the flags by the past presidents. A

CAROLYN CONRAD McCALL
President, 2001

Pioneer flag was presented by Ann Openshaw in memory of her husband, Jay Openshaw. Christina Ploutz sang the National Anthem.

Carolyn welcomed the crowd and introduced the past presidents and the board of the Pioneer Association. Tommy Wilson gave the invocation. Carolyn then honored several special Pioneers by dedicating the new Pavilion in honor of Albert Novo and

Pauline Lownes Novo—truly a well-deserved honor. The Novos and others celebrated by dancing on the new concrete dance floor in front of the Pavilion to the music of "Sound on Sound."

A new area was added to Pioneer Park this year, called Clarence Donati's Hideaway. Carolyn dedicated this area to Clarence Donati, who was in charge of laying out the park from the very beginning. This area has a barbecue pit and tables to accommodate parties of 100 persons.

Jim Gamble was also honored for being in charge of the building of the Pavilion and the concrete dance floor.

Following the dedication, there were songs and dances by the Junior Pioneers, Meghan Olivera, Kevin McCall, Joseph and Jacob Reynoso, Allison Lades, Jenna and Danielle Narron, and Chelsey and Katie Harper. The Senior Strutters, under the direction of Audrey Pezzoni Silva, did several acts that were enjoyed by everyone.

The new Pavilion and concrete dance floor are a very welcome addition to Pioneer Park, and all the volunteers should be congratulated for building such a beautiful building.

A Santa Maria style barbecue, coordinated by Ike Simas, was prepared and served by Joe Hadsell, Jim Erickson and crew at 1:00 p.m.

The annual Pioneer Dinner Dance was held at the Elks Lodge on November 10, 2001, under the direction of chairperson Jean Hadsell.

He Makes Every Picnic a Success

Ike Simas, the "King Pin" in charge of all the barbecue facilities at every Pioneer Picnic, is the one who makes every picnic a success. Don't let that relaxed look fool you—he knows what is going on at all times and will have the meat, beans, and toasted garlic french bread ready at serving time. You just didn't learn that from reading Tesene's book, *Santa Maria Style Barbecue.* Thank you, Ike!

The Pioneer Flag

Ann Openshaw admires the new Pioneer Association flag, dedicated to the memory of her late husband Jay.

The Santa Maria Valley Pioneer Association flag was voted on at the March 2001 meeting of the Board of Directors. Ann Openshaw, wife of former Pioneer President Jay Openshaw, wanted to donate the flag in Jay Openshaw's name. Jay had died just months before. Vicki Anderson Wilson was in charge of getting the flag. She had it made with a white background and military blue lettering and stagecoach logo. The flag was produced by the American Flag Company of Arroyo Grande.

In the parade of past presidents at the 2001 Pioneer Picnic, the flag was carried by Vicki Anderson Wilson, immediate past president and current vice president, and was hoisted up the flag pole for the first time by Clarence Donati. During the program at the picnic, the flag was dedicated to the memory of Jay Openshaw by President Carolyn Conrad McCall. It will proudly fly at all future Pioneer Picnics at Pioneer Park.

The following nine pages are reprinted from the 1997 book
Santa Maria Style Barbecue, *with permission of the author, R.H. Tesene.*
Several minor corrections have been made.

The Santa Maria Pioneer Association's Quest

to find a suitable location and promote a new permanent Pioneer Park

Jim May (above) spent many trying days, weeks and months in charge of promoting the location for Santa Maria Valley Pioneer Park. He also assisted in the trimming of the oak trees when the site was being cleared for the barbecue pit, tables and other facilities. He and the other volunteers learned a few lessons about how to respect the poison oak!

The Pioneer Park was more than six years in the making. During the 1980's, Pioneer board member Pauline Novo plugged for a Pioneer-owned and controlled park for their barbecues and picnics, but without success. For many years they held these barbecues at the Union Oil Company barbecue facility on Orcutt Hill. When Union Oil Company, now known as UNOCAL, decided to sell that and other properties, the Pioneer board made a decision to find a new place for their social affairs. Pauline persuaded the Board to invite Jim May, a fourth-generation Pioneer, former City Councilman, planning commissioner, Realtor, and retired diplomat, to fill a Board vacancy and take on the challenge of finding and promoting a new permanent Pioneer Park.

During 1990 Jim investigated many potential sites. In addition to being generally suitable for a Pioneer

Park facility, it had to be well-located, suitably zoned, environmentally appropriate, economically feasible and politically possible. After much research, the Pioneer Board narrowed their interest to a 13-acre parcel owned by the Santa Maria Public Airport Board at the southeast corner of South Blosser and West Foster Roads —the site of the last California live oak grove on the Santa Maria Valley floor. Subsequently there were numerous meetings, hearings, proposals and counter-proposals with the Santa Maria Public Airport Board, but their decision was that they had other plans for that property.

As 1991 progressed, the focus was on publicizing the Pioneer Park proposal, recruiting more founder-sponsor organizations, firming up the Pioneer Board and general membership support, and gaining the support and cooperation of the City's Director of Parks and Recreation and their commission members, planning commission members, and the Mayor and City Councilmen.

Two new Airport Board of Directors, Ken Bruce and Ed Hennon, had committed to help make the Pioneer Park a reality. Over the next four years they delivered on that commitment.

Several new founder organizations joined the effort. Representatives of the Lions Club Sight Conservation Foundation of Santa Maria, the Noontime Lions Club, and the Santa Maria Valley Jaycees met regularly with the Pioneer Association regarding the new proposed Pioneer Park. It was agreed by consensus that the Pioneer Association would be the lead agency to obtain the land and develop the barbecue facilities, and the Lions and Jaycees would handle the planning and creation of a community center building.

In 1992 the Airport's Land Use Committee agreed in principle to allow the Pioneers, Lions, and others the eventual use of a portion of the 40-acre parcel that contained the oak grove for a Pioneer Park facility. Then a great promotional program developed to get approval of all governmental agencies involved. During the year, the City Recreation and Parks Commission and the City Council gave their unanimous and enthusiastic conceptual approval. A letter was sent to the Airport Board requesting negotiations between the City and the Airport for an appropriate lease.

In 1993 informal "politicking" continued throughout the year.

Experiencing the ambience of the future Pioneer Park location are (from left) Richard Chenoweth, President 1995, Jay Openshaw, Vicki Anderson Wilson and Earl Jennings. The photo shoot was part of a field trip the Pioneers took to explore the site.

The Airport Board decided to postpone all lease negotiations until after the new Airport Master Plan was completed. An election was held for several new Airport Board members, and Muril Clift, a Lion and active member of the Pioneer Park Coalition Committee, won a seat on the Board. This gave the Pioneer Park Committee a solid majority support of the Airport Board.

During 1994 continuing efforts were made to persuade the Airport Board to lease a parcel to the Pioneer Association. The Airport Board members and staff, City Council members and staff worked with the Pioneer Park Association and developed a very attractive lease agreement on 13 acres of land at the southeast corner of Blosser Road and West Foster Road, where the California live oak trees are located. The final lease was signed by both parties,

taking effect in August. The Pioneer Association promptly sealed the contract by delivering a check to the Airport Board for the first year's annual payment of eighty-four dollars and fifty cents ($84.50). The Pioneers wasted no time in starting to improve the site to be known as Pioneer Park and to be administered by the Santa Maria Parks and Recreation Department. Thus this beautiful, well-located park, when completed, will be available for public and private barbecues for parties of up to 1000 persons. What a feeling of satisfaction that must bring to everyone who was involved in promoting the Pioneer Park, and especially to Jim May, the Board member elected to help do the job! Many people say that had it not been for Jim May, we would not have accomplished such a mission.

Santa Maria Valley's New Pioneer Park

by Pauline Novo
Past President, Foundation Board
Secretary and Historian

The thought, or dream, of having our own Santa Maria Valley Pioneer Park started when I was a little girl. My grandmother, Marcia Logan Lownes, used to take me to the annual Pioneer Picnic, which at that time and for many years was held on the Cuyama Highway about twenty miles east of Santa Maria.

The road seemed so long and was so crooked, and I always got carsick. My grandmother said, "Oh, how I wish we had a Pioneer Park down in the Santa Maria Valley."

The thought emerged again when I became a member of the Pioneer Board of Directors in 1979. Later I brought it up several times, but to no avail. Finally in one of our meetings we decided to try.

Pioneer Jim May was asked to find a site, and we picked the southeast corner of West Foster Road and South Blosser Road, because of the beautiful grove of oak trees there. I asked Jim if he would be on our Board of Directors, and the politics started.

For about five years we had working lunch meetings, joined by Lions Club members and Jaycees, who later folded up. We went to meetings of the Airport Board, Parks & Rec, and the Santa Maria City Council, and we wrote letters!

The airport was the last to come around, thanks to Airport Directors Muril Clift, Ed Hennon and Ken Bruce. We acquired 13 acres, leased by the city from the Airport. Park development was to be done by the Pioneers, with the park to be rented out by the Santa Maria Parks & Recreation Department.

We formed a "Pioneer Park Foundation" which applied for non-profit status, wrote by-laws, and got busy. The Lions Club is planning to build a Community Center Building just east of and adjoining the picnic grounds.

Without the men who volunteered, equipment and materials that were donated, the volunteer trucks that hauled it there, and the donated money, it never would have happened.

It was a battle to get rid of the poison oak. The sewer and water lines were put in by May 1996. We paid for the sewer; the water line was installed by volunteers. The pipe was donated.

The tables that are now in place are awesome: they can seat about 700 people. Our thanks to welding chairman Brian Sheehy and his crew! The tables were christened with a festive champagne lunch.

The barbecue pit, built by Jim Gamble and his family, is beautiful. The grills and metal work on the pit were all welded and planned by Fred Hummel, Clyde Stokes and Jessie Garcia. When it was finished, we had another champagne christening to celebrate.

Jim Gamble was in charge of all the concrete work in our new park. With the help of Jimmy Gamble III and Kenny Gamble, he placed forms for pouring concrete. Many helpers assisted in screeding dirt, placing steel and pouring the cement. Two of the main helpers were Ray Smith and Al Smith. The concrete finishers were Jim Gamble, Johnnie Centeno, Joe Centeno, Jim Livesay, R.C. Leffew, Kenny

PIONEER PARK VOLUNTEER WORKERS

All of the Santa Maria Valley Pioneers are very, very grateful for the new park, and would like to thank the following individuals and companies for their part in helping to build this beautiful park in less than a year.

WORK CREW					
Michael Bouquet	Bill Lukeman	Bill Weeks	Dick Donati	Kenny Gamble	David Nivarro
Norman Burke	Frank Marta		Easter Rents	Ronnie Gamble	John Ortega
Clarence Donati	Jim May	*TRUCK*	Engel & Gray		Brian Sheehy
George Donati	Bruce McKibben	*HAULING*	R.C. Leffew	*ACCOUNTANT*	David Souza
Jim Donati	Leo Moore	Monte Epps	Kyle Roofing	Trent Benedetti	Rick Teixeira
Kory Donati	Albert Novo	Mike Gotchal	Able Portable Johns		
Chuck Feliz	Larry Rivas	Gary Murphy	Sheehy Berry Farms	*WELDERS FOR*	*MATERIAL*
Jessie Garcia	Lawrence Rivas	Butch Pope	T&G Water Truck	*TABLES*	*DONATED*
Ernie George	Herschel Rouse	Craig Reed	Service	David Avila	Cal Coast Irrigation
Gordon Gill	Martin Shiffrar			Richard Freitas	Coast Rock
Frank Gomes	Al Smith	*EQUIPMENT*	*BBQ PIT*	Jessie Garcia	Fence Factory
Lillian Hallock	Ray Smith	*DONATED*	*BUILDERS*	Bill Gill	Frazee Paint
Ed James	Alfred Soares	Betteravia Farms	Darrel Gamble	Fred Hummel	Hayashi
Allen Kemp	Clyde Stokes	City of Santa Maria	Jason Gamble	Marshall Munger	Irrigation West
Ron Leon	Steve Tilley	A.J. Diani	Jim Gamble	John Nicely	Pacific Ag Water
	Neil Toy		Jimmy Gamble		Unocal

Gamble, Jimmy Gamble, Emanuel Hamilton and Darrell Gamble. These workers worked on the concrete around the pit, serving lines, dance floor, restrooms and the first speaker's stand, which was removed when the pavilion was built.

The entrance gate was built by Brian Sheehy. Notice the "Pioneer Park" sign he made out of iron and put in the middle of the gate.

The base material was donated by Steve Will of Coast Rock. It covers the road in and all the table areas for easy walking.

There are so many volunteers that I can't list them all here, but their names will be posted at our Pioneer Park.

A few guys—Clarence Donati, Al Novo, Albert Smith, Ron Leon—started working out there. The brush was thick, the trees needed trimming—there was a lot of work to do. As days went by, more Pioneer men appeared, and once they got interested in the project, they kept at it, and many are still working—day after day.

A few strained backs, a few bouts with poison oak, a day off here and there, and right back to work. Talk about a bunch of dedicated Pioneers!

Clarence Donati was chairman of the grounds work, and he did a wonderful job of laying out the park, following through on every detail.

Al Novo was co-chairman, and also spent a lot of time there. Earl Jennings is going to mount all the plaques on the wall.

A lot of man power went into this project. Our retired men really did show us that they aren't done yet! They are proud of their accomplishments. Some of our younger generation got involved, worked hard, and someday will be able to say, "I helped build this park."

The ladies took lunch out once in awhile and got all the mailing done. I was determined to have our first picnic at our Pioneer Park in 1996. They told me it couldn't be done—I was accused of dreaming again. But with this goal in mind, look what our men have done! They built Pioneer Park in one year!

I wrote three newsletters and raised over $40,000, donated by our interested members. Thank you!

For $300 a plaque will be made out of bronze, with your family name or a memorial, and be put on our plaque wall. I'm still collecting donations, because we still need permanent bathrooms, a storage shed, and more. We are looking for grants to help with our ball field and playground equipment.

THE SANTA MARIA VALLEY PIONEER ASSOCIATION

In 1868-69 the first homesteaders came to what is now known as the Santa Maria Valley. In 1923 the descendants organized a group to commemorate and honor the pioneers, holding their first picnic in 1925. The Pioneer picnics first took place on the Alamo Creek, later moving to a site on the Cuyama Highway approximately 13 miles east of Santa Maria. Later they were held at Waller Park, and then for many years at the Union Oil picnic grounds on Newlove Hill south of Orcutt. About five years ago, several of the Pioneers became active in finding a permanent location that would be known as Pioneer Park. By 1996 it finally became a reality.

A grand opening barbecue was held on July 13, 1996, for the 72nd Annual Santa Maria Pioneer Picnic, and 900 to 1000 persons attended. Wow, what a party! It was a beautiful day, with plenty of excitement, entertainment and good food, truly a good place for everyone to see old friends and make new acquaintances.

The Santa Maria Valley Pioneer Association, started in 1925, has never missed having an annual picnic. In spite of depressions, wars, droughts, floods and so on, these Pioneers and their descendants are determined that these picnics and other functions must go on. Thus it has grown to over 1000 members and associate members. Our hats are off to them and the past presidents listed herewith. Large scrap books of pictures and activities during the past years have been made by Pauline Novo and are available to enjoy at the Santa Maria Valley Historical Society Museum.

PAST PRESIDENTS
of the Santa Maria Valley Pioneer Association

1924-1925 . . F.C. Twitchell	1944-1945 . . Walter W. Stokes	1963-1964 . . Marinus Neilsen	1982-1983 . . Curtis Tunnell
1925-1926 . . W.H. Rice	1945-1946 . . Audel Davis	1964-1965 . . Ida Wylie Jones	1983-1984 . . Parnell Tilley
1926-1927 . . W.C. Oakley	1946-1947 . . Raymond Strong	1965-1966 . . Morris J. Stephan	1984-1985 . . Parnell Tilley
1927-1928 . . W.H. Tunnell	1947-1948 . . Ida Hawkins	1966-1967 . . Elizabeth Oakley May	1985-1986 . . Sue Stenner Krafft
1928-1929 . . Judge L.J. Morris	1948-1949 . . Ernest E. Righetti	1967-1968 . . William Elliott	1986-1987 . . Vivian Litten Dutton
1929-1930 . . Judge S.E. Crow	1949-1950 . . Catherine Fickert	1968-1969 . . Glenn A. Roemer	1987-1988 . . Clarence Donati
1930-1931 . . M.P. Baker	1950-1951 . . Marion Rice	1969-1970 . . J. Dorian Davis	1988-1989 . . Clarence Donati
1931-1932 . . H.R. Saulsbury	1951-1952 . . Fred May	1970-1971 . . Emilio Sutti	1989-1990 . . Eddie James
1932-1933 . . H.C. Tunnell	1952-1953 . . Dave Boyd	1971-1972 . . William Ruiz	1990-1991 . . Earl Burger
1933-1934 . . John Fesler	1953-1954 . . Barbara Sumner	1972-1973 . . Leland "Butch" Simas	1991-1992 . . Jim May
1934-1935 . . Alyce Lewis	1954-1955 . . James G. Battles	1973-1974 . . Wilfred "Bull"	1992-1993 . . Oliver Nelson
1935-1936 . . A.F. Black	1955-1956 . . Ellis Fesler	Saunders	1993-1994 . . Betty Haslam Carr
1936-1937 . . Joe S. Calderon	1956-1957 . . Monica Bradley	1974-1975 . . Ivan "Hap" Worsham	1994-1995 . . Jay Openshaw
1937-1938 . . Lou S. Drumm	Touchstone	1975-1976 . . Chester A. Norris	1995-1996 . . Richard Chenoweth
1938-1939 . . Frank C. May	1957-1958 . . George Radke	1976-1977 . . Robert Rivers	1996-1997 . . George S. Hobbs
1939-1940 . . Jack H. Glines	1958-1959 . . Opel Fry	1977-1978 . . Edward "Crow" James	1997-1998 . . Vicki Anderson Wilson
1940-1941 . . Manuel Bello	1959-1960 . . Lesley R. Holland	1978-1979 . . Alex Ontiveros	1998-1999 . . Vicki Anderson Wilson
1941-1942 . . Gaylord Jones	1960-1961 . . Gertrude France	1979-1980 . . Alex Ontiveros	1999-2000 . . Vicki Anderson Wilson
1942-1943 . . Dr. Leland Smith	1961-1962 . . Chester A. Davis	1980-1981 . . Pauline Lownes Novo	2000-2001 . . . Carolyn Conrad McCall
1943-1944 . . Leonald Adam	1962-1963 . . Gertrude M. Clemons	1981-1982 . . Betty McDonald	2001-2002 . . . Carolyn Conrad McCall

Where is Pioneer Park?

The map below shows the location of both Pioneer Park and Waller Park. Each has barbecue pits and tables available to the public. In the photo at right, Santa Maria Pioneer Association members explore the under-construction site of Pioneer Park in December 1995. From left are Gordon Gill, Richard Chenoweth (1995 president), Pauline Novo (Past president and board secretary/historian), and Jim May (past president and board member). Photo courtesy of the *Santa Maria Times,* July 14, 1996.

❶ Pioneer Park
❷ Waller Park
❸ YMCA of Santa Maria Valley

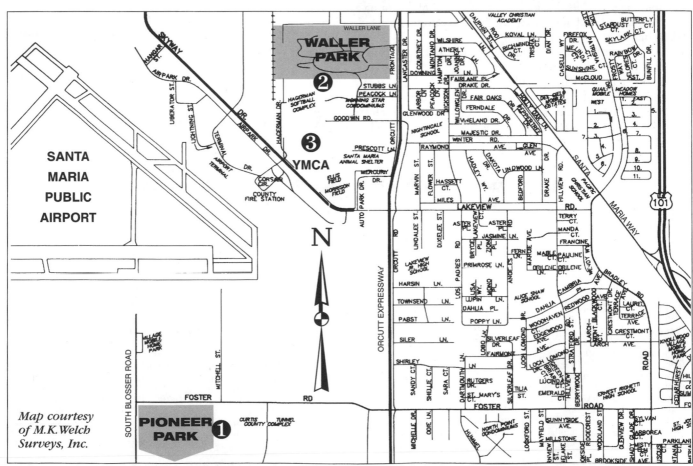

Map courtesy of M.K. Welch Surveys, Inc.

This sign was placed by the City of Santa Maria. A building was being planned at this location for joint use by the Lions and the Pioneer Association.

Santa Maria Valley Pioneer Association
72nd ANNUAL PICNIC
AND PIONEER PARK DEDICATION

Saturday, July 13th, 1996
New Pioneer Park • West Foster and Blosser Road

Headmaster Fred Hummel (left), along with Jessie Garcia and Clyde Stokes, fabricated the steel framework over the barbecue pit and built the mechanism that holds the grates and rods.

Albert Novo (right), co-chairman during Pioneer Park construction, and his grandson, Steven, give a sense of scale to the beautiful hand-made sign provided by Gloria Heide, Regional Chairperson for District 4-A-3, Lions' International.

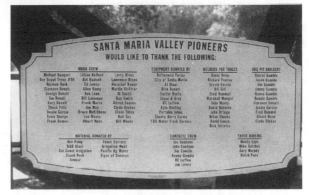

This sign at Pioneer Park thanks the work crews, equipment donors, welders, barbecue pit builders, material donors, concrete crew and truck haulers for a job well done.

This monument will accommodate about 200 bronze plaques for donors to the Pioneer Association. The inset shows some of the plaques to be installed on the monument. Jim Gamble designed the monument and poured the foundation with Kenny Gamble. Jim laid all the bricks; Ray Smith and Clarence Donati were his tenders. The top surface was then poured in concrete by Jim Gamble, Johnnie Centeno, Frank Marta and Jim Livesay.

PIONEER PARK

This beautiful Pioneer Park setting in the shade of well trimmed oak trees with 43 well built picnic tables seating sixteen each could accommodate approximately 700 persons. Between 900 and 1000 showed up for the inaugural picnic on July 13, 1996, but plenty of food had been planned for. This park will be administered by the Santa Maria Parks and Recreation Department.

Clarence Donati (right) was in charge of building Pioneer Park from the ground up over a period of about a year. The park is well planned and everything, including the tables and barbecue pit, are first class. Donati was fortunate to have sufficient equipment and qualified volunteers to transform this sandy brush and poison oak covered area into a most perfect setting for the Grand Opening barbecue.

Co-chairman Al Novo draws attention to the Pioneer Park gate and the cut-out sign made by Brian Sheehy.

Cameraman Rick Fisher caught Joe and Jean Shoup Olivera with their family and friends (left) relaxing after the barbecue. Looks like there's still a cake to be served!

Hungry Pioneer members and friends lined up waiting to be served barbecued top sirloin steak, beans and toasted garlic buttered French bread. Entering the divider is Bob Baker (in the straw hat).

A view from the park looking north shows the entrance gate and a few of the cars parked outside between Foster Road and the rows of eucalyptus trees lining the park.

The beautiful brick barbecue pit at Pioneer Park was built by Darrel, Jason, Jim, Jimmy, Kenny and Ronnie Gamble, Clarence Donati, Jessie Garcia, Fred Hummel, Albert Novo and Clyde Stokes. It can hold 800 lbs. of top block on rods over the fire. Here, author R.H. Tesene tests the mechanism that raises and lowers the separate grate for toasting bread. Both of the other two sections will accommodate rods or grates and can be raised or lowered separately.

The barbecue team on Dedication Day, ready for action: Lawrence Rivas, Steve Reasnor, Carol Sorenson, Dick Malmen, Jim Erickson, Bill Hadsell, Al Smith, Jim Michaels, and chief barbecuer Joe Hadsell all sport Elks' club aprons.

Right: Barbecuers Jim Perry, Carol Sorenson and Dick Malmen (in cap) cut the meat and place it in the pans for the servers. The knives and utensils are kept in the wooden chests in the foreground.

Jim Michaels watches the pit while barbecuers Joe and Bill Hadsell carry pans of sliced steaks.

Right: The Pioneer Park barbecue pit, cutting and preparation tables, with the serving lines at right. Eventually roofs will be installed over these facilities to replace the temporary awning s hown here.

Left: Albert Novo, Ike Simas and Norman Burke (from left) relax after manning the beans, buttering and toasting the French bread, and helping serve the 900 to 100 Pioneers and their guests.

Left: Jim Gamble, who headed the crew that built the brick barbecue pit, points to a special brick marked Rex Café (a café which was a landmark in Whiskey Row, in the 100 block of East Main Street). The brick was made by Jim's father, Harry Gamble.

PIONEER PARK

A champagne toast to christen the 43 new picnic tables! Volunteers included (from left) Al Novo, Al Smith, Ed Hennon (Airport Board), Ray Smith, Ernie George, Clarence Donati, Chuck Feliz, Bill Weeks, and Clyde Stokes.

Tuny Rivas, Les Leal, and Albert Smith cut the top blocks in preparation for the barbecue.

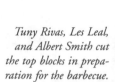

Dick Malmen, Jim Erickson, Carol Sorenson and Bill Hadsell prepare the top block for barbecuing.

Brian Sheehy (inset, left) and his welding crew built the pipe frames for the 43 picnic tables. Lots of fitting and welding was involved. Sheehy also built the entrance gate with the Pioneer Park sign.

Waiting for lunch . . . Clarence Donati, Joe Centeno, John Centeno, Al Novo and Frank Marta display patience.

No more waiting! Pauline Novo shows up with the lunch basket full of good food.

Photos from the Pauline Novo Pioneer Scrapbooks

Bob Leyva, Glenn Roemer, and Fred Buzzini—all faithful Pioneers.

Earl Jennings installed most of the family and memorial bronze plaques on the concrete monument at Pioneer Park.

Clarence Minetti and Butch Simas doing what they liked to do.

Irene and Frank Marta—always ready to help the Pioneers.

Joe and Jean Olivera and their family always have a table reserved at the Pioneer Picnic.

Sheila Bush and Evelyn Muscio—always ready to help at the Pioneer Picnic.

Above: John Wineman and friend. John was still active with the Pioneers well into his nineties.

Parnell and Betty Tilley smile for the camera. No doubt Parnell just made a wise remark about something. He became a two-year Pioneer Association president.

Above: Mr. and Mrs. Bardy Saladin —always at the Pioneer Picnics.

Slim and Kay Juhl, great friends of R.H. and Myrtle Tesene. She was from Hawaii and came to Santa Maria as a teacher. Her father was a perfect host when the Tesenes visited Hawaii.

Below: Joey Buttitta plays "The Star-Spangled Banner" on his saxophone. It is always a pleasure to have the young Pioneers entertain us older ones.

Above: The rest room without the roof was enjoyed by all attending the first Pioneer picnic in 1996. The sunshine and surrounding oaks added to the atmosphere, and gave us the feeling of old ranch and farm days.

Right: Christopher Donati plays the violin to the delight of the other Pioneers.

Below: Tom Urbanske, 5th District Supervisor of Santa Barbara County (left) and former Santa Maria mayor and past Pioneer Association president George Hobbs must be discussing politics.

R.H. and Myrtle Tesene head out for a slow walk at the Pioneer picnic. "People tend to slow down a bit at age 89," says Tese.

Above: The Young Pioneers entertain the crowd by singing a song. (Most of them are singing, anyway.)

Margie Stokes won a prize and is rushing to get it. You never know when your name will be called!

Clarence Donati and John Ruffoni.

Right: Ike Simas and Katherine Brickey Williams in a very relaxed mood at the picnic.

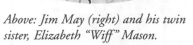

Above: Jim May (right) and his twin sister, Elizabeth "Wiff" Mason.

From left, volunteer workers Jamie Hadsell, Ray Smith, Carol Sorenson, Al Smith, Bill Hadsell, Clyde Stokes and Jim Gamble find a moment to relax.

Above: Christina Ploutz, Carolyn McCall's granddaughter, dances at the Pioneer picnic.

Above: Pioneer Association President Vicki Anderson Wilson and her husband Richard. He is fortunate that she always has to look up to him.

Left: Pearlene Giddings clowns with Ann Openshaw at the picnic. It takes talented people like this to keep us happy.

Dario Ferini enjoys another Pioneer picnic. It looks like cane days for some of us older Pioneers.

Right: Pioneers gather around the barbecue pit. Note the roof structure which shelters the entire pit and serving area. It was built by Pioneer volunteers.

The City of Santa Maria's crew went high into the eucalyptus trees to begin removing the non-native trees that the Pioneers didn't want in the park.

The City of Santa Maria's tree crew prepares to haul away a felled eucalyptus tree next to the bronze plaque monument at Pioneer Park. Thank you, City employees!

Henry "Hank" Datter and Mary Beth enjoy one of the annual Pioneer picnics.

Above: The Boy Scout campfire bowl at Pioneer Park has a firepit with fixed seats on four sides.

This pathway leads to the youth camping area, which includes a volleyball court and five separate camp sites, each with a picnic table, barbecue pit, and water supply. The kids really enjoy themselves here!

For the first time, Louie Avila and Makenzie Novo raise a special American flag on the new flagpole at Pioneer Park. This 48-star flag was the one that covered the casket of Makenzie's great-grandfather, Carl Lownes, in 1920.

Lionel Bowers makes an appearance as "Bud the Cop," an Elks Lodge Kadiddlehopper Clown. Everyone always enjoys the antics these clowns perform.

The 48-star flag flies high on the new Pioneer Park flagpole, which was designed by Louie Avila and constructed and installed by Louie, his son David, and Clyde Stokes.

Rod Rodenberger (left), long-time Santa Maria Recreation and Parks Commissioner, smiles while Ike Simas tries to let everyone know about something. (If you know Ike, it could be about anything . . . or nothing!)

Right: The Junior Pioneers belt out "You're a Grand Old Flag," to the appreciation of all.

Mayor Joe Centeno discusses some important political matters (or something!) with author R.H. Tesene. Tom Urbanske, 5th District Supervisor, smiles in the background. Maybe Joe is asking Tese for another donation for his campaign to take over Tom's job, since Tom announced his decision not to run in 2002.

Jim Gamble's great-grandson and Ron Vertrees' grandson and granddaughter with the Elks Clown at the 2000 picnic.

From left, Carolyn Conrad McCall, Clarence Donati, Nancy Donati and Jim Gamble show off the entrance to Clarence Donati's Hideaway, a section of Pioneer Park where parties of up to 100 can be accommodated.

Some of the past presidents of the Pioneer Association attending the 2000 Pioneer picnic were, from left, Pauline Lownes Novo, Richard Chenoweth, Glenn Roemer, Betty Haslam Carr, Edward "Crow" James, Robert "Bob" Rivers, George S. Hobbs, and Jay Openshaw.

Carolyn Conrad McCall (center), 2001 Pioneer Association president, has just dedicated the new pavilion to Albert Novo and Pauline Lownes Novo. What a surprise for the hard-working and deserving couple! A big thank-you goes out to the Breakfast Rotary Club volunteers who painted the Pavilion, which was designed by Rotary member Jerry Hurley of Hall Hurley Deutsch Architects. Dave Cross of Next Day Signs made and installed the sign—a great addition!

Pioneer Workers Who Donated Their Time on the Construction of the Pioneer Park Pavilion

List compiled by Jim Gamble

Dave Avila
Louis Avila
Dave Cross, *Next Day Signs*
Clarence Donati
Jim Erickson
Jeff Gamble
Jim Gamble
Jimmy Gamble III
Kenny Gamble
Ronnie Gamble
Ruthanne Gamble
Jessie Garcia
Ernest George

Bill Hadsell
David Lorin Hernandez
Jerry Hurley, *Hall Hurley Deutsch, Engineer-Architects*
Kyle Roofing
Les Leal
Frank Marta
Don McCall
Albert Novo
Jim Perry
Rotary Breakfast Club *(helped with the painting)*

Roger Selken, *Santa Maria Noontimers Lions Club*
Ike Simas
Robert L. Simas
Al Smith
Ray Smith
Wayne Souza
Clyde Stokes
Ed Teixeira
Gene Teixeira
Wayne Tiffany

The soaring roof structure over the barbecue pit was completed in 1997.

Onjolee McGill and Meghan Olivera perform a dance to some tap music as part of the entertainment program.

Below: Pioneer children enjoy playing on the new playground equipment.

Abel Maldonado, State Assemblyman from the Santa Maria area, encourages his three children, Erika, Marcus and Nicolas, to smile for the camera.

Right: Jim Gamble mixes concrete for the start of the new Pavilion. Supervising in the background are Clarence Donati and Al Novo.

Below: Jim Gamble's masonry projects at Pioneer Park include this bean bench, specially designed to accommodate large pots of comestibles for the assembled multitude.

The Senior Strutters, under the direction of Audrey Pezzoni Silva (center), perform their dancing act on the concrete pad in front of the Novo Pavilion. Santa Marians have enjoyed the Strutters' colorful costumes and enthusiastic dance routines for over 25 years.

At right, playground equipment furnished and installed by the Santa Maria Parks and Recreation Dept. A substantial donation was made by the Pioneer Association. This was a great addition to the children's playground area. Kevin McCall, at right, tries it out.

The concrete monument on which the 5x7" bronze family and memorial plaques are mounted is almost full. An addition to the monument will be made in 2002. Earl Jennings and others installed all the plaques.

Above, Don McCall hoses off the tables prior to the Pioneer Picnic, while at right, his wife, Pioneer President Carolyn Conrad McCall, helps to clean the picnic grounds. Other volunteers showed that they care and stepped right in to help!

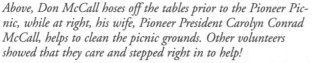

Trent Benedetti (left) has performed an invaluable service by acting as the Pioneer Association's accountant during the process of developing Pioneer Park.

At right: Allene Baichtal, of the Santa Maria Valley Chamber of Commerce, enjoys the Pioneer Picnic at Pioneer Park with a friend.

Left: Joni Gray serves as Supervisor of the Santa Barbara County 4th District. She always supports private enterprise and the welfare of her constituents, and has been a very supportive member of the Santa Maria Valley Pioneer Association. We are very lucky to have a lady of her caliber representing us.

2000 honoree Betty Haslam Carr and family

Honorees

■ Every year, the Pioneer Association dinner dance honors at least one outstanding Pioneer. Here are just a few of the honorees of recent years.

2001 honorees Al Smith (above) and Ernie George (below)

1992 honoree Pauline Lownes Novo (second from left) with her husband, Al, and, at right, her brother Bob Gardner and his wife Patsy.

Above: 1993 honoree Bob Rivers and family.
Below: 1999 honoree Ike Simas and family.

1989 honoree Chet Norris (right) with Glenn Roemer.

THE PIONEERS
GO DANCING

at Annual Picnics and Dinner Dances

Left: Bea Thomas Vallozza dances with her brother-in-law, Eddie Anderson. At right: Alma and Harry Goodchild. Below: Birdie and Bill McDaniel.

Right: Vicki Anderson Wilson dances with John McCurdy. Below: Nancy and Clarence Donati at the 1998 picnic.

Right: Ed and June Parrish Strobridge.

Right: Audrey Silva dances with her son Melvin at the picnic.

■ Dancing and entertainment has always been a special part of any Pioneer function. There has always been music for dancing at the picnics and dinners. In recent years, Sound on Sound has been the popular choice for both picnics and dinners.

Above: Ernie George and Kathy Boyd. Below: Jean and Charlie Denmun.

Peggy Novo Cox dances with her grandson Hayden at the picnic. In the background are Al and Pauline Novo.

Top: Don and Carolyn McCall. Above: Irene and Ike Simas. Below: Bill and Jean Hadsell.

Ann and Jay Openshaw

THE REDHEADS DO THE SINGING

From Julia Beeson Smith, to Peggy Sheehy Bogue, to Vicki Anderson Wilson . . . these ladies' voices have echoed across the valley at the Pioneer Picnics.

From Julia's "Star-Spangled Banner" to Peggy's "God Bless America" and Vicki's "Lord's Prayer," the singing has always been an important part of every Pioneer Picnic.

Julia Beeson Smith in concert (above) and in costume for the title role in Carmen *(left).*

(Left) Peggy Sheehy Bogue with the first Pioneerettes in 1991: Katie and Makenzie Novo and Katlyn Wilson. Below, the Pioneerettes go marching on under the direction of Vicki Anderson Wilson.

Others who have presented vocal solos at the Picnic throughout the years have been Madge Horn, Leah Hatch, Robert Garioto, Rosalee Cutler, Kenneth Hibbard, Margie Stephan and Christina Ploutz.

Vicki belts out her trademark rendition of "The Lord's Prayer" at the 1986 picnic.

Peggy Sheehy Bogue also started the Pioneerettes in 1991. These are the children and grandchildren who perform patriotic songs. This job was taken over by Vicki Anderson Wilson in 1992 and continued through 2001.

Elmore Litten

Four generations of Pioneers! At left, the Glenn girls at Newlove Hill: Gyneth Glenn Carroll, Grace Glenn Vertrees, and Doris Glenn Young.

Below, left: Elmore's daughter Vivian Litten Dutton (center) with Betty Doane Tilley and Pauline Lownes Novo.

Ron Vertrees, son of Grace Glenn Vertrees, with wife Rosalia, daughter Renée Vertrees Reynoso, and grandson Joseph Reynoso III, at the Pioneer Park picnic.

GENERATIONS OF PIONEERS

Below, from left: Katie Novo, Pauline Lownes Novo, Nancy Holloway, Alma Knudsen Goodchild, Aurora Silva Bright, and Grace Barbettini Medina.

Vivian's husband Aubrey Dutton with their grandchild

Collages by Vicki Anderson Wilson

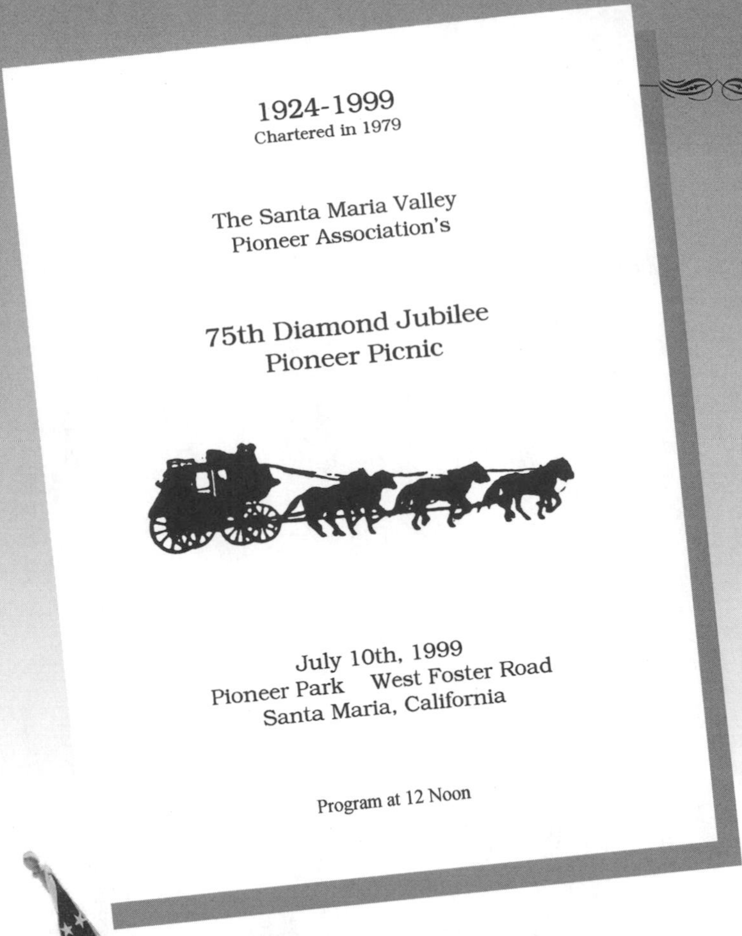

1924-1999
Chartered in 1979

The Santa Maria Valley
Pioneer Association's

75th Diamond Jubilee
Pioneer Picnic

July 10th, 1999
Pioneer Park   West Foster Road
Santa Maria, California

Program at 12 Noon

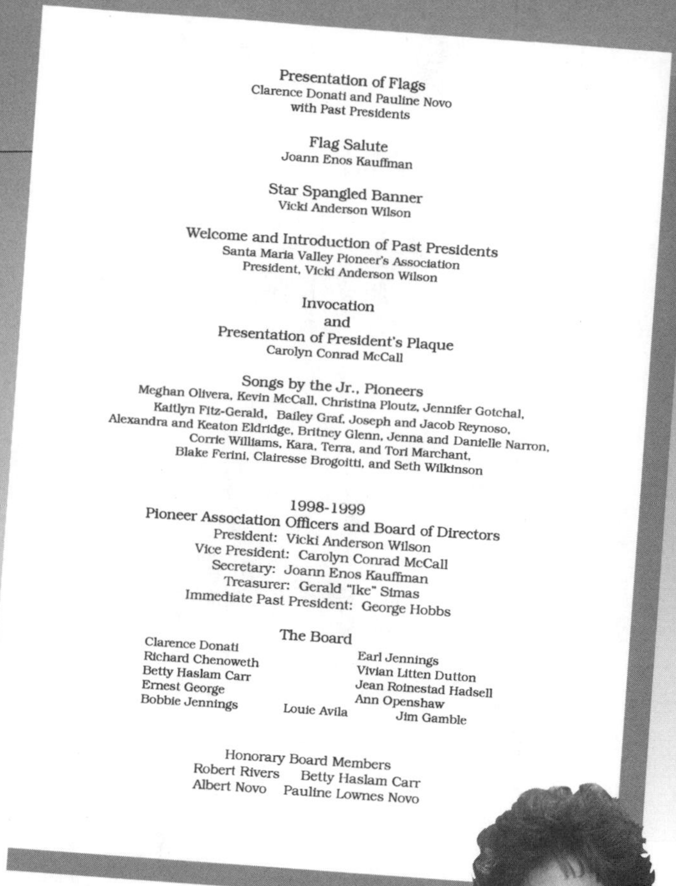

Presentation of Flags
Clarence Donati and Pauline Novo
with Past Presidents

Flag Salute
Joann Enos Kauffman

Star Spangled Banner
Vicki Anderson Wilson

Welcome and Introduction of Past Presidents
Santa Maria Valley Pioneer's Association
President, Vicki Anderson Wilson

Invocation
and
Presentation of President's Plaque
Carolyn Conrad McCall

Songs by the Jr., Pioneers
Meghan Olivera, Kevin McCall, Christina Ploutz, Jennifer Gotchal,
Kaitlyn Fitz-Gerald, Bailey Graf, Joseph and Jacob Reynoso,
Alexandra and Keaton Eldridge, Britney Glenn, Jenna and Danielle Narron,
Corrie Williams, Kara, Terra, and Tori Marchant,
Blake Ferini, Clairesse Brogoitti, and Seth Wilkinson

1998-1999
Pioneer Association Officers and Board of Directors
President: Vicki Anderson Wilson
Vice President: Carolyn Conrad McCall
Secretary: Joann Enos Kauffman
Treasurer: Gerald "Ike" Simas
Immediate Past President: George Hobbs

The Board

Clarence Donati	Earl Jennings
Richard Chenoweth	Vivian Litten Dutton
Betty Haslam Carr	Jean Roinestad Hadsell
Ernest George	Ann Openshaw
Bobbie Jennings	Louie Avila	Jim Gamble

Honorary Board Members
Robert Rivers   Betty Haslam Carr
Albert Novo   Pauline Lownes Novo

*Right: 1999 vice-president
and president, Carolyn
Conrad McCall and Vicki
Anderson Wilson.*

75th
ANNUAL
PICNIC
Santa Maria Valley Pioneer Association

75TH DIAMOND JUBILEE

Above, the parade of past presidents: Glenn Roemer, Clarence Donati, Bob Rivers, Richard Chenoweth, Betty Haslam Carr, Jay Openshaw, and Eddie James. At right, Clarence Donati and Pauline Lownes Novo raise the flag. At left, spectators Kevin McCall and big sis Christina Ploutz.

80

Picnic Production Staff

Barbecue Coordinator..Gerald "Ike" Simas
Barbecue Team...Jim Erickson and Crew
Bread......................................Don & Kirk McCall and Norman Burke
Beans..Eddie James and Crew
Publicity, Program, Jr. Pioneers......................Vicki Anderson Wilson
Servers and Runners...Clarence Donati
Barbecue Tickets......................Betty Haslam Carr & Ann Openshaw
Name Tags......................................Tricia Graham McCall
Raffle......................................Jean Roinestad Hadsell
50/50 Drawing...Jim Gamble
Ticket Printing, Boy Scouts, etc., etc......................Gerald "Ike" Simas
Dinner Ticket Takers....................Joann Kauffman & Carolyn McCall
Greeters.................................Ernie George and Richard Chenoweth
Clean Up..Frank Marta & Crew
Plaques......................................Earl & Bobbie Jennings
Assistants..The Boy Scouts
Music at Picnic.."Sound on Sound"
Membership & Mailing Picnic Letters..............Jean Roinestad Hadsell
Historian...Vicki Anderson Wilson
Printers..Ken Vertrees Printers

Pioneer Scrap Books are on view by the Ticket Sales

Raffle Tickets
$1:00 each or 8 for $5:00

Membership
$10:00 per Family Unit, one time only
NEW STATUS
Anyone living in the Santa Maria Valley
for 30 years can be associate members for $20:00

Remember: Annual Dinner Dance
Elks Lodge: November 27th
Chairperson----Jean Hadsell

Please share your table if it is not full and please pick up all
garbage around you and your table! Thank You

Thank You

Thank you to all the hard working members of this Pioneer Association for making this 75th Annual Pioneer Picnic possible. Thank you to those who have given countless hours to Pioneer Park, working to get the Park ready for today and for the future. Thank you to Ike Simas and Clarence Donati for always knowing what has to be done and doing it. I hope everyone appreciates the hours they give to this organization and to the picnic. At this time I would like to say that the Board of Directors have voted Betty Haslam Carr, Pauline Lownes Novo and Albert Novo, Honorary Board Members for life for their distinctive service to the Santa Maria Valley Pioneer Association. Congratulations! It's great to see everyone here today, and I truly hope that you all have a wonderful time.

Sincerely,

Vicki

Vicki Anderson Wilson
President of the Santa Maria Valley Pioneer Association

*Tommy
Wilson and
Renée Vertrees
Reynoso*

*Below: Past presidents Glenn Roemer, Jim May, Jay Openshaw
and Eddie James. At right, a vocal number from Danielle
Narron and Meghan Olivera along with little Jacob Reynoso.*

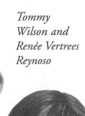

The Pioneer Park
RESTROOMS
COMPLETED 1999

In 1997, Jim Gamble was asked to design plans for the park restroom building. It was designed with block and concrete floors to make it easy to clean and keep up. The sign at right, which is posted in front of the building, thanks all those who worked on the project.

Building Erected By

Johnny Centeno, Joe Centeno, Clarence Donati, George Camacho, Jim Gamble, Sr., Jim Gamble, Jr., Kenny Gamble, Darrel Gamble, Ernie George, Bill Hadsell, Jamie Hadsell, Fred Hummel, Frank Marta, Albert Novo, Bob Simas, Art Simas, Al Smith, Ray Smith, Carol Sorenson, Sam Sorenson, Clyde Stokes

Roofing Tile & Installation donated by Kyle Roofing Company
All electrical material donated by Ed Anderson

Above: The bathroom foundation takes shape, with steel and plumbing in place. At left, Jim Gamble lays the last block on the project. He laid almost all the block, with his son Jimmy and cousin Kenny laying a few of them. Ray Smith mixed all of the mud to lay the blocks.

Clyde Stokes, our Pioneer Park plumber

Above: Ed Anderson and Allan Kyle of Kyle Roofing. At right, Ray Smith helps our Pioneer Park electrician, Robert "Gordo" Simas.

Key Workers on Restroom Project

Below: The Pioneer Park restroom building nears completion. The tile roof was donated by Kyle Roofing; all electrical material was donated by Ed Anderson.

EAGLE SCOUT PROJECTS CREATE
YOUTH CAMPING AREA at PIONEER PARK

Troop 95 was the first youth organization to camp at Pioneer Park on December 14-15, 1996. The tents were set up in the baseball diamond area. Scouts included (from right to left) Jason Tamura, Rick Reynolds, Ian Schaffert, Joey Azar, Jesse Hendricks, Max Ochoa, and others.

The Scouts cooked a Dutch oven dinner for their parents. The cooks were Matt Stroud, Matt Tamura, and Mike Maddux, shown here with parents Jim Stroud and Cheryl Maddux.

BY LAURIE TAMURA

Santa Maria District Chairperson, Los Padres Council, Boy Scouts of America

As the initial plans for Pioneer Park were being considered, one of the Pioneer members, Jim May, had a dream to create an area for youth camping in the City of Santa Maria. Approximately two acres of the oak woodlands was identified for this camping area, and Mr. May knew just who to ask to develop this area.

In the summer of 1996, a group of Pioneers including Jim May, Ed Hennon and Clarence Donati met with several members of the Santa Maria Valley Boy Scouts: Jeff and Laurie Tamura, Thom and Irene Reynolds, and Kathy Chormicle. The group walked the site and talked about the areas for the fire bowl, the campsites and other amenities. Mr. May had a list of projects that he thought would be good Eagle Scout projects.

On Dec. 14-15, 1996, the first youth organization to camp at Pioneer Park was Troop 95 from St. Louis de Montfort Church in Orcutt. The tents were pitched in the area where the baseball diamond is now. The boys cooked dinner for their parents with Dutch ovens; then the boys had to do all the dishes. In the evening, there was a sing-along and a flag retirement ceremony.

As soon as the word about potential Eagle projects at Pioneer Park was announced, a number of Boy Scouts signed up for projects. Laurie Tamura was responsible for assigning projects to the boys and keeping track of the completed projects. In 1997, Mr. Hennon served as the Pioneer Association contact to

The still-rustic surroundings at Pioneer Park made for a rugged camping experience for the Boy Scouts on that first 1996 camping expedition. Later Eagle Project work would develop more civilized camping facilities.

meet with each boy and approve his project. Each boy would then make a presentation to the Association Board. If the board agreed that the proposed project fit in the master plan of the park, the project was officially approved.

Kevin Smith from Troop 91 completed the first project, which included a native plant garden, a trail, and a bench project. Portions of the project were flooded in the winter storms of 1997-98, but several of the plants still remain and are cared for by his family.

Rick Reynolds of Troop 95 started his project in the summer of 1997. His project involved cleaning out the low-lying area to be the new fire bowl. He and his Scouting friends and family cleared out all of the undergrowth, including lots of poison oak, and graded and shaped the bowl. Rick was ready to install the fire pit, but his project was delayed all winter long because of the extensive rain. The fire bowl actually became a pond for about two months. Finally, the fire bowl area was completed in August of 1998.

In the summer of 1998, the park was used for the first time by both the Cub Scout and the Girl Scout Day Camp programs. These camp programs ran for a week each and had over 100 Scouts and adults participating.

In 1998, several other projects were completed. Quinn Capana from Troop 432 completed the first campsite, known as Campsite #2 Eagle. His design for the campsite sign was so well done that it was used

The senior Scouts of the Troop held a flag retiring ceremony. Jason Tamura and Rick Reynolds hold the stripes over the fire while Jason Graham holds the field of stars.

A "Scout's Own" service was held on Sunday morning after that first campout, led by Rick Reynolds.

for all of the other campsites and signs in the project. Adam Boyer of Troop 91 installed the first section of water and electrical lines to the campsites and the fire bowl. Bret Signorelli of Troop 91 installed the asphalt

The fire bowl area was overgrown with scrubs and poison oak. Rick Reynolds' project involved clearing out the scrubs. Scouts helping with this project included Jason Graham, Jason Tamura, Chad Dale, Matt Tamura, Greg Reynolds, Jesse Hendricks and Brent Warner. The area was recontoured using a tractor from U.S. Rental and driven by Thom Reynolds.

Even Rick's mom, Irene Reynolds, helped in laying the gravel area around the fire bowl and watering down the dust.

trail to the fire bowl. This trail was designed to provide handicap access to the fire bowl area. John LaLone of Troop 76 installed the first paths from the campsites to the fire bowl. Shaun Judson of Troop 95 completed the meeting area called the "Rendezvous." This area included tables, a storage box, and a poster board for meetings. By the end of 1998, eight projects were completed, with many more projects just getting started.

In 1999, Clarence Donati was appointed the Pioneer Association contact for the Eagle projects. Jason Tamura of Troop/Crew 95 installed the sixteen benches in the fire bowl area. These benches came in quite handy when the first Cub Scout day camp was held at Pioneer Park and the little Cub Scouts were able have a place to sit around the fire bowl. With the benches installed at the fire bowl, this area has become a very important part of the youth camping experience in the Santa Maria Valley.

The first Eagle Court of Honor, for Jason Tamura, was held at the fire bowl on October 10, 1999. Over 125 people attended this event, sitting on the benches Jason installed. A wonderful BBQ dinner was served afterwards.

Jason Graham, Brent Warner, and Greg Reynolds helped rake the gravel for the walkway. This Eagle Project was completed in August of 1998.

Below: Building the sixteen benches for the fire bowl was Jason Tamura's Eagle Project. Here, the first row of benches is set. The footings include concrete in five-gallon pickle barrels. Jason is helped by his dad, Jeff Tamura, and brother Matthew.

Other projects in 1999 included the completion of Campsite #3 Aquila by Jason Graham of Troop/Crew 95. This is the biggest campsite, and is very popular for most groups. Eric Streng of Troop/Crew 95 extended water and electrical lines and installed the water fountain near the campsites. Daniel Silva of Troop 95 installed the volleyball court near the campgrounds. Andy Ostapiuk of Troop 96 installed Campsite #1 Quail, and Seth Lieshman of Troop 96 completed Campsite #4 Hawk.

In other areas, Max Ochoa of Troop 95 installed more benches in the area of Kevin Smith's Garden; this small circle of benches has become a very special place for small groups to meet under the oak trees. This area is now called the Owl's Nest. Jason Beres of Troop 91 installed decorative rocks and plants along the asphalt trail. Aaron Cota of Troop 72 found some telephone poles and used them as the edging for the big trail from the campsites to the bathrooms. Kyle

Jason's friends Rick Reynolds, Matt Swann, and Jason Graham helped install the benches and level out the area.

Right: In June 1999, Troop 95 held a Leadership Training Program days after the benches were installed. As part of their program, they weight-tested the benches. Scoutmaster Elie Azar is in the foreground. Some of the Scouts at this training included Max Ochoa, Alex Ochoa, Joey Azar, Corey Manley, Tom Stroud, and other Scouts from Troop 95.

The first Cub Scout Day Camp was held in the summer of 1998. Nancy Newton led the group in closing ceremonies. That year there were no benches yet.

A group of first grade Tiger Cubs sings a song in the closing ceremonies in 1998.

By 2000, the fire bowl area also included the flag poles from Jordan Hettinga.

Daniels of Troop 96 installed the gravel road to several of the campgrounds.

By the end of 1999, ten more projects were completed at the park. In November of 1999, the Eagle Scouts of Pioneer Park were recognized by the City of Santa Maria Parks Commission and the City Council as "Volunteer of the Month." The resolution noted that there were twenty completed projects and over 3,000 man-hours of work at the park, with very little cost to the City of Santa Maria.

As with many programs, there was a lull in 2000. However, one unique project was unexpectedly completed. Jordan Hettinga of Troop/Crew 95 had signed up for the flagpole project in 1997, but because of a

Many Scouts attended the Eagle Court, including (first row) Jason Tamura, Chad Dale, Aaron Kloch, Greg Reynolds, Matthew Tamura, Daniel Silva (volleyball court), Ian Schaffert, Jesse Hendricks (campsite #6), Corey Manley, and Alex Ochoa. Second row: Aaron Cota (pathway), Jason Graham (campsite #3), Eric Streng (water lines), Rick Reynolds (fire bowl), Jarod King, Jordan Hettinga, Joey Azar, and Max Ochoa (Owl's Nest). Third row: Chris Silva, Matt Stroud (water lines), Tom Stroud, Brandon Hendricks, Brent Warner, David Betten, Brian Betten, and Jeremy Frickman.

number of other commitments with sport and school, wasn't able to finish his project before his eighteenth birthday in February of 2000. However, during the summer of 2000, Jordan purchased and installed the flagpoles and completed his project, all the time knowing that he would not get his Eagle Scout award. Jordan is considered an honorary Eagle Scout by many of his friends and has set an example that all should try to follow.

In 2001, the Pioneer Association appointed Jim Gamble as the contact for the Boy Scouts. Chris Head of Troop 91 completed Campsite #5 Raven. Chris was the first Eagle Scout for this Troop. Chad McCray of Troop 91 did a massive clean-up project throughout the campsite area, and removed several truckloads of concrete and junk from the outlying areas of the camp.

In 2002, Jesse Hendricks of Troop 95 completed Campsite #6 Phoenix. Matt Stroud of Troop 95 added more water and electrical lines to Campsites 4 and 5. Andy Kruger of Troop 93 completed the retaining wall project for the flag pole area.

Eagle projects in process in 2002 include the entrance monument sign being done by Jay Pontos of Troop 93. Matthew Tamura of Troop/Crew 95 has

The first Eagle Court of Honor was held in October of 1999 for Jason Tamura. Members of the court included Jason Graham, Lindy Judson (Scoutmaster of Troop 95), Jason Tamura, Thom Reynolds (Scoutmaster of Troop 95), Aaron Cota, and Kevin Smith.

designed a plan for the flatwork around the flagpoles at the fire bowl. Brandon Espinosa of Troop 76 completed the flagstone work around the fire bowl.

In the first five years, there was a total of 27 Eagle projects and over 4,500 man-hours of work done by over a hundred boys in the Santa Maria area. These projects are part of the continuing effort to improve the campsites at Pioneer Park for youth camping in the Santa Maria Valley. Each project was designed to stand the test of time, and hopefully these boys will be able to bring their own children to Pioneer Park and show them what they have built.

The Scouts, volunteers and parents of the Santa Maria Valley Boy Scouts would like to thank the Pioneer Association for the opportunity to be part of the effort to provide youth camping in the Santa Maria Valley.

Jason Graham was attested by his father, Glenn, and his grandfather. At right, Jason pauses in front of his completed project.

Santa Maria Times, April 3, 1993

■ BOY SCOUTS

SM leader elected to head Boy Scout council

Santa Maria community leader Jim May has been elected president of the county-wide Mission Council, Boy Scouts of America. He will lead an executive board of 50 members who give leadership to more than 5,000 young people registered in 45 Tiger groups, 65 Cub packs, 46 Scout troops, 12 Varsity teams and 34 Explorer posts. The council has more than 1,500 volunteer leaders giving support to youth membership.

The board is responsible for the management of the council and the implementation of the policies of the National Council, BSA.

May earned his Eagle Scout rank in Santa Maria, Rotary Club sponsored Troop 1, in October of 1939. He received National Scouting's highest council award, the Silver Beaver, for outstanding service to youth in 1991 and is a long-time member of the Order of the Arrow, a national honor camping society. His son, Fred L. May, received his Eagle Scout award in 1991.

May served as Santa Maria district committee chairman for four years and was responsible for the district financial program for two years. He was serving his third term as council vice president when elected to the presidency of Mission Council.

His principal role is to lead the consolidation of the San Luis Obispo Council and the Mission Council into a new Los Padres Council.

Jim May

About Laurie Tamura

Laurie and Jeff Tamura have taken the Boy Scout program to heart. In 1989, when their first son, Jason, was old enough, they signed him up with Pack 95 at St. Louis de Montfort Church. Within a year, Laurie was asked to serve as the Pack Committee Chair. She held this position for four years. When their second son, Matthew, bridged into Troop 95, Laurie resigned her pack position and moved on to the troop. While Jeff served as the Assistant Scoutmaster, Laurie was asked to serve as the Troop Committee Chair, a position she held for two years.

When the District Chair, Alex Ochoa, passed away unexpectedly, the District Executive, Kathy Chormicle, asked Laurie to serve as the District Chair to complete Alex's term. For a number of reasons, Laurie served as the District Chair for four years (1998–2001). During this tenure she assisted in many successful programs, including Scouting for Food, Pinewood Derby, and Camporees. She served as the Eagle Scout Project Coordinator for Pioneer Park for five years.

She was awarded the District Award of Merit in 2000 and the Council Silver Beaver Award in 2001. She also completed the Wood Badge (Owl Patrol), Ordeal and the Brotherhood in the Order of the Arrow.

As their sons complete Eagle and move on to college, Laurie and Jeff continue to serve as volunteers in the Scouting program.

Laurie and Jeff Tamura with their sons Jason and Matthew

PART SIX

Family Histories

of the

SANTA MARIA VALLEY PIONEERS

Compiled by
Pauline Lownes Novo

Nellie Clark Adair

Grandfather Lafayette "Laf" German and grandmother Priscilla German were both born in California. "Laf" was born near Stockton, and Priscilla in Geyserville. They were married in San Luis Obispo on March 6, 1882, and moved to Point Sal, which was then a thriving port that supplied Santa Maria and from which products were shipped. He drove teams hauling to and from Point Sal. They moved to Santa Maria after a year and a half; then he worked as a stagecoach driver for some time. After that, he farmed in the Garey area, and lastly worked for Pacific Coast Coal and Lumber Company until he retired in 1937.

They purchased their home at 1000 West Barrett in 1906 and resided there until his death in 1943. Priscilla passed away in 1947. She had been living with her daughter Edithe Clark.

They raised four children, James Andrew German, Edithe German Clark, Lottie German Potter, and Lee Morris German. James married Myrtle Mathey, also a Pioneer. They had two sons, and took a girl to raise as their own daughter. James passed away in 1932 while living in Paso Robles. Myrtle returned to Santa Maria, passing away in 1974. Both of their sons have passed away.

Lottie married Jerry Potter of Santa Rosa and left the area, but visited often. She passed away in 1956. Lee married Lillie Morris, also a Santa Maria Pioneer. They had three sons. Lee died in 1936 as the result of an accident while working for Pacific Freight Lines in Santa Maria.

Edith married Frank Clark, who came to this area in 1899 from San Joaquin County to work at Jesus Maria Ranch. They were married in 1906 and lived in Santa Maria all their lives. He farmed, and was active in agricultural activities in the community. They celebrated their 50th wedding anniversary in 1956, and seven months later he passed away. She passed away in 1960. She was active in gardening, winning many prizes at the fair. She was also active in Pythian Sisters and Native Daughters. They had three daughters: Vivian Clark Brickey, Nellie Clark Adair, and Lela Clark Fox Lavigne. In 1928, Vivian married James Howard Brickey, son of the William Brickey family. Howard worked for Union Oil until retiring, and then continued to raise cattle on their ranch near Sisquoc. He died in 1985. Vivian was active in Farm Bureau Home Department, and also taught Tailoring to Adult Education classes at Hancock College.

Lela Clark married Huxley Fox. They had one daughter, Sandra Tamar Fox. After a divorce, Lela married Albert Lavigne in 1951. They lived in Santa Maria and then Arroyo Grande until his death in 1983. In 1988, Lela, now in ill health, moved to Felton to live with her daughter. Lela has five grandchildren.

Nellie Clark married Fred M. Adair in 1932. Fred moved here with his parents in 1920. Fred's family went to Mariposa County during the Gold Rush with John C. Fremont. When the mines closed, his father came to Orcutt to work in the oil business. Nellie and Fred built their home at 201 E. El Camino in 1938 and have lived there ever since. Nellie has worked as a bookkeeper and secretary. She was active in community affairs, while Fred worked for 32 years for Southern California Gas Company.

July 1, 1989

The Anderson Family

Edward Harrison Anderson and Alma Hammer Anderson came to Santa Maria in 1926 with their children Maxine (born in 1912) and Edward (born in 1920). That same year, they opened the business of Anderson Electric, which went on to become one of the oldest electrical companies in the state. Edward, Jr., purchased the business which bore his name from his father and operated it until the day he died, November 18, 1999.

Edward, Jr., known as Eddie, was the only son of Alma and Edward, Sr. He lived in Santa Maria his entire life, attending local schools and graduating from Santa Maria High School with the class of 1939. He served in the U.S. Navy during World War II, and married Alice Thomas of the pioneer Thomas family on June 13, 1944, at St. Mary's of the Assumption Catholic Church. The union brought forth three children:

• *Victoria (Vicki)* was born on June 1, 1949. She attended local schools and graduated from Santa Maria High School in 1967. On June 10, 1972, she married Richard Wilson, an engineer, at St. Mary's of the Assumption Catholic Church. They have one son, Thomas Anthony Wilson, who was born in Santa Maria on June 21, 1983, attended local schools and graduated from St. Joseph's High School on June 10, 2001.

Vicki Anderson Wilson has owned and operated The Academy of Dance Arts for 24 years and has performed as a singer and dancer at Pioneer Picnics since the age of four. She served three terms as Pioneer Association president, from 1997 to 2000. Thomas ("Tommy") Wilson has participated in many Pioneer Picnic programs, as well as helping to clean up Pioneer Park before the big Pioneer Picnic.

• *Teresa (Teri)* was born on November 5, 1953. She graduated from St. Joseph's High School and married Joseph Buttitta on January 7, 1978, at First Christian Church in Santa Maria. They have one son, Joseph Edward ("Joey"), who was born May 25, 1989.

• *Thomas Edward* was born September 9, 1963. He married Lori Michael of the pioneer Lawrence Michael family on May 4, 2002, and lives in Santa Maria, where he works as a musician and personal trainer.

The three daughters of Edward, Sr., and Alma Anderson were Maxine, Mary Dena, and Joan.

• *Maxine* was born in 1912; she graduated from Santa Maria High School in 1930 and married Charles Kertell. They had one daughter, Joan Kertell Weismann.

• *Mary Dena* was born in 1924 in Santa Maria. After graduating from Santa Maria High School in 1942, she married B.J. Bonham, and they had two children, Dena Bonham Kirk and Douglas Edward Bonham.

• *Joan* was born in 1930. She graduated from Santa Maria High School in 1948 and married Robert Goodall. Their three children are Robert, Jr.; Rebecca Goodall Nelson; and Janice Goodall Wilhelm.

Edward Anderson, Sr., died in 1963, followed by his wife Alma in 1969, daughter-in-law Alice in 1998, and son Edward, Jr., in 1999. All four are buried in the Santa Maria Cemetery.

Alice Thomas Anderson and Edward Anderson, Jr.

Juanita Avila

Juanita Avila lived on a Spanish land grant that was given to her family. That is where the town of Avila Beach got its name. Her children sold off the land, piece by piece—the last one was Juan Avila. The last time he was seen, he was fishing off the Avila Pier, basically broke.

Juanita married a man whose last name was Bunch. They had one son, Henry Bunch. He worked the railroad crew in Los Alamos, where he married Mary Ontiveros Filionchais and raised her daughter from a previous marriage. Juanita's daughter, Maclovia, married Louis Silva. It was a short marriage, but they had two daughters, Marjorie Silva, Santa Maria High School Class of 1937, and Jessie Silva, Class of 1937.

Jessie Silva married Al Allen of Nevada, and resides in Santa Maria. Marjorie married Earl Lapp, and had one son, Thomas Earl Lapp, Santa Maria High School Class of 1957. He married Jeanne Baker, Class of 1959, and they live in Newbury Park, California.

Marjorie's second marriage was to Max E. Faulkner; they had three children, who are all graduates of Santa Maria High School and all live in Santa Maria. They are Theresa McGrew, Max Faulkner, and Elison.

—Tom Lapp

Arthur and Elsie Baker

Arthur and Elsie Baker left North Carolina in 1947 with their three daughters—my two sisters and me—a new Ford Convertible, and a little Prell trailer with treasured things.

We stopped at Harley Estabrook's big truck stop at Battles Road and South Broadway for gasoline. We also ate at their coffee shop. Our friendly daddy, in talking to Mr. Estabrook, discovered that his night employee had cleaned out the till and left!

Estabrook talked Daddy into working for him, which he did for many years, until he leased Bob Nolan's service station at El Camino and Broadway. When Nolan sold out, my dad went to work at Home Motors, then located downtown. He retired from Home Motors after many years, having also taught night classes in body shop at Allan Hancock College. We lost our daddy on May 30, 1989, about a month before his 80th birthday.

Mother still lives in Santa Maria but is not in good health.

I met my husband, Bob Cassidy, in 1951 while he was attending Hancock College and also drove the school bus. We were married in 1952. We are still happily married, and have two adult children. We have a granddaughter whom we take care of daily.

As far as North Carolina goes, it's a good place to visit. Santa Maria is home, and always will be.

Bob is retiring on January 3, 1993, from the Marshal's Office in Santa Maria. He has worked there since 1969, serving as Marshal for the last four years.

Elizabeth Giovanacci Barca

My father came to America six months before we did. My mother, brother and I, accompanied by a friend, Mr. Talevi, took the boat from France to New York, arriving in ten days. I remember saying to my mother, "Mama, see the pretty lady!" It was the Statue of Liberty. I was six years old.

We took the train to Santa Barbara, arriving in five days. My father was working, so we were met by my grandparents and my uncle.

We rented a house in Montecito. My mother cooked for three men, and my father worked for the railroad. Leaving there in one year, we moved to Goleta. There my parents learned to milk cows. They had never seen cows before. From there we moved to Guadalupe, working for Mr. and Mrs. Rusconi on a dairy farm. My father did the milking and my mother cooked for the family.

The eldest daughter was Mayme Rusconi, who later married Anthony Caroni. After one year, we moved to a Los Alamos dairy. My father leased that dairy for two years, but stayed only one, quitting after the first year.

From there we moved to Garey, where my father bought a small ranch. It was here, at the age of ten, that I started school. I did not speak English, but I had a good teacher, Linda Pertusi Ontiveros, who helped me a lot. She still lives in Tepusquet and is still active.

The ranch was too small, so after three years Father sold it to Mr. and Mrs. Ardantz, Nick Ardantz's parents. We moved to Fletcher Ranch, dairying and farming. We had twenty-five cows at that time. I went to Rice School on Prell Road, graduating from there. Our neighbors were Mr. and Mrs. Medeiros and their two daughters, Mamie and Palmara. Palmara was my best friend. We went to the Saturday night dances and had so much fun. We met the Cossa family, and together we would all go to the Pismo Saturday dances, chaperoned by the Patocchi brothers.

Each month we would get together to party and dance with other families, the Bettigas, Linda Pertusi, John Spazzadischi, Uncle Battista Fumia. It was at one of these dances that I met Peter Barca. He had a sore throat—and two weeks later I came down with the mumps. Peter apologized. We were married a year later, with just family attending.

We moved to the old family home on Todos Santos Ranch. Bob Barca was born three years later; four years later Nadine was born; and two and one-half years later Dorothy was born. We lost a daughter, Elsie, at 17 months old. Peter and his brother Albinio went into a business partnership on the ranch and were partners until they died, four months apart, in 1972. I have one brother and his wife, who are wonderful to me. They took care of Mother until she died.

I have eight grandchildren and five great-grandchildren, whom I love dearly.

Peter was an Elk for many years.

I live in my nice home in Santa Maria, and attend the Elks as often as I can.

—*Elizabeth Barca, 1990*

Manuel and Mary (Niverth) Bello

ary Ellen Niverth, who was born on August 13, 1899, the third daughter of Stephen and Rachel Niverth, grew up in Garey. She attended elementary grades at Garey School and graduated from Santa Maria High School in 1917. She worked as a bookkeeper for W.A. Haslam Company until her marriage to Manuel Bello on August 12, 1920, at her parents' home in Garey.

Manuel Bello was the fifth child of Antonio and Maria Bello, born on March 13, 1900, at their ranch in Oso Flaco. He attended Oso Flaco School and worked on area farms. He and his brother-in-law, Eddie Goodchild, farmed his parents' ranch. He also worked for his father-in-law, Stephen Niverth, when he and his wife lived in Garey. A daughter, Yvonne June, was born and died in August 1925.

Manuel and Mary built a home on Palm Court Drive in Santa Maria, a site she had selected from a strawberry field when she was in high school. There a second daughter, LaVonne Jeanette, was born on November 6, 1926.

Manuel worked for Novo's in Guadalupe, and then had the Cletrac agency at Novo Bros. blacksmith shop on West Main Street in Santa Maria. After a year as co-owner of the Cletrac agency in Riverside, he returned and purchased the National Cleaners. He later returned to the farm equipment business and worked for John Deere and Caterpillar companies—Thomas Luke Tractor Company, Holt Brothers, and Joseph G. Moore Company, from which he retired in 1952.

After his retirement he worked with the Santa Maria Soil Conservation District and was instrumental in the construction of its building on Foster Road.

He was also active in Santa Maria Indian Baseball and the establishment of Elks Field. He was a member of the Santa Maria Elks Club, Santa Maria Rotary Club, the Historical Society, and the Salvation Army Board.

Manuel died on March 15, 1980. Mary still lives in their Palm Court home.

—1991

Mary Linman Benton

ary moved to Santa Maria with her dad, Roy Linman. They lived with Mrs. Lawson until he married, and the family moved to 601 Park Avenue in 1932.

Roy worked at the Santa Maria Ice Company. Then he worked for the Department of Employment as a farm labor advisor, and later as manager of Santa Maria Valley Farms. He took time out and enlisted in the Army during World War II, and was an aircraft warning sergeant in Orange County.

Mary and her husband, Bill Benton, had one son and two grandchildren.

Mary graduated from high school in Santa Maria, and in her later years moved to La Mirada, California. Her husband, Bill, died of kidney failure, and Mary died on May 3, 1995. Her son joined the Pioneers when his mother died.

Bibiana (Vivian) Valenzuela Bianchi

by Ted Bianchi

This portrait is of our mother at 17 years of age, just before her marriage to our father on May 15, 1893. The wedding was in San Luis Obispo de Tolosa Mission.

Mother was born at Sisquoc on September 14, 1876, to Alfred and Maria Jesus Valenzuela. She was baptized on January 14, 1877, in San Ramon Chapel. This small chapel, with its graveyard, is located at the top of the hill at the entrance to Foxen Canyon, about two miles south of Sisquoc. It was built by Ramona Foxen in 1876.

During the early years of her married life, Bibiana gave birth to thirteen babies—eight boys and five girls. Mother was happy with her large family; however, there were times when sadness would come from the death of one of us.

Mother was a good cook and housekeeper. Baking twelve to fifteen loaves of bread on a wood stove was no easy task. She scheduled her wash day on Saturday so we could help her. It was fun being around so many brothers and sisters.

During the summer and early fall, Mother kept herself busy canning fruit, jams and jellies for the winter ahead. These would be stored in an underground cellar with other foods and Dad's wine. Still, Mother found time to rest and sew, and enjoyed a social life.

Sadness came to us and to her friends when Mother died from breast cancer on December 23, 1944. The funeral mass was held in St. Mary of the Assumption Catholic Church on December 26, 1944, followed by burial at a local cemetery.

Theodore A. "Ted" Bianchi and Mary Eunice Araujo Bianchi

Born right here in Santa Maria, Ted remembers growing up in a community of a few hundred people. He knew Santa Maria back at the turn of the century, when it had dirt streets and wooden sidewalks. It was a time when he carried out his errands on horseback or by horse and buggy. He did his homework by the light of a kerosene lamp.

In 1930, Ted married Mary Eunice Araujo of Hanford, California, and they became parents of three children. Ted A., Jr., is a corporate representative of General Dynamics at the Kennedy Space Center, and lives with his family at Cocoa Beach, Florida. Mary Jane, now deceased, was a teacher for eighteen years, and sold real estate in Montecito. Antonia, the youngest, teaches in Guadalupe and resides with her family in Santa Maria. Ted and Mary have been blessed with nine grandchildren and five great-grandchildren.

For 37 years, Ted owned and operated a grocery-meat business at the corner of Broadway and Stowell Road. In those days, it was at the very edge of the city limits.

Ted is a 50-year member of the Knights of Columbus Council 2475, having received his third degree in 1935 at Watsonville, California. He held several offices in our council before serving as Grand Knight in 1939-40 and 1941-42. The Council selected him as their Knight of the Year for 1967-68.

Ted is also active in Fourth Degree Activities. He is a charter member of Archbishop John J. Cantwell Assembly, and served two terms as Faithful Navigator.

For 35 years Ted was an usher at St. Mary of the Assumption Church. He helped raise funds for the first playground equipment at St. Mary's School. He helped in fund drives for the new St. Mary's Church, as well as Catholic Hospitals.

As president of the Santa Maria Historical Society, he spearheaded a successful drive to raise $105,000 to build a new museum.

From 1922 to 1927 he was Scoutmaster of Troop 5 and is past president of the Santa Maria Council for Campfire Girls. He was a member of the Rotary Club and a 41-year member of the Elks Lodge.

Photography was Ted's hobby. He has faithfully recorded the community's growth and development, an important part of our Historical Museum.

He produced the first Chamber of Commerce film in 1955, the Golden Anniversary of Santa Maria's incorporation. In 1965, he produced the documentary film, *From Darkness into Light,* for the Santa Maria Council for Retarded Children.

For 25 years he filmed the annual Elks Parade and Rodeo, and the annual Trek for Vaqueros de los Ranchos.

According to Ted, living in Santa Maria has been an enjoyable experience. There was a lot of hard work, but along the way he was privileged to meet a lot of wonderful people. In his words, "I owe thanks to our Blessed Lord for giving me a good and loving family."

J. Miles Boothe

J. Miles Boothe came to Santa Maria in 1926 with his wife, Litta, and two daughters, Janice, age seven, and Betty Ann, age one. They rented a house across from the high school in the two hundred block of West Morrison Avenue.

Mr. Boothe taught biology, botany, math, and agriculture at the high school. He graduated from Oregon Agricultural College at Corvallis in 1915, and completed his master's degree there in 1916. At this time he married Litta Christine Welch.

He retired in 1958 after 32 years of teaching. That year the school annual, *The Review,* was dedicated to him. He was the advisor for Future Farmers for many years. He instituted and taught the first photography class at Santa Maria High School until his retirement. He was nicknamed "Jasper" by his students, and was also called "Barney," for Barney Oldfield, the racer, because he was given a ticket for speeding one night returning from a Santa Barbara football game.

Mrs. Boothe was the organist at St. Peter's Episcopal Church and pianist for the Community Orchestra. She was the floral division director at the Santa Barbara County Fair for seven years.

The Boothes were members of the Santa Maria Goodtimers Club, Eastern Star, Masons, Toastmasters, Camera Club, Minerva Club, Daughters of the American Revolution, Daughters of American Colonists, Farm Bureau, and Department of Agriculture Home Advisor.

Their daughter, Janice, was State College Champion of women's tennis, Oregon State. She was a flutist with high school and community orchestras, and spent two years with the All-County Orchestra in Santa Barbara. Janice graduated from Oregon State College, and then married a Lompoc boy, Robert J. Pattee. Their one daughter, Joan Boothe Pattee, graduated from Santa Maria High School, attended Chico State College, and married Keith Berry of Santa Maria. They had two children, Janice and Marc.

Betty Boothe also played the flute as well as the violin, and studied voice with Irene Mesirow. She did solos for the Presbyterian Church, Eastern Star, and other groups. After World War II, Betty married a Marine who was stationed at Goleta Marine Corps Air Station, where she worked. William "Bill" Brozowski worked for the City of Santa Maria as assistant athletic director under Paul Nelson, and was a Boy Scout leader after his discharge. After graduating from UCSB, he became a special agent for the FBI, living in Washington, D.C.; Minneapolis, Minnesota; Sioux Falls, South Dakota; Detroit, Michigan; and finally, in 1960, back in California, where he worked with the space program in government security for North American (Rockwell).

Betty and Bill had a son, Miles Brozowski, in Santa Maria, and a daughter, Christine Anne, in Sioux Falls, South Dakota. Betty worked as a volunteer art teacher in a Lutheran school, did advertising for the *Anaheim Bulletin,* and volunteer reporting and photography for Texas and Florida newspapers. She was secretary for the Episcopal Church in Texas and California, and was involved with the Daughters of the American Revolution and American Colonists in several states.

Miles is an electrician/computer specialist at Port Hueneme for the Navy as a civilian, and is a ham radio buff (N6ADA). He married his high school sweetheart, Sue Dunley of Anaheim, after his tour of duty and discharge from the Vietnam War. They have adopted two girls, Jennifer, age 5, and Kathleen, age 3, who came from Korea.

Christine married a young man from El Cajon, California, Kevin Michael DeLaFont. They have two sons, Joshua, 9, and Jason, 2½.

—*Betty Boothe Brozowski*

Charles Bradley and Elizabeth Booth Bradley

Charles Bradley was born in South Wingfield, Derbyshire, England, in 1839. At the age of twelve he began work in the coal mines of Oakerthorpe. On April 5, 1857, he married Elizabeth Booth, also a native of South Wingfield, who was born in 1840. At this time he went into his first business—breaking coal for market, which he continued until 1868.

At the encouragement of an uncle in Monterey County, California, who needed help with his stock, Charles left England with his wife and five children, Mary Jane, Annie, Louise, Agnes and Charles William. The family sailed to New York on the *City of London,* and from New Jersey down to Panama on the *Ocean Queen.* After crossing the isthmus, they sailed up the west coast on the ship *Colorado,* which landed in San Francisco in November of 1868. They traveled on to Monterey by boat, and then were outfitted for the 160-mile trip south to Santa Maria. In the Salinas Valley en route, a sixth child was born—a girl named Ellen.

The family came to Charles' uncle's homestead in Bradley Canyon. Charles worked for him in his sheep raising business endeavors for four years. In 1872, he struck out on his own and purchased 160 acres of land. As crops and flocks flourished, he added by purchase and homestead until he became the owner of 2720 acres. (This is still held by the Bradley Land Company.) When open range for his stock became more restricted, he turned to other lines of activity. The Bradley ranch was well improved, and in 1873 a fine home and farm buildings were erected.

Charles became interested in the town of Santa Maria, and purchased the Hart Hotel. He remodeled it and renamed it the Bradley Hotel. It stood at the corner of Broadway and Main Street, and was known throughout the state as an up-to-date hostelry of its time. (It burned down in 1970.)

He was a member of the Hesperian Lodge #264— F&AM of Santa Maria. He was instrumental in the founding of Santa Maria High School in 1891. He and William Hickman Rice furnished the bonds necessary to insure the success of the new institution. He was a board member from 1891 to 1912. He was also a stockholder and director in the Santa Maria Bank, and in 1904 was elected president of the bank, a position he held until his death.

Charles and Elizabeth had five more children after their arrival in Santa Maria: Rachel, Elizabeth, Sadie, Alyce, and James Frederick. They were preceded in death by their son Charles in 1901, and Louisa Janes in 1902. Mother Elizabeth died in 1903. They were survived by nine children: Mary Jane Tunnell, Annie Long, Agnes Elliot Forbes, Ellen Elliot, Rachel Niverth, Elizabeth Singleton Howerton, Sadie Kelley, Alyce Lewis, and James Frederick Bradley.

Marshall Lawrence Brumana

Marshall was born February 16, 1927, in Los Alamos, California. His father was Giovanni Bultisto Brumana, born April 1, 1891, in Indovero, Como, Italy. He died May 5, 1969, in Santa Maria. He was married at the Santa Inez Mission to Antonia Rosalia Ybarra, who was born June 13, 1888, in Arroyo Grande, and died June 13, 1977, in Santa Maria. Other children included Frank, Louie, Andy, Pete, John, William, Kate Brumana Jensen and Lucille Brumana Welch.

The boys were all good athletes, especially star baseball and softball players in Santa Maria.

The Brumana family lived in Los Alamos and Santa Maria for years.

Belle LaFontaine Buck
Mrs. Charles Buck

Mother of Lorraine Buck Chadband.
Belle was born in Santa Ynez in 1898.
She moved to Santa Maria in about 1903.

BELLE'S ANCESTORS:
Father: Gueremon La Fontaine
Mother: Josephine Fernandez LaFontaine
Paternal grandfather: Roman LaFontaine, born in France
Paternal grandmother: Josefa Bravo Fernandez, born in Santa Barbara.
Maternal grandfather: Jose Pedro Fernandez, born in Spain.
Maternal grandmother: Refugio Pico LaFontaine

Bill Burgett

Santa Maria 1911 to 1933

I attended a small grammar school in the oil fields near Sisquoc, and attended Santa Maria High School from 1922, graduating in 1926, the year I was also student body president. I entered the University of California at Berkeley, where my fraternity brothers included Jack Glines and Paul Oakley. I set the batting record in baseball at U. of C. in 1929, which was for a single season, and it still stands.

I spent nearly four years in the Navy in World War II. The last three years I was a commanding officer, and I was discharged as a lieutenant commander.

I retired from Union Oil Company in 1967. I had been the Los Angeles resident sales manager for several years. Since retiring, Mary Jane and I live seven months at our home in West Covina, California, and five months at our summer home in Montana. I had two brothers, Maxwell F. Burgett and Byron Charles Tunnell. My stepfather was Charles Tunnell, the nephew of George Tunnell, father of Curtis Tunnell.

—Bill Burgett
Stryker, Montana, September 9, 1986

Donald G. Caroni
and Frances Caroni

My father, Anthony N. Caroni, came to America from Switzerland in 1916. He settled on the Tognazzini property three miles south of Guadalupe. Here he worked making butter for the Golden Eagle Creamery.

Later he married Mayme Rusconi, and operated the dairy on the property until 1975. I became a partner of the operations in 1946.

I graduated from Santa Maria Joint Union High School in 1941½. I retired in 1988.

Frances and I had two children, Donald and Jean.

—Donald Caroni

José Carranza and Agapite Torres Carranza

José Carranza, ancestor of the Carranza families, pioneers of the Santa Maria Valley, was born in Mexico near the home of General U. Carranza of Mexico fame. He was educated in Mexico, and there he married Agapite Torres, and soon afterwards the young couple came to California to seek their fortune.

They settled in San Bernardino County and farmed for a time. Saturina and Geronimo were born there. Later they moved to San Luis Obispo County, and continued raising stock. There Miguel, Feliz and Dolores were born.

Then the family moved to southern California, where José Carranza bought a large ranch and engaged in the stock business on a large scale. Their five children were educated there.

Saturina, their daughter, married Feliciano D. Esparza, who became secretary to General Castro, governor of Lower California. When General Castro was killed, Feliciano became governor. While affairs were progressing nicely, a revolution occurred. The governor was banished to Mexico, and José Carranza's property was confiscated, and he and his family were also banished.

They all embarked on a vessel to the island of Guadalupe, where they concluded to land and await developments. The island was uninhabited by people except for the Carranza family. It was a desert waste with thousands of wild goats roaming over its expanse.

Thus began a Robinson Crusoe life which continued for one year and eleven months before they were rescued. They existed on goats' flesh and milk, a native date, and the pulp of a species of palm, out of which they made bread.

When their clothing wore out, José fashioned clothing for his family out of goat hides. They trapped the goats by building a stockade with runways up to the top where the goats would go in search of the date fruit used as bait. Once they got inside, it was impossible to get out. Many of the hides were spotted with black and white and made very beautiful clothing. José also made shoes that were tied with thongs.

One day they spotted a passing schooner, and attracted its attention with a large fire. They were rescued and taken to the Port of San Quentin, and from there back to San Diego. There Mr. Carranza died, date unknown. The rest of the family came to the northern part of Santa Barbara County, where Agapite Torres Carranza died on April 29, 1896, at the home of her son, Geronimo, on Suey Ranch. She was 88 years old.

—Genealogy in Pioneer file

Mamie V. Carroll

My parents moved to Santa Maria in 1895 with three children who were born in Park City, Utah. My mother and father had been married there in 1889. I was born in Santa Maria on July 2, 1903.

We farmed two 20-acre parcels in the Santa Maria city limits. We grew small white beans without irrigation.

I attended the Mill Street School for first through fourth grades, and then moved on to Main Street School, where I graduated in 1918.

In high school I took a college prep course, and graduated in 1922 as an honor student. Four years of English taught by Ethel Pope will always bring pleasant memories.

I married in 1922 and my first son, James, was born in 1924. He was killed in an auto accident in 1947.

My second son, Pat, was born January 16, 1935. He is retired and lives in Phoenix, Arizona, with his wife of 32 years.

My third child is a daughter, Susan, born September 23, 1940, also in Santa Maria. She has been an emergency room tech clerk at Marian Medical Center for the past twenty years.

I have three grandsons and one granddaughter. Two of the grandsons are presently captains and pilots in the U.S. Marine Corps, stationed at Camp Pendleton. There are six great-grandchildren.

My granddaughter is enrolled at Arizona University in Tucson, and is a wildlife biology major. Her brother is also a graduate of AU, a business administrator, and is manager of a K-Mart store on Tucson's Miracle Mile.

In 1950 I began as proofreader at the *Santa Maria Times,* and was later named Women's Page editor, a position I held for almost twenty years. I've had a happy 88 years in Santa Maria, and loved every day of it.

—Mamie Carroll

Frank H. Chadband Family

rank Harold Chadband was born in 1891 in Warwick, England, to Henry and Mary Louise Chadband, who owned and operated a bakery and pork shop, and raised eleven children in the upstairs rooms.

Frank sailed from England around 1912 at the age of 21. He landed first in Canada, then went to Nebraska, where he was employed on a cattle ranch.

Lily Violet Haines was born near Warwick in 1891. Frank and Lily made plans to meet in America. Lily was employed by a wealthy family who traveled back and forth from England to America. They were among the survivors of the wreck of the *Titanic* in April 1912. Lily stayed in New York and traveled to California, and she and Frank were married in San Diego on April 5, 1914.

They moved to Piru, in Ventura County, where two children were born to them: Richard Thomas Chadband in 1915 and Amy Louise Chadband in 1917. In 1917 they moved to the oil fields south of Orcutt. Frank worked for the Union Oil Company. There they had two more children: Edna Mae Chadband in 1922, and James Frank Chadband in 1927. They lived on the Hartnell lease at the foot of Squire's Grade.

The children all attended Orcutt Grammar School and Santa Maria Union High School. Dick and Amy graduated from Santa Maria High. In the 1920's, they purchased land in a redwood grove near Felton in the Santa Cruz Mountains. Frank and son Dick built a cabin there, where they spent their yearly vacations.

In August, 1934, Frank, Lily, Amy, Edna, James, and Amy's friend Louise Schultz were returning from one of these vacations when they were struck by a truck on Highway 101 near Shell Beach. Frank, Lily and Edna were killed instantly. Amy, Jim and Louise were injured.

Dick had remained home, because after graduating, he was employed at Johns Manville in Lompoc.

Dick, Amy and Jim continued living in the family home in the oil fields. Dick was then working for the Union Oil Co.

Dick married Lorraine Buck in 1938; they had three children, Susan, Tom, and Rick Chadband.

Amy married Keith Crain of Orcutt in 1944. They had four children: Jim, Steven, Lauralee and Lu Ann Crain.

James married Connie Fait of Idaho and they had two boys, Cory and Craig Chadband.

—*Amy Chadband Crain*

The Cole Family

David and Barbara Cole brought their young family to Santa Maria in February of 1961, when the General Telephone company transferred Dave north from his native city of Santa Barbara. Within about three and a half years they were settled in the Cape Cod-style cottage on South Speed Street where they still live today. They also still own the 1932 Ford coupe that Dave bought before he graduated from high school in 1949, and the 1940 Lincoln Continental convertible that he and Barbara acquired after they were married, a fact which has garnered them some minor notoriety in town as "the family on Speed Street with all the old cars." Over the years, several other vintage Fords and Lincolns have populated their driveway, followed by a Volvo that is about the same age as their children.

Both born in 1931, Dave Cole and Barbara Bruce (she formerly of Schenectady, New York) met at UCSB in Santa Barbara when they were the only two students in an advanced Spanish class. They were married (by Barbara's grandfather, the Rev. Robert B. H. Bell) at Trinity Episcopal Church, Santa Barbara, in 1953. Their lack of a honeymoon was somewhat compensated for a couple of years later by a two-year sojourn in Munich, Germany, at the behest of the U.S. Army. Their '40 Continental made the trip with them.

Dave's automotive interests led him to active membership in the Lincoln Continental Owners Club, the Early Ford V-8 Club, and the Lincoln-Zephyr Owners Club, where he became known as an authority on the authentic restoration of Fords and Lincolns of the '30s and '40s. After his retirement from General Telephone in 1985, he became the editor of the Zephyr Club's magazine, *The Way of the Zephyr.* He also found time to pursue his interest in other aspects of automotive history, including early roads, highways, and gas stations. In the mid-1990's he published a series of articles on the string of Richfield Beacon service stations that were built in 1929, including the one in Santa Maria, just south of Betteravia Road, whose beacon tower with blue neon letters spelling out RICHFIELD was a prominent local landmark for many years. The series of articles was later reprinted as the centerpiece of R.H. Tesene's book, *The Beacon Story.*

Dave and Barbara are both active in the Santa Maria Valley Historical Society. Barbara has served as editor of the Society's *Quarterly* for a number of years and has prepared several research projects for presentation at Society convocations.

The Coles raised three children: Richard, born 1954; Elaine, born 1959; and Kathleen, born 1962.

Richard graduated from Santa Maria High School in 1972 and married the former Catherine Banta of Pocatello, Idaho, in 1978. They have three daughters: Caroline, born 1982; Claudia, born 1985; and Cecily, born 1986. Richard's high-school dabblings in art and journalism directed him to a career in graphic design, and in 1980 he founded Graphics LTD, where over the years he has designed logos, publications, and other print material for numerous local businesses, including Allan Hancock College and Marian Medical Center. He has also worked on *The Way of the Zephyr* with his father since 1989, and was responsible for the design of R.H. Tesene's books *Santa Maria Style Barbecue* and *The Beacon Story,* as well as several others.

Elaine graduated from Santa Maria High School in 1977 and spent several years working with the Mark Evans family at their South Broadway eatery, Markee's Open Pit Barbecue, before joining Richard at Graphics LTD in 1986. A student of American Sign Language, she also enjoys a second career as a sign language interpreter for the deaf.

Kathleen graduated from Santa Maria High in 1981 and worked for seventeen years at Graphics LTD with her siblings before joining the City of Santa Maria's Public Works Department as a clerk and graphic artist. In 2001 she married local contractor Daniel Villegas, scion of a long-time Santa Maria family that the Coles have known for forty years. Her children from a previous marriage are David Wilson, born 1990, and Corinne Wilson, born 1995.

Pirky Colvin's Pioneer Connection

Pirky came to Santa Maria in 1975 with no knowledge of her pioneer family connection with the Santa Maria Valley.

Her mother, Jeanne Stowell Southworth, mentioned a vague recollection that her father, Floyd Stowell, may have been born in Santa Maria. Nothing was investigated until 1990, when Pirky received from her mother some photos which were made by a studio in Santa Maria, California, called McMillan Bros.!

Upon joining the Santa Maria Valley Genealogy Society, Pirky met Barbara Cole, who publishes their periodical and does the research on the various local pioneer families which are a feature of each issue. Barbara instantly provided Pirky with the entire history of her pioneer ancestors—Henry Stowell and John and Jane Leigh Hopper. Henry Stowell's son, Frank, married the granddaughter of John and Jane Hopper, whose father, Greenberry Hopper, had a blacksmith shop at Broadway and Chapel in the 1880's.

The best fun from this connection came when Pirky called Pauline Novo to join the Santa Maria Valley Pioneer Association and make reservations for that year's November dinner dance. She mentioned that she was qualified for membership as a descendant of John and Jane Hopper. Pauline replied with delight (and goose bumps)—"We're cousins!"—which gave Pirky great happiness (and "hair standing on end"!)

Pirky enjoys her friendship with her newfound cousin, Pauline, as well as her relationship to two wonderful pioneer families in the Santa Maria Valley.

J. C. Conn Family

J.C. and Mary Conn were married during World War II. Settling in Santa Maria, they raised four children on East Mariposa Street, where they still live. The children all went to Santa Maria schools, all graduating from Santa Maria High School.

Dusty Jay Conn was born in 1944; he married Brenda, and their children are Shannon, born 1966; Lisa, born 1969; Mardelle, 1971; Sky Lee, 1983; Dustin, 1984; and Charla, 1986.

Jimmie Conn married Catherine; their children are Shann, born in 1969; Aaron, 1971; Kellie, 1989; and Terra, 1991.

Janice Conn, who was born in 1947, married Bernard Carreira. Their children are Lalanya, born in 1969, and Bernard, born in 1974. Lalanya had three children, Bryon, Matthew and Christine.

Scott Lewis Conn was born in 1950; he married Georgina Duran Conn, and they have one son, Nicholas, born in 1983.

J.C. worked in refrigeration, retiring from Lompoc Federal Prison. Mary stayed home and raised her children, and is now enjoying her great-grandchildren.

J.C.'s father was foreman at Casmite Oil Refinery. After retiring, he and his wife moved to Los Osos. After his death, she returned to Santa Maria to live until her death, near J.C. and his family. They will celebrate their 52nd anniversary on April 1, 1995.

"We all had so much fun when we were young people in Santa Maria. We all loved to dance, sing, and run around with our very active 'gang.' There's nothing like old friends—and a lot of us are still having wonderful times together."

Russell and Erla Slater Cook

y father, Russell Cook, was born in Santa Maria on December 14, 1909, to Eral and K.B. Cook. She taught at several local schools; her parents were Richard and Amelia Holland. Russell married Erla Agusta Slater of Nipomo in 1930. She is the daughter of Steven and Erla Kelley Slater. (The Slaters' history is in this book.) Erla was born in Graciosa, south of Orcutt, in 1912.

Russell worked for the Union Oil Company from the age of 17 until his retirement. He worked mostly in the Santa Maria Valley, but also did work in Creston and Shandon. I started school in Shandon. Russell died suddenly in Santa Maria in 1993.

My mother Erla was very ill around 1940 owing to complications of childbirth. The baby was stillborn. My sister Joan and I went to live with our grandmother, K.B. Cook, who taught school in a two-room schoolhouse in Creston, California. Later we stayed with my mother's sister on a ranch north of Los Alamos—Cathy and Everett Brickey. Erla recovered, and we moved back to Santa Maria. Joan and I both attended Fairlawn School, on West Main Street, followed by El Camino Junior High School and Santa Maria High School.

Joan married Rudy Dyck of Templeton. They had three children, and now, in 1995, live in Winters, California. The children, Cathy, Mike and Jane, gave them five grandchildren.

I married Grady Claborn in 1953. We had four children: Russell (1954-1974), Bill, Julie and David—they also have five children. We owned Grady's Auto Painting Shop, from which Grady retired. We then sold our home in Santa Maria and bought a mobile home at Del Cielo, south of Santa Maria. Soon after, Grady was killed in a horrible motorcycle accident.

I still live there. My daughter Julie and her son live with my mother, Erla, in Santa Maria. Julie takes care of her while attending Hancock College. I also spend a lot of time with my mom and stay there when Julie goes to college.

—Told by daughter Jerrie Cook Claborn, 1995

Marshall Cooper

Parts of a letter written to Pauline Novo in 1985

any years have passed since my school days in Orcutt, but we still keep in touch with my sixth-grade teacher, Miss Hilda Van. She is living in San Jose in a teachers' retirement home.

I am retired now, so my wife, June, and I travel a lot. On our way south from Oregon we stopped in San Jose and had a very good dinner and visit with Mrs. Gann. We then stopped by Grover City and had a nice visit with Paul and Norma Twyford. We also visited Minnie Tonnelli and Rowene Spears, who were both in my sixth-grade class in Orcutt. We live in Fontana, California.

Leota Pollard Clark Crawford

At Easter time, 1929, I arrived in Santa Maria with my family, from Fresno, California. My father went to work for Mr. Filiponi, who had a garage and service station on West Main Street. We resided at 621 South Lincoln Street, and I attended Santa Maria High School, graduating in 1932, followed by one year of junior college, which, at that time, held classes at the high school.

In July of 1933, I married Paul Clark, a resident of Orcutt, and we lived in the area where Paul was employed by Union Oil Company. He retired in 1968, and we moved to Guerneville, California, where I now reside.

My three children were born at Grigsby's Hospital on South Broadway in Santa Maria. Our youngest, Mac Clark, lives on Hobbs Lane near Orcutt, and is deeply involved with the Elks Club. He is currently going through the chairs.

Paul passed away in 1980, and I married Douglas Crawford, also a former Santa Maria resident, who had been an employee of Union Oil for 40 years.

Louis and Winifred Crawford

Louis Noiré Crawford and his wife, Winifred Kittredge Crawford, came to the Santa Maria Valley in 1920. They lived in Lompoc in 1919. They came from Berkeley, California, where Mr. Crawford taught at the University of California. He was a manual training teacher at Santa Maria Union High School, coaching football and other sports while completing his Architect degree.

He received his Architectural Certificate from the State of California in 1920, and opened offices in the Gibson-Drexler Building. He became known as the Architect with the Spanish Influence. Many of the schools he designed, from northern San Luis Obispo County to Santa Barbara, became well known schools. He designed Santa Maria City Hall and the Santa Maria Public Library, as well as many homes up and down the coast.

In 1938, at the age of 48, he had a stroke, paralyzing his right side. He passed away in 1946 at the age of 56.

Winifred Crawford made her mark as an educator. She taught English and journalism at Santa Maria High School. *The Breeze* won many awards for being an outstanding high school newspaper. She was also responsible for the annual, *The Review.*

In 1953 she married Henry W. Dixon and went to Hancock College as Dean of Girls (Women) before she retired in 1957, after almost 35 years as an educator.

She passed away in 1968 at the age of 75.

Two daughters came from this union: Dorothy, born in Santa Barbara in 1919, and Marjorie, born in 1921 in Santa Maria.

William "Bill" Dalessi

Maternal grandparents: William and Frances Davis Tunnell

On my father's mother's side (Adele Rojas), the family traces back to Don Manuel Boranda, who came to Monterey as a corporal in the Spanish Army with Father Serra. He later became the first schoolteacher in California in the Monterey and San Francisco area. His old adobe still stands in Monterey, and is the oldest adobe there.

My father's sister, Marie A. "Mollie" Knotts (Mrs. Jocko Knotts) was a Dalessi. I have lots of cousins in the Santa Maria Valley.

The Dalessi family came from Cavergno, Canton Ticino, Switzerland. My paternal grandfather was Alexander A. Dalessi, Sr., and my father was also Alexander A. Dalessi. Both of my parents lived in the Santa Maria area—my mother all her life. My father lived in the Long Beach area during his later years. Both are deceased.

Prior to 1900, my grandparents had a ranch in the Manzana area, but they moved to Santa Maria around 1900.

I live in Huntington Beach with my wife, Margo. We have three children: Theodore Dalessi, who is single, and William and Pamela, who are married. I graduated from Santa Maria Union High School in 1940½ and was very active and popular. I am now a lawyer in Huntington Beach, California.

Chester A. Davis, Jr.

My great-grandparents and my grandparents came to Santa Maria Valley in the early 1880's. My father, Chester A. Davis, Sr., was born in Garey in 1890. My mother was born in Los Olivos in 1896.

I was born in Santa Maria in 1921, and lived there in the valley-Orcutt Hill area continuously until 1974.

The year my father was president of the Pioneers, 1961-62, I was secretary-treasurer. That was the year we moved the location from Cuyama Road to the Union Oil Picnic Grounds. I now live in San Diego, California.

Mary Dudley Davis

My parents, George and Florence Robinson Dudley, were both born and raised in Humboldt County, California. They were married in 1905, and gradually migrated south, arriving in Santa Maria on January 13, 1910. They came from San Jose with all their possessions by Southern Pacific to Guadalupe; there they transferred to the electric car, which brought them into Santa Maria, where they were met by Marriot's transfer wagon. Mr. Domingues was the motor man and Mr. Gillespie the conductor of the electric motor car. Mr. Bill Yarnell drove Marriot's transfer wagon.

George Dudley was a brother of Albert A. Dudley, owner and founder of Dudley Mortuary. Until a house could be found, they stayed with brother Albert at 427 South Lincoln Street.

George was hired by T.A. Jones and son Jeff, who had begun this business in the late 1800's or early 1900's in a small building which they erected on the corner of Broadway and Church, having the "good earth" as a floor.

Their first home was on West Cypress. Later they built a new home at 506 South Lincoln Street. About 1920 they built a home in the country—about where Kmart is now, on Orcutt Road. At that time there were three children. They all went to Washington School, a one-room school which stood on Orcutt Road south of the Freeman property and across from the Toy property.

We made another move, settling again on Orcutt Road, where my father had a feed store and raised chickens for meat and eggs. Later he raised turkeys, until the government came in World War II and bought land right up to the Dudley property line, putting in an air field. This was no environment for turkeys, so we had to move. I went off to college after graduating from Santa Maria Union High School in 1932. I was back in Santa Maria for my marriage in June, 1937. I have two brothers: Donald, of San Jose, and John, of Visalia, California.

Joseph M. De Rosa

On May 13th, 1887, José, age 5, his sister Isabella, age 7, and their mother, Isabella Adelina Rosa, sailed to the United States from the Azores Islands, putting ashore in Boston Harbor.

Their father, Francisco, a carpenter by trade, had been at sea on a whaling ship. When they put into Morro Bay for repairs, around 1882, he never returned to the ship, and made residence there in Morro Bay. He built a home and many rentals on his property, which still stand today on Morro Bay Boulevard.

It is believed that Joseph, his sister and mother took another ship around South America to Port San Luis (Avila). Sisters Laura (Perry), Lenora (Simas), and brother John were born in the United States.

Francisco later owned a wharf and boats. He rented the boats for fishing, and Joseph's job was to catch bait for the fishermen. The "Portagee" joke told by my grandfather was that when they arrived at a good fishing spot, he told his son Joseph to mark the spot on the bottom of the boat.

In the early 1900's, Joseph drove wagons with teams of horses or mules. At one time he drove the Borax mule team through Death Valley—a very, very hot trip. He also hauled sugar beets for the Union Sugar factory in Betteravia.

In 1915 it took Joseph most of the day to drive a wagon from Morro Bay to Guadalupe for the Saturday night dance. It was worth it, because he met my mother there—Refugia Evangelina (Eva) Garcia. They married on November 1st, 1915, and lived in Santa Maria until 1934, when they moved to Betteravia with daughters Lorraine, born 1920, and Ruth, born 1927, and son James, born 1929. They lost a daughter, June, born in 1918, to pneumonia in 1923.

Joseph worked most of his life for the Union Sugar Company in Betteravia. He drove Caterpillar tractors and trucks, Jim and Ruth got to ride along with Dad on Saturdays to deliver beet seed to the farmers who contracted to grow sugar beets. Jim always had to ride in the middle, because the truck had no doors.

Dad became field foreman for Union Sugar, which meant a lot of visiting with farmers to get them to sign contracts to grow sugar beets. He had many friends in the valley; some remember him to this day. He already spoke Portuguese and Spanish, as well as a little Swiss-Italian. He retired in 1954 and moved back to Santa Maria with his wife, Eva. Lorraine had married Gerald George in 1938, and had five children; Ruth had married Ray Thornton in 1953 and had one daughter. Jim had married Jeanne Jackson in 1953 and they had three daughters.

In May of 1955, Joseph went by airplane to the Azores Islands. When applying for his passport, he was told that his father had not completed his citizenship papers. He had married Eva, who was born in Pozo, so he was legally a citizen. On Joseph's return from the Azores he applied, and in June 1955 he officially registered his name as Joseph Machado De Rosa.

Joseph died on December 27, 1961, and is buried by his wife, Eva, in the Mission Cemetery in San Luis Obispo, along with daughter June and his parents Frank and Isabella De Rosa, as well as his sister, Isabella (Mammie) Silveria.

—*Ruth De Rosa Thornton, 1994*

G. Keith Diamond

rt and Hazel Diamond moved to the Santa Maria Valley in 1936. They had two sons, Vic and Keith. Vic was born in 1933 in the Los Angeles area, and Keith was born in 1943 in Santa Maria.

Art worked at an auto parts store on East Church Street. Later he took on a partner and formed Valley Auto Parts in the 400 block of West Main Street.

In 1957 Art and Vic opened up Diamond's Auto Supply in Guadalupe. Keith got involved in the business when he was fourteen with after-school hours. In 1961, Art and Vic opened their second store in the 600 block of West Main Street in Santa Maria. Keith worked there throughout his high school years.

Keith went to grade school at Alvin Street School when it first opened. After that he attended El Camino Junior High School. He played the trombone in the El Camino band, led by Lester Hayes. He also played in the high school band under Mr. Baldwin. He graduated from Santa Maria High

School in 1961. He attended Hancock Junior College until he was called to active duty in the U.S. Air Force in 1964; he was honorably discharged in 1968.

Keith met his bride-to-be in Colorado. They married in 1966 in Colorado Springs. Their first daughter, Nanette, was born there. Their second daughter, Michelle, was born in Santa Maria.

After Keith was discharged from the service, he and his family returned to Santa Maria, where he went back to work in the family business.

Mrs. Art Diamond passed away in 1998. She had a good life.

In 1990, Keith and Vic sold their business.

Keith now works for a forklift dealer in Santa Maria, managing the parts department. After hours, Keith has a hobby business, building and repairing custom fishing rods and reels.

Keith's wife has been a beautician for thirty years. She owns her own business.

Donati Family History

Samuel (Sam) Donati was born in the town of Broglio, Canton Ticino, Switzerland, on April 29,1853, and moved to America in 1872, settling at Cayucos, California. At the age of nineteen he married Maria Bassi, who was born in Canton Ticino, Switzerland, on November 11, 1865, and died June 4, 1892, at 27 years of age. Sam and Maria were married at the San Luis Obispo Mission on July 2, 1883. Sam was a dairyman farmer and Justice of Peace in Cayucos. In 1881, Sam and Maria purchased 1,200 acres along the coast near Cayucos. He raised cattle, hogs and over 120 dairy cows. Sam and Maria had seven children: Virginia, Flora, Louis, Arnold, Priscilla, May and Ida.

Louis C. Donati, Sam and Maria's third child, was born in Cayucos on March 1, 1887. When he was twelve years of age, Louis was sent to Switzerland to attend school. He returned to Cayucos at the age of twenty and worked at his father Sam's ranch. In 1904, Louis met Lillian Becwar, formerly of Wisconsin, who was a school teacher in Arroyo Grande, California. They were married at the Catholic Church in Arroyo Grande in 1906. From 1906 to 1920, Louis had various jobs—he worked at a meat market in Arroyo Grande, raised pigs in Betteravia, and worked at the Guadalupe Creamery. In 1920, Louis started a dairy in Oso Flaco on Highway 1 at the base of the Nipomo Mesa. In 1929, Louis and Lillian bought 160 acres of farmland in Santa Maria. The ranch was bordered by Alvin, Blosser, Donovan and Railroad. Louis eventually sublet the dairy and continued operating the ranch until he retired in 1939. Louis passed away in 1970 and Lillian in 1971. Louis and Lillian had seven children: Samuel, Clifford, Margaret, Edith, Evelyn, Louis Jr. and Clarence.

LOUIS AND LILLIAN'S CHILDREN:

Samuel (Sam) is a retired electrician in Santa Maria and has one son, Mark.

Clifford married Elsie DeMartin and farmed in the Santa Maria Valley until his death in 1980.

Clifford and Elsie had four children: Catherine Allen, Fred, Richard and David. Elsie died in 1999.

Margaret married Bob Corcoran of San Luis Obispo. They had two daughters, Peggy Lambert and Mary Ellen Corcoran.

Edith married Baldwin Handel of Shafter. They had two children, Judy Casey and Tim.

Evelyn married Oscar Liebert. They had two children, Bruce and Carlyn Liebert.

Louis Jr. married Evelyn Poletti from San Luis Obispo. They had two sons, William and Thomas. Louis Jr. farmed and raised cattle until his death in 1973.

Clarence married Nancy Boden. Nancy's parents came to Santa Maria in 1925, and had three daughters, Patricia Dudley, Nancy Donati and Sally Testa.

Clarence and Nancy raised six children: Jane Rouse, Leslie Webb, George, James, John and Patricia Bouquet. Clarence farmed for thirty years in Garey, California. He then managed the Santa Maria Chili Dehydrator from 1979 to 1987. In 1996, Clarence and Al Novo co-chaired, with the help of numerous Pioneers, an ongoing project to design and develop the Pioneer Park on Foster Road. The Park has become a very popular gathering spot for groups of all sizes. Clarence is a past president of both the Pioneer Association and the Pioneer Foundation.

The Diani Family

Lorenzo Diani, born on October 15, 1882, in Figione, Switzerland, immigrated to America in 1919. He soon sent for his fiancée, Mary Dolinda Balzani, and they were married in San Francisco in 1920. After a short stay in San Francisco, they moved south to Greenfield, California, where he worked in the dairy business. In 1928 Lorenzo brought his family to the Santa Maria Valley community of Betteravia to operate, in partnership, a dairy with the Union Sugar Company. In 1939 he bought out Union Sugar and moved the dairy to a new location just west of the city of Santa Maria.

Lorenzo and Mary raised two children, A.J. and Madeline. Madeline married Woodrow Bianchi and worked for Union Sugar Company for 43 years. A.J., after serving in the Navy during World War II, established a grading and paving business, A.J. Diani Construction Co., in 1949.

A.J. and the former Margaret Bowden of New Zealand raised five children, Cecilia, Bob, Susan, Jim, and Mike. All the children were born at Sisters' Hospital, attended local schools, and still reside in the area. A.J. married the former Gayle Winger in 1979 and Margaret married George Paden in 1993.

Cecilia married Allan Teixeira of the Santa Maria Valley-based Teixeira Farm family and has three children, Steve, Christy, and John, and six grandchildren. Bob married the former Julie Koop of Lakeview, Oregon, and has two children, Tony and Mary Beth. Susan married Don Ward of Olton, Texas, and has four children, Justin, Jody, Jill, and Jeff, and three grandchildren. Jim married the former Teresa Galyardt of Russell, Kansas, and has two children, Jason and Missy, and one grandchild. Mike married the former Marty Ashwanden of Galt, California, and has three children, Nick, Laura, and Katie.

A.J. Diani Construction Co., Inc., celebrated its 50th anniversary in 1999 and is currently owned and operated by Jim and Mike Diani and Don Ward. The company also has four third-generation family members in its ranks: Justin and Jeff Ward and Jason and Melissa Diani.

The Diani family has been noteworthy for their civic, educational, and business leadership and for their quiet but generous contributions to many important local projects and charitable organizations that improve the quality of life in the Santa Maria Valley.

Dunlap Family

The Dunlap (or Dunlop) family came from the early Celtic tribal chieftainship. The forebears of our local Dunlaps moved from Dunlap, Scotland, located in Ayrshire, to Londonderry, Ireland, to Londonderry, New Hampshire, to Cherry Valley, New York, to Dunlap, Illinois, to San Francisco, California.

Ralph Stuart Dunlap married Caroline Agnes Covell in San Francisco. They were in San Francisco during the 1906 earthquake. Their two sons, Jim and Don, were born in Palo Alto, California—James in 1908, and Donald in 1910. The family moved to San Luis Obispo, and then to Creston; from Creston to Orcutt in 1917 on the narrow-gauge railway.

Ralph Dunlap's family descended from Reverend Samuel Dunlap, who was born in 1690 and graduated from Trinity College, Dublin, Ireland. He came to the United States: first to Londonderry, New Hampshire, and then in 1714 to Cherry Valley, New York. A gentleman learned in the classics, as well as in the modern literature of the day, he erected a log church and schoolhouse combined. It was the first church west of the Hudson River in which the English language was preached. In the winter of 1743, the first classical school west of Albany was founded: the Cherry Valley Academy.

A part of the Dunlap family moved to Illinois and settled there in about 1838. They deeded land for a church and a school, and later built an Academy on their property. Ralph Dunlap was born there, in Dunlap, Illinois, in 1881. He graduated from the Dunlap Academy.

Ralph Dunlap was on the Orcutt School Board from 1918 to 1924, and was the main worker in establishing the Orcutt Union School District, and in building the new Orcutt school. The district was organized mainly to provide an education for the children of Union Oil Company employees, who lived on Newlove Hill and in the town of Orcutt.

Donald Dunlap, Ralph's son, also worked for Union Oil Company, and served on the Orcutt Union School Board from 1950 to 1959. He was chairman of the board when the new school his father helped build was torn down. He did not want to have it torn down, but was made to believe that it would be his fault if an earthquake came and destroyed the building.

Donald was six years old when he came to Orcutt. He attended the old original school in the 300 block of West Clark Ave., and then walked to the other side of town when the new school was built in 1920.

Donald worked before and after school and on weekends for Jack Jullian's service station. Then he worked for years for Charlie Webb at the Orcutt Mercantile. Then he worked for Union Oil Company for thirty-nine years, retiring as water superintendent.

Donald married Marie Sweet, and they have two daughters, Diane and Debbie. The girls were well known for their dancing ability in the Santa Maria Valley. As late as 1991, Don and Marie were still living in the Orcutt area; by 1994, Don had died and Marie had moved to live with her daughter Diane in southern California.

Isaac and Nancy Fesler

Isaac and Nancy Fesler arrived in this valley with their eight children in 1869. Isaac was born March 13, 1818, in Winchester, Kentucky. He was the tenth of thirteen children born to John and Catherine Fesler, natives of North Carolina. While still a boy, Isaac and his family moved to Pike County, Illinois, and it was there that Isaac met Nancy Barnes, daughter of James and Mary Barnes. Nancy was born on February 12, 1822, in Tennessee. They were married October 28, 1841, in Griggsville, Illinois, and that is where their first four children were born: James K., Silas W., Emily J., and Stephen A.

Isaac Fesler moved his family to Linn County, Missouri, in about 1855, and farmed there for the next ten years. Three more children were born there: Austin R., Sterling O., and Edward L.

Many families from the Midwest were moving on to the west coast, having heard of rich, fertile land for good farming. The need for farmers there was due to the large influx of gold seekers and business people in the 1850's.

Isaac Fesler, with dreams of a better life, moved his family and possessions in a covered wagon and headed west in a wagon train in 1865. Their trip to California was long and arduous, the older children walking most of the way. They first settled in Sonoma County; it is not known how long they stayed there. However, it is known that they were living in Solano County by May 19, 1867, for it was on that day that their last child was born. Mary Catherine was born in a covered wagon. They remained there until 1869, when word began circulating that there was good farming land to the south, which the government was granting for homesteading. Isaac Fesler was now 51 years old, and he felt the need to settle down and build a home for his family.

On arriving in Santa Maria by covered wagon, he wasted no time taking up a quarter-section of land to homestead. He chose the northwest section of what was later to become Central City. They built their home on what is now the north side of the 100 block of West Fesler Street. Isaac Miller, John Thornburg, and Randolph Cook took up the other three quarter-sections. Soon these four homesteaders had a meeting to decide on plans to develop a town site on their property. They each donated land for two wide streets to be named Broadway and Main. The site was surveyed in 1874 and was named Central City.

A deed of sale was signed by Fesler on January 31, 1875, to L.M. Kaiser of Guadalupe, for a piece of property (107x140) bordering Broadway and Main. The price: "Three Hundred Dollars—gold coin of United States of America." The Kaiser brothers built a clothing store. Fesler also donated the right-of-way to the Pacific Coast Railroad during this period.

All had not gone well for the Fesler family during these years. Soon after their arrival in our valley, their elder daughter, Emily, died in December, 1869. She was eighteen years old. This was followed by the death of their second son, Silas, in April of 1871, at the age of 21. Again in December, 1872, they lost another child: their oldest son, James, who died at the age of 26. Isaac and Nancy had great faith in God, which helped them to accept their losses. Stephen, their fourth child, was now 17 and able to take on a man's chores.

In 1882, when Central City applied for a post office, it was required that the name be changed. The name Santa Maria was chosen, after the Santa Maria Rancho and the river north of town.

As the town grew and families moved closer together, the townspeople started meeting at picnics, band concerts, and so forth. One by one, the young people began to pair off. Isaac and Nancy's children began to marry. Stephen was first. He married Olive May Johnson in 1876. Austin married Sarah Couch in 1882, and Sterling married Frances Culp in 1883. Mary Catherine married James C. Martin in 1885, and Edward married Charlotte Gressby in 1888.

Isaac Fesler died on July 24, 1891, twenty-two years after coming to our valley. He had prospered, and saw many of his dreams come true.

Nancy Fesler died on August 22, 1895, at the home of her son, Stephen. Her obituary reads, "Mrs. Fesler was highly esteemed by all who knew her . . . she was devoted to her children and grandchildren."

There are many descendants of Isaac and Nancy Fesler living in the Central Coast area. Among them are these great-grandchildren:

- Ellis Fesler, *Santa Maria*
- Norman H. Thole, *Nipomo*
- Glenn Fesler Thole, *Nipomo*
- Pauline Thole Brown, *Nipomo*
- Martin H. Brisco, *Arroyo Grande*
- Richard Fesler, *Arroyo Grande*
- Elizabeth Thole Farrar, *San Luis Obispo*

July, 1987
Submitted by Mabel Kraft Brisco
and Rosemary Thole, 1990

Everyone—Remember the Egg Man?

by Robert Flint • "Senior Beat," Santa Maria Times, 1995

They don't play "kick the can" anymore. Most of you Seniors who are in my age group will probably recall how many times you played this game.

Can you remember the egg man? He came to our house once a week. If Mom had to be away, she would leave the money on the kitchen table to pay for the eggs. He would leave the eggs in the "ice box," collect his money, and leave. If he was hungry, maybe he would have a doughnut and a glass of milk—for this he would leave an extra egg or so.

Strange as it may seem, the egg man could do this because we never locked our doors; it wasn't necessary. Maybe it was the era we lived in, or perhaps the people were different. I don't know. It was not because everyone was honest; they were not. We had our share of crime, but it was different from what we have today. As I look back at this, I think it was because we were in the same boat, so to speak. To say it was a good time might be a little exaggerating. There was hunger, want, and sickness. There were not enough doctors, but they did make house calls, and the people had each other to depend on.

I can recall when Mom was baking a cake, or pie—she would run out of flour. She'd hand me a cup and tell me to go to the neighbors and "borrow a cup." If that person was not home, I would get a cup of flour from the flour bin, and close the door on my way out. This was a common occurrence that everyone did.

I remember that when I came down with the measles, the whole house was quarantined. Neighbors would come to the door and ask what we needed. They'd place boxes of food, fuel and sundry items on the steps for our needs. This was a system that worked—for the simple reason that to survive, we all had to stick together. It was called love of our fellow man. When the man of the house became disabled, everyone in the neighborhood would pitch in and help.

There was no welfare system in those days to help. Only through the help of others did we survive. I think, as I look back, that we had one common factor that helped us: we were all poor. Most of the country was. We had just survived the war to end all wars, and the Great Depression was upon us.

As I reminisce about this time, there is one thing that stands out above all else. I'm proud of the people who lived then, and many are still with us.

They persevered in the face of overwhelming odds to help bring this nation into the affluent position it now holds. I'm very grateful to have lived my youth in that generation.

Now there is a new generation—I wish them well. I would like to think they will profit from our mistakes. Soon most of my generation will be gone. I have but one regret. They don't play "kick the can" anymore.

* * * *

Reading this article in "Senior Beat," I decided that it really rang a bell. First I gave it to my eleven-year-old granddaughter Makenzie to read, which she did with interest. I grew up in Orcutt—east end—the last house on Union Avenue. A hill across the street went down to the creek that ran in wintertime. A large oak was there; this is where we played "run sheep run" and "kick the can." We rolled tires in from the dump, and had huge bonfires. This we could do in those days.

Most families went to the movies in Santa Maria on Saturdays. We went in our Model A Ford. Those days, and our friends and neighbors, I will never forget.

I love to remember . . .

—*Pauline Novo*

James F. Forbes

James Forbes, of Orcutt, California, erected the fourth building in the town, and became a builder in commercial, in the oil fields. He was born in Nova Scotia in 1859, son of a sea captain. He followed the sea for many years, going to sea on his father's ship, the *Alexander*. He became first mate and worked his way to the top, as master mariner. In 1854 he married Jessie Crow from Nova Scotia.

Forbes became acquainted with Mr. W.W. Orcutt, and bought two lots, where he erected a wooden store building in what is now downtown Orcutt. He was the first merchant. He served as Postmaster from 1905 until his resignation in 1913.

In 1910, the building and its contents were destroyed by fire, a loss of $52,000, with only $12,000 insurance. Mr. Forbes then organized the Orcutt Improvement Co., and they erected an 80- to 90-foot building at the cost of $10,000. The second floor is used for a public dance hall. The lower floor is occupied by Orcutt Mercantile. Officers are F.C. Twitchell, president, C.E. Webb, and Mr. Forbes.

They were the parents of eight children, four of whom died in early childhood: Aubrey D., Stella, Edward and Willard. Willard lived, worked, and died in Orcutt. He and his wife Stella had two children.

As of 1997, Eda Mae is married, and lives in the old Forbes home, a very nice two-story home at 255 Pinal Avenue in Orcutt. She is married to Charlie Atkins. They are very well known in their community. Willard's wife, Stella Forbes, ran the Orcutt Post Office for many years, and Willard worked for the Union Oil Company, from which he retired. They lived all their lives in Orcutt, as their daughter, Eda Mae, is doing.

The Randall Froom Family

The Froom family has a long history in the Santa Maria Valley. My father came from Shanley, Ontario. Look around and perhaps you'll still see an A.H. Froom oil or water tank. His sheet metal shop was originally in Guadalupe, and following his marriage to Annie Saulsberry there in 1894, they relocated to Santa Maria. A team of horses hauled lumber from Point Sal for the home they built, which is still standing at 324 West Church.

My sister Gladys was the first child, born in 1897, followed by Darrell three years later. I was born in 1910 in the same room. When I was six, my dad moved his skating rink on North Broadway around the corner on Mill Street to make room for a two-story addition to the California Hotel. Below was the sales room for Rickenbacker cars, with a garage in the rear.

At Main Street Elementary School, I was awarded the high point medal at a track meet for three counties in the 50-, 100-, and 220-yard dash, and third in the shot put. I was class president in 1927 at Santa Maria High School, and took part in football and track. You'll see my mark in the block letters I designed for sports. Attending junior college, I did my homework while working in Jeff Cochran's garage. Then I went to San Jose State, where I earned a teaching credential in Industrial Arts in 1939. I first worked at Hoover High School in Glendale. My son Doug was born there in 1942. Following a tour of duty as an officer in the Marine Radar Maintenance Group during World War II, I returned to teaching in Glendale. I established a tank (model airplane) business on the side.

The hobby was just starting, so I added spinners of all sizes to my line of tanks. (A spinner is the pointed nose that streamlines a plane.) I sold to dealers world wide, and to the Navy for a drone plane. With these spinners, speed records were broken.

It was a lucrative business, but the interest in model planes fell off with the advent of television. After sixteen years, I sold out and moved to Sacramento, where I contracted and built a first-class mobile home park, the first one in the area.

A third generation has followed similar pursuits. Doug has said he acquired his mechanical abilities from me. In my retirement, I can enjoy my son's achievements when Ethel and I aren't RV'ing from our home in Folsom four or five months out of the year.

I am pleased when I think of being born and raised in the Santa Maria Valley, where I could make so many good friends from different ethnic groups.

—*Randall Froom*
Approx. 1989

Gamble Family History

James Harrison ("Harry") Gamble was born on September 22, 1892, in Los Angeles, California, to James Mitchel Gamble and Margaret Ann Harrison. The Gamble family already had seven children when they came to Los Angeles from Cleveland, Ohio, in 1885; five more were born in Los Angeles, with Harry being the last. He grew up to be the fourth generation of Gamble brick makers.

In 1920 the Faulstich Bros. Masonry Co. of San Luis Obispo, California, who were contractors, decided to make their own brick, in order to save the cost of hauling bricks from Los Angeles. Accordingly, they added San Luis Brick, Inc., to their business, but they were unable to get their new brick machine to work properly, so they contacted the Gambles, who were noted for making brick in Los Angeles, and asked for help. Harry Gamble took on the job, bringing two of his brick-making brothers and a brother-in-law to San Luis Obispo to teach the Faulstich Bros. how to make brick. They did such a good job teaching that the Faulstich Bros. asked them to make brick for them all year.

When they finished in the fall of 1920, the Faulstich Bros. offered to teach the Gambles how to lay brick if they would stay in town (for you can make brick only when there is no rain). Most of them did stay. Later, when Harry Gamble came down to Santa Maria with the Faulstich Bros. to work on a brick job, he was introduced to city leader C.L. Preisker as "the man who taught the Faulstich Bros. how to make brick." Right away, Preisker asked Harry if he would like to buy a brickyard. Harry told Preisker he didn't have enough money to buy water to make brick, let alone buy a brickyard. The next day, Preisker came back and offered a deal: he and five other men would buy 50,000 bricks right then, before they were even made, so that Harry could buy the defunct brickyard

at 700 South Blosser Road, which had been owned by the Hill Brothers. It was an offer they couldn't refuse, and Harry and his brothers Elroy Taylor (E.T.) Gamble and Henry Morton Gamble moved in during the spring of 1921.

The Gambles made brick by hand until they were able to obtain their father's old Machine Witch that was still in the family; their brother John Archibald Gamble came with it. John had been married but was divorced. After John A. Gamble, another brother, Wilbur Davis Gamble, came to work in Santa Maria. He was married to Ruth Farrell Bryan. They had four children, but only the oldest one, Alvah Kenneth Gamble, came to live at the Santa Maria brickyard.

All five of the brothers built homes and lived and died in Santa Maria. Wilbur's son, Alvah, also built homes in Santa Maria when he came back from World War II. He had two short marriages with no children before marrying Opal Hawthorne of Los Angeles. They had four children: Kenneth Elwood, born June 23, 1954; Beverly Jean, born August 21, 1955; Dean John, born February 28, 1961; and Ruth Tabitha, born November 20, 1962. They all still live in the Santa Maria area.

Harry was divorced and had three boys: George Harrison, Kenneth Wilson, and Charles Morton. The two oldest came to Santa Maria with him, but since the youngest was only a year old, he did not come until he was 15 years old. Harry also brought with him a new wife from San Luis Obispo who lived across the railroad tracks from the brickyard.

Harry's second wife, Louise Cattaneo Guerra, was born September 19, 1906, in Cambria. Together they had two sons, James Harrison Gamble, Jr., and Jack Robert Gamble. All five of the boys went to Santa Maria High School.

• George Harrison Gamble, the oldest son, was

born April 13, 1916. After leaving high school, he went on to the Navy for a hitch. He married Vera June Hegwood and they had a son, Ted Harrison, born May 22, 1940, and a daughter, Peggy June, born February 20, 1945. After World War II they all lived in the Los Angeles area.

• Kenneth Wilson Gamble, the second son, was born May 2, 1918. After high school he married Betty Jane Towner. During the war he served in the Navy. They had a son, William ("Bill") K. Gamble, born March 3, 1939. After the war they also moved to the Los Angeles area. Bill came back to Santa Maria and lived with his uncle James Harrison ("Jim") Gamble three different times for several years at a time until he got married and moved to San Francisco to finish law school. After working as a lawyer in Los Angeles for a few years he came back to Santa Maria, and today he has law offices in five different cities in the Central Coast area.

• Charles Morton Gamble, the third son, born on October 22, 1919, came to Santa Maria in 1939. He married Louella Mae Cottle on October 5, 1940, and worked in the tile business for his father. He then became a pipefitter and worked for Union Oil Co. and other oil work companies. Charles and Louella had three children: Christine Marie, born February 12, 1942; David Charles, born April 30, 1944; and Eric Dennis, born June 15, 1948.

• James Harrison Gamble, Jr., the fourth son, was born on December 3, 1924. On April 9, 1944, he married Lucille Phyllis Silva, born December 1, 1928, and they had five children: Charlotte Mae, born January 5, 1945; Eileen Carol, born September 8, 1946; Ronald Harrison, born November 25, 1948; James Harrison III, born December 17, 1949; and Darrell Harrison, born January 9, 1958.

Jim Gamble, fourth son of Harry Gamble, has been very active doing masonry work at the new Pioneer Park during the past five years. In May 2001

Jim took Clarence Donati's place as president of the Pioneer Park Foundation. He hopes to finish all the projects laid out by the Pioneer Association during his term as president.

On July 29, 1962, Charlotte married George Wright, born August 30, 1943. They had two children, Teresa and George. They all now live near Sacramento.

On October 20, 1962, Eileen married Harold ("Butch") Rios, born March 30, 1943. They had two girls, Tamara Lynn ("Tami"), born September 1, 1963, who married Lance Lodes of Lompoc, and Cheryl Antoinette ("Toni"), born October 6, 1965, who married Larry Lane of Lompoc. They all live in the Santa Maria area.

On August 9, 1969, Ronald married Ruthanne Maretti, born December 24, 1947. They had a daughter, Stacy, who married Kenneth Shaw, and a son, James, who is not yet married. All but Stacy and her husband live in the Santa Maria area.

James III never married.

Darrell married Joan Abaffi, born September 14, 1955. They had two boys, Jason Michael and Bryan Mathew, and two girls, Kaelyn Maria and Madison. The two boys live in Santa Maria, while the rest of the family lives in Idaho.

• Jack Robert Gamble, the fifth son, was born on December 5, 1925, and married Francis Freitas from Hanford. They had four children, Jackie, Robert, Dennis, and Jeffrey. After the children were born, they all moved to Grass Valley, including Jackie and her husband Larry Azcarate. Jack was killed in a car accident on September 21, 1968. At that time all of them came back to Santa Maria.

Most of the Gambles have been very active in the Santa Maria community. They have always donated much in the way of time and skills to local clubs, schools, parks, sports, churches, and the Santa Barbara County Fair, and raising money for worthy causes.

The First Black Family to Settle in Santa Maria Valley

by Kenneth Gatewood
Submitted by Leander Gatewood, 1992

It wasn't until the late 'twenties and early 'thirties that blacks were attracted to Santa Maria. The first were Bill and Mabel Wilfred. Bill operated Bill's Taxi. A Mr. Messina went to Bakersfield in search of an employee. He met Mr. Loudon Gatewood, and offered him the job of shoe shiner. Mr. Gatewood accepted, and after working for awhile, he found a place for his family to live. He went to Bakersfield and loaded up all the Gatewoods' belongings, his wife and five children, and moved to Santa Maria.

Loudon Gatewood started life in Santa Maria in 1932 with his family. He was born in Pueblo, Colorado, in 1900. As a boy, he moved to Needles, California. It was there that he learned the trade of shoe shining. Work was hard to find, so he moved around a lot, using shoe shining to support himself. He met his future wife in Chehalis, Washington. They were married in 1926. There they had three children. Then they moved to Bakersfield, California. Two more children were added to the family there.

Moving to Santa Maria in 1932, he worked for Mr. Messina for two or three years; then he opened his own business. At first, shoe shining was all he offered, but in 1938, with the business well established, he went to selling books, magazines and candy.

When World War II began, business became very good because of the military bases in the area. "Gatewood's Shine Parlor" polished many military boots. Mr. Gatewood worked as many as twelve hours a day. Some days, due to military blackouts, he had to quit early. Blackouts meant lights out to prevent attacks at night upon our town. Mr. Gatewood had a wife and eight children to support, so he was not drafted into the service. During the War his children proved to be a great asset to him by helping in his business. After the War, his shop closed, and he worked for other businesses and shops.

After the children had grown older and gone their own ways, Mr. Gatewood went into semi-retirement and worked only when he wanted to. He also began to travel, and turned the family home over to the oldest children. Mr. and Mrs. Gatewood had six sons and three daughters. All of them attended local schools and were very well known, especially for their athletic abilities. Santa Maria proved to be home to all the Gatewoods. Some of the children have left the area, while others remain.

Clyde, the oldest child, was born in Chehalis, Washington. He graduated from Santa Maria High School and worked in his dad's shop after school and on weekends. He was drafted into the service. After his discharge, he returned to Santa Maria for awhile, after which he moved to San Francisco, where he raised a family—four sons and one daughter.

Annabelle, the second child, was also born in Washington and went through the Santa Maria school system. She was very active in sports. After school she worked at the shop, keeping business records and selling candy, magazines and books. After graduating from Santa Maria Junior College, she married Eric Tell. They had six children: four sons and two daughters. They all attended and graduated from Santa Maria schools and are still living in the area. Eric worked for Bill's Taxi in the 'thirties. He also owned his own trucking business for a while. Then he drove for a local trucking firm until he retired in 1980.

Le Roy was also born in Washington. When he became old enough, he helped his father in the business. "I became my father's right-hand man," recalls Le Roy. He could not get involved in school sporting activities because he worked after school. Le Roy was a Boy Scout, and during the War he had the job of telling people on his block to turn out their lights. He had to let the government know that he was buying a bike for a "war effort" job—a paper route. The paper informed people about the War. Le Roy went into the military for a while, after which he returned to Santa Maria. He worked for several jobs prior to going to work for George Sousa's Music Center. He was there for twenty-five years when the business closed. He is presently living and working in the Santa Maria area.

Urelalee was the fourth child and second daughter. She was born in Bakersfield shortly after they moved there from Washington. Several years after she graduated from the Santa Maria school system, she married Connie Seymore. She raised seven children, and later moved to Guadalupe, where she lived until her death in 1978. Several of her children are still living in the Santa Maria Valley.

Leander, the fifth child, was born in Bakersfield in 1932. He was five months old when they moved to Santa Maria. He went clear through Santa Maria schools, and was involved in many activities. When he was twelve years old, he joined the Boy Scouts' Troop 2, sponsored by the Kiwanis Club. He became the first black child to qualify as an Eagle Scout. It was stated that he won more awards than any other Scout between Los Angeles and San Francisco. He also was selected for the "Order of the Arrow" as a charter member of northern Santa Barbara County. He also advanced to the rank of Assistant Skipper in Explorer Scouts.

Leander graduated from Santa Maria High School in 1950. He then went to Santa Maria Junior College during the time it was located at the high school. He was drafted into the Army during the Korean War. He

stayed in the military for 22½ years, retiring as a Master Sergeant. Then Leander returned to Santa Maria and continued his education at Allan Hancock College. Presently he lives in the Santa Maria area and is employed by a local school district.

Geraldine was the sixth child and third daughter. She was born in the Grigsby Hospital in the 300 block of East Church Street. At that time the family lived in the 200 block of East Church Street. Geraldine was the first black child to be born in Santa Maria, on March 21, 1935. She attended local schools, as did her brothers and sisters. She married Emanuel Manson and moved to northern California, where she raised seven children. She is now living in southern California.

Geraldine related the fact that Mr. Langenbeck, the principal of El Camino Junior High School, had taught all of the Gatewood children.

Norman, the seventh child and fourth son, attended local schools and was active in sports as well as other activities. He was active in Boy Scouts. In high school, he was very active in the school band, orchestra, and a dance band, in which he played the trombone and drums. He was voted All-Conference player of the year in football. He graduated from Santa Maria Union High School in 1955, and while attending Hancock College in 1956, he was voted most valuable player on the Hancock football team. As a young man he worked with his father at the shoe shine parlor; later he worked for the Roemer and Rubel Buick auto dealership on North Broadway. He delivered several newspapers. He was in the local Navy Reserve for eight years prior to going on to active duty. After being honorably discharged from the Navy, he settled in Los Angeles. In 1959 Norman married Mae Reed of Paso Robles, California, who is now a professional Gospel singer and recording artist. They raised three children and now have three grandchildren. Norman has been a member of the Los Angeles County Sheriff's Department for sixteen years. He now works for United Parcel Service, and is an ordained deacon and the financial secretary of the Friendly Missionary Baptist Church.

Donald was the eighth child and the fifth son. He attended local schools and graduated in 1957, after which he attended Idaho State College. While attending Santa Maria High School, he was the first black student body president. He was active in youth programs in Santa Maria. He taught at St. Joseph High School and served as football coach there.

Don Gatewood and daughter

He sold newspapers on the street corner and to local businesses, a popular pursuit at the time. He graduated from Santa Maria High School in 1961. During Kenneth's early years his father had retired, so he didn't get to work for the family shoe shine parlor. But he did work; he learned the business and followed in his father's footsteps. He didn't really like it, though, so he went to work at a local department store.

Kenneth met and married Nora Pennington in 1968. They are raising three children in Santa Maria. He is employed with a local oil company.

While he was in college, Donald married Alice Anderson, of Washington, D.C. They raised two children in the Santa Maria area. He is now employed and lives in southern California.

Kenneth was the ninth child and the sixth son. He was very active in school sports. During the 'fifties he participated in local Little League and Middle League baseball.

Although Eula and Loudon Gatewood have passed away, in 1953 and 1957 respectively, the Gatewood legacy lives on in the Santa Maria Valley. Five children have left the area, but four remain, raising families and passing on the legacy of the Gatewoods—the first black family to settle in Santa Maria.

Glines Family History

Cassius Henry Glines (1850-1928) was a resident of Santa Maria Valley for over a half century. During this time he achieved noteworthy success as a farmer and stock raiser, and at the same time contributed to important work in the field of public service. He was a school trustee of Pine Grove for a quarter of a century and aided in establishing Santa Maria High School. Cassius was born November 5, 1850, in Salt Lake City, Utah, to John Henry Glines and Mary Ann Evans Glines.

Cassius Henry Glines and Sarah Belle Martin were married on September 22, 1872. Along with his parents, they moved to Santa Maria in 1879. Although the outlook was discouraging, father and son set to work farming after purchasing a tract of one hundred and sixty acres from a squatter. Cassius also filed on a pre-emption claim and from time to time would add to his holdings, becoming the owner of a ranch of twelve hundred and twenty-five acres situated near the headwaters of Alamo Canyon, and also a tract of one hundred and twenty acres six and one-half miles south of Santa Maria. He produced the crops best adapted to the soil and climatic conditions of this region, and also raised cattle, horses and hogs. The Orcutt ranch owned by the Glines family was sold and is now known as "Oak Knolls." It is a housing development, and one of the streets is named Glines Avenue.

Cassius Henry and Sarah Belle Glines were the parents of eight children: Charles Henry, John Thomas, Robert Cassius, Anna Belle Glines MacDonald, Huldah Araminta Glines Purkiss, Eva May (unmarried), James Leroy, and Sarah Lavina Glines Goodwin.

• Charles Henry Glines (1873-1949). Charles ("Charlie") worked very closely with his father as a cattle rancher on the Alamo property twenty miles northeast of Santa Maria. This ranch later became the home of Charlie and his family. Charles Henry was married to Annie Purvis on April 9, 1913, in Santa Maria. They had two children: Charles Purvis Glines and Dorothy Belle Glines Young. Dorothy married Kenneth Young. They had two children, David Kenneth Young and Elizabeth Ann Young. In later years, the Alamo ranch became the home of Charles Purvis and Gladys Nadine Johnston Glines, where they reared their two children, Charles Herbert Glines and Charlene Glines. Charles Herbert ("Chuck") Glines married Linda Riley. He worked for the U.S. Forest Service and as a firefighter at Vandenberg Air Force Base. Chuck and Linda have the following children: Timothy Scott Giovanacci, Tami Michelle Traylor, Tandi Marie Hester and Gina Jenette Jimenez. Charlene married Phillip Baczkiewicz. They have two children, Cody Sean Baczkiewicz and Courtney Kelley Baczkiewicz. Charlene is a teacher and administrator in the Santa Maria Bonita School District. Both Chuck and Charlene, along with their families, continue to raise cattle on the Glines Ranch, which makes four generations who have occupied the Alamo property.

• John Thomas Glines (1875-1949). John Thomas married Dora Beatrice Holloway in Los Alamos on December 10, 1895. John Thomas had a homestead on the Alamo Creek in San Luis Obispo County, a branch of the Santa Maria River, in about 1895. He later bought up a number of other homesteads on that creek to give himself a cattle ranch which became known as the Rock Front Ranch. John and Dora had the following children: Vera Lucille Glines, Melba Violette Glines, Rebecca Belle Glines, Denzil ("Denny") Cassius Glines, and Jack Holloway Glines. Vera Glines married Frank Audel Davis. They had one child, Audel Glines Davis. Audel married Virginia Lynne Showers. They had the following children: Rebecca Barton Davis, Stephanie Lucile Davis, Trevor Glines Davis, and Jane Showers Davis. Melba Violette Glines married William Hobson Hughes.

They had the following children: Anabel Tress Hughes and William Glines Hughes. Rebecca Glines never married.

Denzil ("Denny") Cassius Glines married Ellen Lanza. They had one child: John H. Glines. Denzil later married Margaret Loretta Shields. They had two children: James Denny Glines and Margaret Anne Glines.

James ("Jim") married Mary Ann Beaver from Porterville. They had the following children: John Thomas Glines and Patrick James Glines. In 1986 Jim married Kathryn A. Blevins, who had a son, Caden James Blevins, and daughter, Dannica Nicole Lippincott. Jim is the President and CEO of Community Bank of Santa Maria. Margaret ("Anne") Glines was the first full-time secretary of Maintenance and Operations and later joined the custodian staff at Allan Hancock College.

Jack Holloway Glines married Frances Baril. Jack was the city attorney for the City of Santa Maria and practiced law for over 60 years. They had the following children: Patricia Glines Rees and Pamala Glines Jordan.

• Robert Cassius Glines (1877- 1933). Robert married Cordelia Victoria ("Cora") McCroskey on March 1, 1898. Robert was a park ranger, and later owned and operated the Orcutt Boiler Works. Robert and Cora had the following children: Neal Cassius Glines, Lemuel Elza Glines, Ariel Reberta Glines and Robert Cassius Glines, Jr. Neal Cassius Glines married Ruby Barr. They had the following children: Henry Cassius Glines and Jacqueline Glines. Henry Cassius Glines married Lois Lloydene Swattord. They had one child, Cindy Leigh Glines. Henry ("Casey") was a professor and teacher of music and language. Jacqueline ("Jackie") married Aud ("Ace") Clarris Welch. He worked for oilfield servicing companies. They had the

James Denny Glines and Kathryn Blevins Glines

following children: Gregory C. Welch and Neal C. Welch. Jackie worked in administration for major oil companies in California. Gregory ("Greg") married Debbie Powers. They have one child: Nichols ("Nick") James Welch. Greg works as a firefighter for the City of Santa Maria. Lemuel Elza married Dorothy Nicholson. They had the following children: Margie Coreen Glines, Robert Rolland Glines, and Betty Williams. Ariel Roberta married James Rolland Nicholson. They had no children.

• Anna Belle Glines Mac-Donald (1878-1968). Anna Belle married William Grant Mac-Donald on April 27, 1910. They had no children.

• Huldah Araminta Glines Purkiss (1880-). Huldah received her primary teaching certificate and taught until she was married on June 28, 1905, to Myrton Marcus Purkiss. They had the following children: Albert Cassius, Cassius Myrton and Huldah Constance ("Connie"). She married Peter Dillon Kelly, Jr. They had the following children: Peter Dillon Kelly, III, Thomas Myrton Kelly, and Craig Allen Kelly.

• James Leroy Glines (1885-1933). James was employed as the vice president and manager of Bank of Italy, which later became Bank of America. He and Ethel Dream Dempster married on January 14, 1911. To this union one son, Dempster Cassius, was born.

• Sarah Lavina Glines Goodwin (1888-). Sarah ("Sadie") became a secretary to the Union Tool Company and later a secretary for the Fairbanks-Morse Company. Sarah married Guy Leonard Goodwin on November 14, 1917. They had the following children: Sarah Belle Shelton, Maryly Eva Darsie and Elizabeth Ann Ditz.

This information was researched and assembled by Charlene Glines Baczkiewicz.

Oscar F. Glenn Family

Oscar Glenn, his wife Maude, and their four daughters moved to the Santa Maria Valley in 1923. He was a retired Illinois farmer. He and his family had spent two years in Mississippi, one of those years on a plantation.

The Glenn family traveled west to California in the fall of 1921, coming to Santa Maria after a stint in Long Beach. In the spring of 1923, Mr. Glenn bought the New and Used Furniture Store at 209 West Main Street. The family's first home was located at the corner of West Cypress and South Lincoln, where the Santa Maria Post Office later stood for many years.

Mr. and Mrs. Glenn owned and operated their furniture store until their retirement in 1943. At that time, they moved to a new home at 205 West Cypress.

Maude was a member of the Republican Central Committee for a number of years. She served on the Santa Barbara County Hospital Board while Leo Preisker was supervisor. She was also active in the Community Club for many years.

Mr. and Mrs. Glenn were members of the First United Methodist Church. Four of their grandchildren and one great-grandchild were married in this church. All nine of their grandchildren, two great-granddaughters, and one great-great-granddaughter were all baptized in the same church. Grace Vertrees and Doris Young are still active members of the church.

At the time of Mr. Glenn's death on October 18, 1960, he owned and managed seven rentals throughout Santa Maria.

Oscar and Maude's four daughters were Gladys, who married John Anderson, Jr., in 1924, and had two daughters, Doris and Marilyn; Doris, who married Bert L. Young in 1929 and had one daughter, Grace; Grace, who married Kenneth M. Vertrees in 1931 and had four children, Richard, Ronnie, Rosalie, and Robert; and Gyneth, who married William J. Carroll in 1934 and had two children, Glen and Nancy.

Before moving to Santa Maria, the Glenns had lived in seven different places. Grace and Doris had attended eight different schools. Mrs. Glenn had always said that she wanted to live in California. When they arrived in Santa Maria, she said, "This is the last move—this is perfect."

R.H. Hanson

Mr. Hanson drove the horse-drawn street car in San Luis Obispo for several years. He came to the Santa Maria Valley and started farming in 1906. The Hansons and Thompsons have been farming there and in the surrounding area since that time.

Norma James Rice Goodbrod

Norma James Rice Goodbrod moved to Santa Maria in August of 1935 after attending San Diego State College, receiving teaching credentials. She was on the faculty of Santa Maria Union High School, teaching girls' physical education and general science. After one year, the general science class was dropped, so Norma went full-time into physical education. She was the advisor of the Tri-Y Club, an organization for high school girls connected with the YMCA.

In 1936, Norma married Owen S. Rice of the pioneer Rice family. She retired from teaching in 1941, and her daughter, Carolyn Marie, was born on December 17 of that year. Four years later, she had a son, James Owen, who was born on December 1, 1945. Norma divorced Owen Rice in 1959.

For two years, Norma worked as a substitute teacher at El Camino Junior High School, and then returned full-time to Santa Maria as Dean of Girls in September, 1959. In June, 1963, she married Oliver Goodbrod.

In 1965 Norma resigned her position at the high school and moved to Marin County, where she continued her career in substitute teaching. In 1970 she moved to Caldwell, Idaho, and in 1985 moved back to Santa Maria. She was active in the Minerva Club, A-Z Club, and the Santa Maria Country Club, where she enjoyed frequent rounds of golf.

Carolyn is married to Stanley Ball; they have two sons, Michael, a student at Cal Poly, and Darrell, a student at the University of California at Santa Barbara. James Rice is married to Linda, and has a step-daughter, Stacie, age 16, and a son, Andrew James, age 9.

Gularte Trucking Company Is Valley Asset

Printed in the Santa Maria Free Advertiser, 1932

The Gularte Trucking Company, established in Santa Maria in 1927, is an outstanding example of successful business management under modern facilities serving the people of Santa Maria Valley today.

Frank Gularte, president and manager of the business bearing his name, has made a reputation by making his word good! Shippers have learned to depend upon this service. Antone Olivera, vice president, has added considerably towards the building up of this concern by taking an active part in the business and is on the job at all times.

M.F. Madruga, secretary and treasurer, completes the officers of the organization, and knows every detail of the business. During the last year the salaries have expanded to $28,000, which has added materially to the welfare of the Santa Maria Valley.

In speaking of the success of this trucking company, it is estimated that most of its popularity comes from the direct contact and service that they give between the shipper and the receiver—the quickest and most dependable service that is possible to provide. Thus the popularity of shipping by truck.

Cappy Harada

Cappy Harada was born in Santa Maria on October 16, 1920. He lived his life in a home on South Blosser Road. His first grammar school was Agricola School, at the corner of Main Street and Blosser Road; then he attended Fairlawn School and El Camino Junior High School. At Santa Maria High School, he graduated as the Outstanding Student of his senior class. He was also captain of the football, basketball, and baseball teams, and served as editor-in-chief of the school newspaper, *The Breeze*. He was a member of the Quill & Scroll Society for outstanding work in high school journalism.

Cappy's education was interrupted due to World War II, but he was awarded a graduation diploma for outstanding scholastic record before entering into the service in 1941. He attended and graduated from Military Intelligence Service School in Savage, Minnesota. Cappy volunteered on December 7, 1941, to enter the United States Army, where he served until 1950; the highest rank he attained was that of captain. He was wounded three times while serving in the South Pacific and in the Philippines, and was honorably discharged as a Purple Heart veteran. He terminated active duty during the occupation of Japan, serving as aide-de-camp to Major General William F. Marquat, chief of the Economic and Scientific Section, G.H.Q. SCAP. He also served as special assignment officer to General of the Army Douglas MacArthur, and served as interpreter for a meeting between MacArthur and His Highness the Emperor of Japan.

In 1945-46 Cappy attended the University of California and earned a Master of Science degree in Journalism. From 1946 to 1949, as a member of the occupation force of Japan, he attended Meiji University, graduating in 1949 as a language specialist.

In 1949, Cappy went to Maizuru by special order of General MacArthur, and assisted the Japanese government in negotiations of returning Japanese repatriates from Nakhodka. He assisted the Japanese government in establishing a re-indoctrination center at Maizuru. It was at this time that Harada was responsible for having the Yomiuri Giants manager, Shigeru Mizuhara, released for a return to Tokyo where he addressed the fans at Korakuen Stadium.

In 1949 Harada was appointed by General MacArthur to head the Joint Committee of the U.S.-Japan Goodwill Baseball Tour of the San Francisco Seals. He was appointed to rehabilitate sport in Japan in the post-war years, and fought many hours with high officers of the U.S. Forces to preserve athletic facilities so that the people of Japan could rehabilitate themselves in sport programs.

Harada was also responsible for making night baseball in Japan possible by securing from MacArthur's headquarters a permit for the Korakuen Stadium to procure vital electrical cables to install lights for Japanese professional baseball.

The people of the industrial city of Osaka, Japan, refer to their Osaka Stadium, which stands in the center of the city, as "the stadium that Harada built." They credit him with securing the necessary material to construct the stadium.

While serving as aide to General Marquat, Harada supervised the economic rehabilitation of Japan. He conducted high-level meetings at ESS between General Marquat and Prime Minister Shigeru Yoshida, as well as the finance minister, Hayoto Ikeda, and many other Japanese cabinet members.

In 1960, Cappy organized and led the San Francisco Giants' goodwill tour to Japan, and was cited by the Congress of the United States for promoting goodwill between the U.S. and Japan through the medium of baseball.

Harada returned to the United States in 1966 and was appointed director and general manager of the Lodi baseball club of the California League, thus becoming the first Japanese-American to hold such a position in baseball. In December, 1966, he was selected by *The Sporting News* and the National Association of Professional Baseball as Executive of the Year for his outstanding leadership and promotion of professional baseball in Lodi.

In 1976, Harada joined the Office of the Baseball Commissioner as Director of International Division for Major League Baseball Promotion Corporation. There, he supervised international negotiations of foreign merchandising and promotion of major league baseball.

Harada's position with the San Francisco Giants, and later with the office of the Baseball Commissioner of the United States, is the first for any Japanese-American.

In 1980 Harada incorporated Cappy Harada Associates, Inc., and became its president and chief executive officer. The company is engaged in national and international public relations, marketing and lobbying, serving clients such as Tuji Television, Pete Rose (personal management), and Hollis Stacy, and numerous other clients.

In 1979, Harada was appointed Athletic Commissioner of the State of Washington by Dixy Lee Ray, governor of Washington State. This made Cappy the first Japanese-American to hold such a position in government. He still holds this position.

In 1980 Harada became a charter member of the Republican Presidential Task Force, as well as the Republican Senatorial Inner Circle.

Since 1976, Harada stages an annual Baseball Celebrity Golf Tournament and Banquet each January to raise funds for Hancock College's baseball program to grant a Japanese high school student a scholarship to play baseball in the United States.

Cappy is widowed and has three children. His parents were from Wakayama, Japan; he is a citizen of the United States.

Harada was responsible for securing permission from General Douglas MacArthur to raise the Japanese flag and have the Japanese national anthem played for the first time in the post-war era during the opening ceremonies of the San Francisco Seals Goodwill Tour of Japan. As aide to General Marquat, Cappy was responsible for rehabilitating many Japanese industries, including trading companies, banking, insurance, and so forth. He served on the advisory board of the Japan Tuberculosis Association with Her Highness Princess Chichibu, and served on the advisory board of the Japan Crippled Children's Association with His Highness Prince Takamatsu.

And so much more! Cappy Harada has had a very successful life, helping so many people and promoting baseball. He has settled in the Santa Maria Valley, in the beautiful Foxenwoods area, and is still very active.

Charles Matthew Hinds and Alice (Niverth) Hinds

Alice Niverth was the first daughter born to Stephen and Rachel Niverth, on June 15, 1891. She grew up in Garey, where she attended elementary grades at the Garey School, and then went to Cal Poly at San Luis Obispo. She worked as a bookkeeper for W.A. Haslam Company, Herron & Baker and Holser & Bailey.

She married Charles Matthew Hinds of Felton on November 18, 1913. They first lived in a home owned by her parents on the corner of Lincoln and Church Streets. There a daughter, Lucille Rachel, was born on July 11, 1914. They later bought a home on Tunnell Street.

Daughter Lucille died on July 24, 1925. Matthew died April 12, 1947, and Alice died April 21, 1955.

Henry A. Hoeger

I came to Santa Maria in the summer of 1929. My father, H.J. Hoeger, became superintendent of the *Santa Maria Times* job department, and I also worked there part time.

I entered Santa Maria High School in the fall of 1929 as a member of the junior class, transferring from Chaffey High School in Ontario, California.

We remained in Santa Maria until my father's death in October 1932. After that, my mother wished to move back to southern California, to be nearer to other family members.

I transferred from Santa Maria Junior College to Pasadena Junior College.

—July 1991

The Settlement of the Holland Family

Amelia Ann Calaway's folks came to San Luis Obispo by wagon train in 1851. They settled in See Canyon, named after her grandfather, Joseph See. It was here that Amelia was born and reared. She and Richard Holland met at a house party, and after a brief courtship, they were married. In 1881 they moved to the desert region of Santa Maria. The small village was called Central City. They went to the upper part of the valley, and filed a homestead in Cat Canyon at the foot of what is now known as Holland Grade. They lived there for 25 years, engaged in dairy farming. Richard Holland and his father hauled their grain to Shute Landing to be shipped. Part of it went to McNeil's flour mill in Santa Maria.

The roads were so gullied, and houses so far apart, that Mrs. Holland and her children went visiting on horseback. She sat on a side saddle and wore a long black riding skirt. A child rode behind her, holding onto the back of the saddle or to her dress. When they went to town, Central City, they went in a spring wagon drawn by two horses. It took a whole day to make the trip. The children rode horseback to school, five miles to Olive School House. This was also the community center.

In 1898 three of the Holland children graduated from grammar school and were taking post-graduate courses while waiting to enter high school. In 1901 the three were placed in care of a Santa Maria family so they could attend Santa Maria High School, a two-story building. Amelia Holland had a desire to become a teacher, but as the eldest of twelve children (as it happened in those days), she had to help at home—all work was done by hand.

Many years later Amelia saw her desire partly fulfilled when she managed to help four of her daughters to become teachers: Mrs. Emily Jane Yelkin, Mrs. Kittie Bessie Cook, Miss Alice Amelia Holland, and Miss Elizabeth Holland. Two boys, Leslie and John Holland, became prosperous by farming and working in the oil fields. A fifth daughter, Hazel Shamhart, became a bookkeeper.

They build a home in 1907 on South Pine Street in Santa Maria after selling the ranch in Cat Canyon to an oil company. Richard Holland died in June, 1945, at the age of 84. Mrs. Holland's life was not dull; she enjoyed reading, listening to the radio, watering and weeding her flowers, taking auto rides, and entertaining friends. Amelia died on June 5, 1952. They are both buried in the Santa Maria Cemetery.

—Submitted by Jerrie Cook Claborn

The Hopper Family

Eight Generations in the Santa Maria Valley
by Pauline Novo—the great-great-granddaughter of John and Jane Hopper

The original Hopper family settled in Virginia early in the 17th century, hailing from England. Later the family began to work its way westward, along with other hardy pioneers. My great-great-great-grandfather, William Hopper, father of the four Hopper boys, was a native of North Carolina who had moved to Lawrence, Indiana. At the time this story begins, Hopper brothers William, Ary and Tom (born in Indiana) and a cousin named Charlie all moved to Lone Jack, Missouri. In 1846, Charlie formed a wagon train to California. When complete, it consisted of fourteen picked men and their families, and the best equipment money could buy. The wagon party included Sam Young, Cyrus Hitchcock, John Young, Sam Gans, and John Yount, who later settled and founded Yountville in Napa Valley.

In this party, John and Jane Hopper (my great-great-grandparents) traveled with their three children, Sarah, Greenway, and baby Donald, and John's youngest brother, Tom Hopper. On the trail, at the Platt River, Tom married Minerva Young, daughter of Sam Young. When the party arrived in Salt Lake City, Utah, the group split up, and some went to Oregon while the others, including the Hoppers, were to continue on to California.

Charlie Hopper was captain, and John Hopper was second in command. They traveled and entered the land of promise by the route taken by the ill-fated Donner Party just a few months earlier. The evidence of their tragedy, all frozen, caught in a hard winter, was plain to be seen.

From Donner to the valley below was the hardest and most hazardous part of the trip. They had to literally cut their way through brush and undergrowth. They made a road through those high rough mountains. Reaching Sutter's Fort, the party divided. Some went north to Oregon; the Hoppers continued west and reached San Jose in 1847, six months after leaving Missouri. John and Jane built the first wooden house in San Jose out of redwood trees. They later moved to Sonoma County and went into the cattle business with John's brother Tom. Tom later became a millionaire and founded the Bank of Santa Rosa. He was president of this bank for many years. John settled in Potter Valley, and prospered from the beginning, raising cattle and farming.

Their first son, George, was the first white child born in California, according to the *San Francisco Examiner,* December 12, 1848. He later had a string of race horses and settled in Santa Maria and Ballard. He was the city's caretaker, under whose personal direction the modern and well-equipped Buena Vista Park became a big attraction to travelers and was known from Canada to Mexico. He died in Santa Maria at the age of 82.

Another son, John, worked for a brother, Greenway Hopper, who had a blacksmith shop in Santa Maria. In 1888 he sent for his family in San Miguel and they made the trip in a big double-decked Concord stagecoach *(see the next story).*

John and Jane had eight children: Emma, Greenway (who owned the blacksmith shop at the corner of Broadway and Chapel), William, Sarah Jane (who died in Santa Maria), John II, George (who died in Santa Maria), Luther, and Donald (who died as a child).

Luther Hopper was well known in the Santa Maria Valley, and ran the Broadway Bootery in the 100 block of South Broadway for many years. He died in 1940 at the age of 85. "California has lost one of its oldest native sons, the last living child of John and Jane Hopper," noted his obituary. "The books are closed on that pioneer generation."

Sarah Jane Hopper married Sam Logan. They had seven children, one of whom was my grandmother, Marcia Leigh Logan. As a young lady, she was voted the prettiest girl in the Santa Maria Valley, and sang with the Santa Maria Municipal Band at the flagpole in the center of town at Fourth of July celebrations. She sang "The Star-Spangled Banner" to open the festivities. She married Isaac (Dick) Lownes, and their first home was in Orcutt, where Grandpa Lownes built the first house in Orcutt.

They later moved to Bicknell, where they had a small grocery store and ran the post office, while Grandpa also worked in the oil fields. They had four children: Neil Wade Lownes, Audell Verde Lownes, Annette Leigh, and my father, Carl Dewey Lownes— fourth generation residents of the Santa Maria Valley.

Carl married my mother, Hazel Virginia Slater, in 1919, after a stint in the Air Force during World War I. Before my parents could establish a home of their own, he was killed in an auto wreck south of Los Alamos. I was three months old, having been born May 26, 1920, in my grandparents' home in Bicknell. They tell me that my dad was the life of any party: a singer who played the piano, the violin, and the mandolin. He loved to dance, and carried me around the dance hall on a pillow.

My mother, Hazel, remarried when I was three or four. We lived in Orcutt, and Mama died in 1982.

I married Albert Novo in Reno, Nevada, on July 4, 1942, during World War II. Albert served in the South Pacific, and while he was gone, our daughter, Peggie Annette Novo, was born on April 7, 1945. We took her home to the house I was born in. It had been moved from Bicknell to Orcutt in 1938, and is still there today on Union Avenue. Wayne Stanley Novo

was born on August 26, 1946. Carl Lewis Novo was born on December 4, 1953. All of the children were born at Sisters' Hospital in Santa Maria, grew up in the Santa Maria Valley, and attended Orcutt and Santa Maria High School, with the exception of Carl, who graduated from Righetti High School.

I still live in the Santa Maria Valley. I play the piano and the violin by ear, as I did all the way through school, and have been a tap and ballet dancer since I was ten years old. I danced in programs and recitals all over our valley. I was also active in all kinds of sports; I pitched softball in the Santa Maria Softball League (our sponsor was the Union Oil Co.) from 1937 through 1939, and was chosen to play on an all-star team with members from San Luis Obispo, Pismo Beach, Arroyo Grande, and the Santa Maria Valley. We played at the San Francisco World's Fair on Treasure Island in 1939. We won the game, and were named Central Coast All-Stars.

Later, after Peggie and Wayne were born, I opened Pauline's School of Dance, which was very rewarding. After Carl was born, I tried to teach for a while, but retired to raise my family.

In 1978 I got involved with the Santa Maria Valley Pioneer Association, and served as secretary-treasurer for two years, followed by a year as president, and have served on the board of directors ever since. In 1979 I started Pioneer Membership, and as of this writing, 1992, I have almost 1000 families signed up, and have been collecting family histories all these years, which I'm compiling in this book. My husband, Al, and our son, Carl, have worked right along and done their share in our growing Pioneer Association. Our Pioneer Picnic has grown from two to three hundred to between eight and nine hundred attending. We are working this year, following my idea of having our own Pioneer Picnic Grounds. Time will tell.

When I was 65, I started teaching tap dancing and exercise to Seniors. I volunteered my time, and we had a wonderful time dancing for different organizations and anyone that would have us. In 1991, Al and I danced in the "Alumni on Parade" program at Ethel Pope Auditorium, a restoration fund raiser. We waltzed together, and I tap danced.

We all still live here in the Santa Maria Valley, with the exception of our daughter, Peggie, and her husband Jim. He is in the aerospace industry, and they live near Denver, Colorado.

Al and I have been married fifty years on July 4, 1992. Our family gave us a big anniversary party at the old schoolhouse on Orcutt Hill. My mother went to school there as a little girl, and we have many memories of parties there. In 1993, at the age of 72, I joined the Silver Liners, a dance group. In 1995 I danced with the Pikake Hawaiian dancers.

Our daughter Peggie married Jim Cox, and they have two children, Melissa Cox Wiseman and J. Douglas Cox. Our first great-grandchild was given to us by J. Doug Cox—his daughter Tiffany, followed by Kayla Cox, Wyatt Cox in 1996, and Cayden Cox in 1998. Melissa has a son, Cody Wiseman.

Jim retired in Denver, and he and Peggie moved home to the Santa Maria Valley in 2001, buying a home in the Nipomo area. They are enjoying their whole family—mainly their grandchildren.

Our son, Wayne, married Barbara Berg, and they have two children, Cheryl Novo Stafford and Steven Novo. Cheryl has seven children: Anthony, April, Andrew, Ashley, A.J., Allison, and Abigale Pauline, who was born in 2001 and named after her great-grandmother.

Our son, Carl, married and had two daughters, Makenzie Novo and Katie Novo, who, at this writing, are six and eight years old. Carl divorced and later married Nadine Vanderli, who had two sons, Blake and Ryan, thus giving us two more grandsons.

Recently, I went to the Santa Maria Cemetery and found the graves of John and Jane Hopper. John's headstone bears the dates 1821 to 1887; Jane's, 1814 to 1898. Their daughter Sarah, my great-grandmother (1840-1925), is buried next to them.

On their tombstone are these words:

> *A precious one from us has gone*
> *A voice we loved is stilled*
> *A place is vacant in our home*
> *Which never can be filled.*

Santa Maria Valley is our home. Living in a small town has been a big plus to us. It is so nice to be around people you have always known. Many have moved away; many, many have moved here, and changed our valley into a big, fast, busy place.

2001: Al and Pauline will be married sixty years on July 4, 2002. Pioneer Park is reserved for a celebration. They have three children, ten grandchildren, and twelve great-grandchildren.

The Gentleman Stage Robber

by Kenneth C. Hopper
Sent to a fifth generation Hopper, Pauline Lownes Novo

MOVING TO SANTA MARIA IN 1888

In spring 1888, when California was just beginning to emerge from the pioneer stage, I was a lad of eight summers, living with my parents in San Miguel, California.

My father, who was a blacksmith by trade, had gone to Santa Maria to work for his brother, and had sent for us to come. San Miguel was a little Spanish town, and the southern terminal of the railroad. From there it was sixty miles to San Luis Obispo, and one had to travel by stagecoach. The stagecoach—the last word in luxury! They were big double-decked Concords, with the body resting on rawhide straps running fore and aft and powered by six spirited horses.

The driver was Jim Myers, one of California's most renowned "knights of the ribbons." The railroad was gradually cutting down the stagecoach runs to extinction.

My mother, my five-year-old sister and I took the stage in the early afternoon with five other passengers, Mother being the only woman aboard. The first few miles were a thrilling experience for an eight-year-old lad. The roads were dirt, full of ruts and chuck holes, over which we rocked and rolled. I got hot and clammy, and Mother got my head out the window just in time.

At dusk we reached the foot of Cuesta grade, over San Luis Mountain. This was a steep, winding road of some four miles to the summit, and the same distance on the south side.

All the passengers had got acquainted, and it was jolly company as the stage wound its way up the grade in the bright moonlight. Talk drifted to stage robberies. I stuck my head out the window in time to see a robber jumping down from the bank to the road in front of the leaders. "Robbers!" I shouted out.

By this time the stage was halted, and the robber was holding a big six-shooter trained on the driver. He told Jim to get down and to tell everyone to be quiet, and ordered him to throw the Wells Fargo strongbox down to the ground.

The robber told my mother and us to stay in and to be quiet. He wore a hood with eye holes, and produced hoods without eye holes for all the men.

Young as I was, I was impressed with the gentleness of his voice. He was a man of some education and refinement. I was all eyes and ears, and didn't miss a thing. (As a matter of fact, the reporters in San Luis Obispo got a clearer story from me than from any of the others!)

He frisked all the men and took what he wanted. He was taking a small gold watch from one man, a Mr. Long, when the man broke down and said, "My God, mister, please don't take this watch. It was given to me by my wife, and I'd just as soon have you kill me as take it." The robber paused and said, "I'm sorry"—and he put the watch back into Long's pocket.

He broke open the Wells Fargo box with a short-handled axe. As I remember, it yielded about $3000.00.

My mother said, "If I had a gun, I'd shoot you!"

I was tired, cold and hungry, so I got right down to brass tacks. Gathering my courage, I burst forth with, "Say, Mr. Robber, won't you please hurry? I'm tired and hungry, and we want to get to San Luis Obispo tonight!"

Of course, everyone laughed.

"All right, sonny," said the robber. "I'll hurry—it won't be long now."

He then got the mail bags, scattering them all over

the road.

Presently we realized that all was quiet. After a few minutes the robber was gone. Jim could not leave his horses, so all the men gathered the mail and returned it to the mail bags.

Jim made a record-breaking run down the grade into San Luis Obispo.

The robber had disappeared without a trace, and I was glad. It was thought by many that he was Black Bart, the notorious California highwayman who made life so miserable for Wells Fargo.

We had a big story to tell when we reached Santa Maria the next day!

Jamison

Mary Jamison Sweet was born in Hemet, California. She had three sisters and four brothers. They moved to Santa Maria in 1899, one year after her mother died. They lived at the end of Lakewood Road and attended the Washington School at the corner of Orcutt Road and Foster Road, a one-room school. Mary's father was Francis Marian Jamison.

Olive and Walter Johnson Family
1936-1956

Olive and Walter Johnson, with their five children, moved to Santa Maria early in 1936 and purchased a home at 321 West Hermosa Street. Walter worked for Mr. Miller at the Santa Maria Furniture Company. He later worked for the elementary school system as a maintenance man. The children—daughter June and four boys, Bill, Jim, Dan and Ron (Bucky)—all attended Santa Maria schools. The family was active in the First Presbyterian Church, where Bill was later ordained a minister.

In 1943, Olive started working as a secretary for the Army Air Corps at Allan Hancock Field. After a while she was transferred to a new building in Washington, D.C.—the Pentagon. The family moved to Washington for a year until the end of the war. During this time, June married Peter Ellena, who was in the Navy, and they moved to Hawaii, where he was stationed. They stayed on in Hawaii after the war and Peter worked for the Federal Aviation Administration, returning to the mainland in 1986 and retiring in Paso Robles.

In 1945 the family moved back to Santa Maria and settled at 814 South McClelland Street. Bill had joined the Navy while the family was on the east coast, but he returned west to attend college and ultimately settled in the Los Angeles area. Bill left the ministry after awhile and is now teaching school in Laguna Hills, Orange County, California.

Jim graduated from Santa Maria High School, and then attended California colleges. He was in the 40th division National Guard, and made a tour of the Far East before settling in San Diego, where he manages a Longs Drug store.

Dan, after completing school, settled in the Santa Barbara area, where he runs his own County Carpet Cleaning business. He is a drum major for the Santa Barbara Elks Drum & Bugle Corps that participates in Santa Maria's annual Elks' Rodeo Parade.

Ron graduated from Hancock College in 1955, worked for Knudsen's Creamery for awhile, and then joined the Navy. He served 26 years as a fighter pilot and now resides in Irvine, California. He plans on moving back to Santa Maria in the future.

Olive and Walter moved to Santa Barbara in 1956, and later to San Diego to be near their grandchildren. Olive passed away in 1970, and Walter in 1976; they are buried in San Diego. While they lived in Santa Maria, Olive was active in the American Legion Auxiliary and Native Daughters. Walter was a member of the Odd Fellows Club.

Growing up in Santa Maria had a profound effect on the family, giving it a balanced, stable view of life. The area and the people, through their friendship and work ethics, have left a lasting impression on the extended family of Olive and Walter Johnson.

—*Ronald J. Johnson*
Irvine, California

Ruthe Suggs Jones

I graduated from Santa Maria Union High School in 1939. Some of my classmates were Larry McGinley, Lorna Houghton Rice, Marjorie Crawford Martin, Marilyn Mason O'Neal, James and Elizabeth May Mason, Louise Sutter Hapgood La Barge, and many others. When I came to Santa Maria from West Texas in 1930, we stayed temporarily with my mother's family, John and Ethel Hutchison, on East Cypress Street. When my father's leg injury became too painful for him to work, in 1931, he went back to live with his parents in West Texas. My older sister finished junior college and married Paul Yarnell. Mother and I lived together until I went to Santa Barbara State College. I was graduated in 1943 and taught at Redlands Junior High School, 1943-44, and was wed to my college sweetheart, A.M. Rasmussen,

Lt. A.A.F., on June 24, 1944, at the age of 23. He went overseas in October, 1946, with a B-29 squad, to return in January, 1947. I worked as in my college years at the *Santa Barbara News-Press*.

During this time he finished undergraduate school and got his master's degree at U.S.C. I taught 10th and 11th grade students at Santa Barbara High School. we lived in Los Angeles for three years, from 1949 to 1952, and then returned to Santa Barbara, where he taught at Santa Barbara Junior High School and I taught at La Cumbre Junior High School. After years of trying to be parents, we finally got our adoptee in 1959, and our own child in 1960. The boys are now 33 and 34 years old.

We divorced in 1981. He remarried in 1983 and I in 1987.

Daniel H. Ketcham

The advent of Daniel Ketcham in Santa Maria occurred in March, 1881. Doctor Ketcham had been born in Albany, New York, on July 15, 1820. He married Harriet Price in 1848, and was practicing medicine in Michigan when he made his first trip to California with a wagon train. He spent some time in the gold fields and in San Francisco, and then returned home, crossing the isthmus in Panama via "Donkey Express." He rejoined Harriet, and they moved to Eau Claire, Wisconsin. Their only surviving child, Edward Thomas Ketcham, was born there on July 15, 1867. He was four years of age when the family traveled to Gallatin Valley, Montana, where they remained for several years. The severe winters and the decreasing mining productivity constituted enough reason for the family to come west to Santa Barbara, California. Dr. Ketcham opened his practice in September, 1875, in Goleta, and remained there until March 1881. Edward recalled years later that upon their arrival in Santa Maria, his father built a small house where Scaronis' home is now (1940) on South Broadway. There was only one house south of that, as far as you could see. His father died in Santa Maria on November 2, 1886, and is interred in the Santa Maria Cemetery adjacent to his wife, Harriet, who died March 27, 1907.

Following his graduation from Santa Maria High School, Edward attended Baltimore Dental College in Maryland. He married Julia Isabelle Merritt of Santa Maria on January 19, 1893. Their only child, Donald Edward, was born November 6, 1894. Edward practiced dentistry until 1902 or '03, at which time he became editor of the weekly newspaper, *The Santa Maria Vidette.*

As a staunch Republican, Edward Ketcham was rewarded with an appointment as Santa Maria's Postmaster, which position he retained until President Roosevelt took the position out of politics and put it under civil service. By that time, Edward was over 65 and ineligible to apply for examination. Julia died on January 8, 1930, at the age of 61; Edward's second wife, Lucy Kirkwood, died January 18, 1951.

Donald—or "Doc," as his family and friends called him—continued his education at Stanford University following his early school years in Santa Maria. He graduated in 1917 with a degree in Chemistry. He served in France with the 1st Gas Regiment during World War I. He was then employed by Standard Oil Company until his retirement. He had married Gladys Lavene Froom on July 20, 1920. They were living in Los Angeles when their son, James Gordon, was born on April 5, 1922.

Jim spent many happy summers with his maternal grandparents, Acel and Annie Froom, in Santa Maria. He enlisted and served as a Naval Air Corps flight instructor during World War II. He married Edith Kayser in Altadena on October 22, 1944. He was employed in the construction industry, and, with two small daughters, moved to Sacramento in 1950. Donald Robert Ketcham was born September 13, 1956.

Jim's parents were temporarily living in Sacramento when both died in 1975. In compliance with their wishes, they were both buried in the Santa Maria Cemetery. Jim's love of flying never faltered, and his ashes were scattered at sea following a courageous year-long battle with melanoma that ended in his death on March 28, 1982.

—Submitted by Edith Ketcham
September 1992

James and Mae Lapp

James Lapp was born in Templeton, California, on June 6, 1906. He attended schools in San Luis Obispo County, graduating from Templeton Union High School in 1924. His first trip to Santa Maria was to attend a Christian Endeavor convention in 1923. He moved to Santa Maria in 1925 and went to work for La Brea Securities Company. In 1935, he went into business with B.J. Piercy as the General Refrigeration Service Company.

James and Mae Thompson were married in 1936. Mae was one of the best-known ladies in this valley. She was always helping any situation that needed her—the U.S.O., the Boys and Girls Club, the Cancer Society, and many more.

James joined the Navy in 1943 and served in Alaska and the South Pacific. He got out of the Navy in 1945. In 1946 he joined the Masons, and was raised to Master Mason in 1947. He served as president of the Santa Maria Rifle Club in 1947-48. In 1951, he went into business in Morro Bay to serve commercial fishing boats from Alaska to San Diego. He sold out in 1973, dissolved his partnership with B.J. Piercy, and retired after 47 years in the refrigeration business.

James and Mae bought a home at 210 Palm Court Drive in 1944. They enjoyed many nice hunting and fishing trips throughout the western United States. Mae passed away in 1982 and is buried in the Santa Maria Cemetery.

Charles Laskey and LaVonne Bello Laskey

LaVonne Bello was born to Manuel and Mary Bello on November 6, 1926. She attended local schools—Miller Street Elementary, El Camino Junior High, and Santa Maria High School—graduating with the class of 1944. She attended Stanford University, and after graduation in 1948, married Jack Gunter, and had a daughter, Cassandra Ellen, on July 9, 1949. They lived in Long Beach and Costa Mesa for short periods. In 1953 she returned to college work at the University of California at Santa Barbara for her teaching credentials and subsequently taught third grade at Fairlawn School on West Main Street.

In 1954 she married Charles Dodge Laskey of Massachusetts, and a son, Kim, was born to them on August 11, 1955. After Charles completed his M.A. at Cal Poly, San Luis Obispo, they moved to Ceres, near Modesto, where Charles became head of the Mathematics Department at Ceres High School. He retired from there in 1986 after 31 years.

LaVonne has been an active volunteer in P.T.A., American Field Service, Junior Women's Club, Persephone Guild, Sierra Club, League of Women Voters, Ladies' Aid to Retarded Children, Delta Blood Bank, and Memorial Hospitals Volunteers. She has worked more than 7000 hours for the hospital, and is now on the Memorial Hospital Foundation board for her second term.

She was awarded the P.T.A. Honorary Life Membership in 1967; the School Bell Award for outstanding contribution to education by the Ceres Teachers Association in 1976; the Soroptomists Award for outstanding non-member in 1977; the Association for Retarded Citizens individual award for outstanding service in 1981; the Soroptomists Women of Distinction in Health in 1987; and was named one of the ten Outstanding Volunteers in Stanislaus County in 1987.

Her daughter, Cassandra, graduated from the University of California at Santa Barbara and is now a Learning Consultant at Sylvan School District in Modesto. She is married to Steven Sparks, a claims adjuster for State Farm Insurance Co. They have two sons, Nathan Charles and Anthony Bello Sparks.

Her son, Kim, graduated from the University of California at Santa Barbara, got an M.B.A. from San Jose State University, and, after working for Allstate Marketing Research Institute in Palo Alto for three years, is now Director of Marketing for two casinos and a hotel for Summa Corporation in Las Vegas. He was married to Lisa Strawick on May 23, 1987.

The Loring Family

James Russell Loring moved his family to the Santa Maria Valley in 1934 from Canton, Illinois. The family consisted of his wife, Nellie May Loring; their daughters, Ellen, Ruby, and Charlotte Lee; and their son, James Grant Loring.

Mr. Loring was employed by the Casmite Oil Refinery, and settled his family on the oil lease until moving to Orcutt in 1936. In 1937, the family moved to a home they purchased at 625 South Lincoln in Santa Maria, and opened a family restaurant in Orcutt, which the family ran until his retirement in 1944. At that time, Mr. and Mrs. Loring moved to Clear Lake, California. Both are now deceased.

Ruby Lucille Loring married John L. Spears, a member of a Santa Maria pioneer family. They are both deceased.

Ellen Loring married Richard Struss during the second World War, and is now living in Port Byron, Illinois. They have three children.

James G. Loring lives in Saugus, California. and has three children.

Charlotte Loring married Clifford Owen of Carmel, California. She is now married to Ray Standly and living in Yuba City, California. She has two children.

All of the Lorings graduated from Santa Maria High School, and they return for class reunions as often as they can.

Isaac Richard "Dick" Lownes

by his granddaughter, Pauline Lownes Novo

Isaac "Dick" Lownes came to Santa Maria in 1885 at the age of 15. He followed a wagon train south from Mendocino County, where he was born on Foster Mountain in 1870. He acquired a job in a livery stable owned by Wilt Riley, located in the 100 block of North Broadway.

Dick grew up in this valley, and there are many stories about him. He was a Pony Express rider, carrying mail across the Santa Maria River at full flow.

Dick married Marcia Logan, granddaughter of John and Jane Hopper, and they had four children: Neil, Audell, Annette, and my father, Carl Lownes. Dick built the first house in Orcutt, and moved his family there. Later they moved to the Bicknell oil lease, a small town east of the Righetti Ranch in the hills south of Orcutt. He worked as a well driller, and they also had a small grocery store and post office. My great-grandmother, Sarah Hopper Logan, lived with them until she died in 1925.

I was born in that house in 1920. The house was moved to Orcutt, and my daughter, Peggie, was the fifth generation to live in it.

Dick Lownes' ancestors came to America from England in 1620 and lived in caves in Pennsylvania until they could get established.

When Dick Lownes died in 1934, he was living in Atascadero with his son, Neil. He was retired from the Division of State Highways, where he had worked for many years.

In 1961, I received a letter from Luther Hopper.

He shared these recollections about Dick Lownes:

"Dick and Kale Lownes were two of the best men it was ever my pleasure to know. They were both very thoughtful, and very kind to children. When I was a kid working at the Sisquoc mines, Dick took me hunting on horseback, and with his 30-30 rifle, I killed my first deer.

"Kale Lownes died in a horrible accident south of Orcutt. He was caught in the wheel belt of a threshing machine engine and was badly mangled.

"One time, Jim Glines and I started to the Glines Ranch in the Alamo Canyon in an old repossessed Model T Ford. It was after a heavy rain, and the Alamo Creek was swollen. A hundred and fifty yards away from the Oakley ranch house, we dropped into a hole in the creek and found ourselves hub-deep in the sand. Jim waded out and came back with Bert Lownes and two of the largest horses I have ever seen, named Tom and Jerry. Bert hooked them to the front axle of the Model T and yelled, 'Tom! You, Jerry! Get 'em out!' The horses pulled, and out came the whole front end, wheels and all. We ended up spending the night. The horses belonged to Ed Norris, who was married to Mary Frances Logan. They were the largest horses in Santa Barbara County."

In 1908, the Lownes family lived on West Cypress Street in Santa Maria. They bought a horse named Bird. It ran away, and Dell Lownes walked clear to Sisquoc and three miles beyond to get the horse. It had found its way back home.

Marlett Family

by Ben Marlett, 1990

Benjamin and Alice Marlett moved from Elyria, Ohio, to Avila Beach, California, in 1905. Later they moved to Sisquoc, California. They had ten children: daughters Maud, Jen, Pearl, Bea, Belle, Alice and Grace, and sons Benjamin ("Frank"), Gordon and Dorman. Grace married Charles Marston and lived in Orcutt; her daughters were Doris and Ruby.

Ben and Alice celebrated their 50th wedding anniversary in Sisquoc on December 29, 1925; all their children and grandchildren were present.

Ben "Frank" and Lettie Marlett had nine children. They lived in Sisquoc, where he worked for the Gilmore Oil Co. All nine children went to Santa Maria High School.

Berthena graduated in 1924. She was a fine student, and enjoyed reading. She worked in Santa Barbara. She now lives in Angwin, California, with her husband, Clyde Hazen.

Grace graduated and went on to college in Moscow, Idaho, and San Diego State. She is a retired school teacher and lives in San Diego. She is the widow of Perry Shannon.

Walter graduated in 1928. He played on the greatest football team ever recorded at Santa Maria High School. The coach was Walt Herreid. Some of the players were Les Hayes, Fred Haslam, Roemer, Rusty Gill (All-American), and Earnest Gardner. Walter also played for Hancock College. Walter went to U.C.L.A., where he played football as a guard. Walter lives in Santa Maria with his wife, Espy. He is a retired teacher-coach. He has a real estate business.

Bruce graduated in 1933. He was a fine musician, and played all kinds of instruments, from bassoon to saw and comb. Bruce passed away in 1956. He lived in Santa Barbara and was a carpenter-contractor.

Louise and Margaret both graduated in 1935 from Santa Maria High School. They both played in band and orchestra. Louise lives in San Jose with her husband, Gilbert McEnroe. Margaret lives in Prescott, Arizona, with her husband Robert Thomas.

Marvin graduated in 1938. He played trumpet in band and orchestra. He lives in Santa Maria with his wife, Tillie. He is a retired minister and carpenter.

Ben graduated from Santa Maria High School in 1940 and served in the U.S. Navy during World War II. He played football and was active in F.F.A. He lives in Santa Maria with his wife Helen. He is retired from the grocery business.

Jimmy was active in plays all through high school. He died in 1974. He was a barker for lumber mills in Ukiah, California.

Ben and Helen's daughter, Kathleen, graduated in 1964 and is an insurance agent for Joel Byars in Orcutt. She lives in Santa Maria with her husband, Mark Swihart.

Eugene D. Martin

Eugene Martin and his wife, Muriel Rose (Cochran) Martin, arrived in Guadalupe in 1926 from Helena, Montana. He was told of a job opening with the Waller-Franklin Seed Company. They brought with them Hazel Mae, age 7, and Douglas Harold, age 6. The move to Guadalupe was difficult for the young family from Montana. He worked his way up in the company and became their president and general manager. He was with Waller-Franklin for 23 years. In 1949 they moved to Santa Maria to work for another seed company as vice president. This position he held for eight years. They moved to Gilroy in 1958 to work again as vice president and general manager for Pieter-Wheller Seed Company. He was with them until he retired, and moved back to Santa Maria to live out their senior years. Mrs. Martin was a homemaker. They both lived to just short of 92 years.

Elizabeth May Mason

I have many happy memories of the yearly Pioneer Picnics, starting when I was very young. I remember games with prizes at the old Pioneer Park in Cuyama, and the programs—Jim, my brother, and I performed a piano and violin duet one year. Also, what fun we kids had when the wax was spread on the dance floor, and we ran and slid on the floor to work the wax into the surface. I remember the barbecues and all the good food. It seems the family groups were tremendous. We watched the opening grand march and learned the varsouvianne, the schottische, the rye waltz, the two-step, and many others. My great-uncle Ace Oakley loved to dance "Put your little foot."

Later it was time to go home to rest a bit and clean up for the evening dance in the high school gym. I can remember feeling so grown up the year I wore a long dress for the first time.

I have four children: Janet, Elizabeth, James and Barbara. We live in San Anselmo, California.

—*Mr. and Mrs. R.L. Mason*

John and Mary McCurdy

Vandenberg brought John and Mary McCurdy to Santa Maria in 1958. John, an engineer, was employed by Lockheed and Martin Marietta. Mary owned and operated a ladies' ready-to-wear shop in Santa Maria for 35 years. The shop, known as "Town Togs," supplied fine fashions to many Santa Maria ladies. The slogan "For ladies . . . with men in mind" will long be remembered in this valley.

John and Mary had two children, Felicia Kae Rogers and John Michael McCurdy. The children are both deceased and are interred in the Dudley Hoffman columbarium.

Right: John and Mary McCurdy

148

May Family Pioneers

Robert May, a farmer's son and a tailor, and his wife, Ann Rowe, immigrated from Launceston (near Plymouth), England, to Buffalo, New York, in 1837. They had two daughters, Amy and Elizabeth, and six sons: John Curtis, Robert, William Henry Scott, Oscar George, Richard Rowe and Erie Alanson. John Curtis May married Rebecca Trekel and had three children: Ida Kate, Frank Curtis and George Arthur. Frank Curtis May and his wife, Mary Lyon, moved to Santa Maria around 1890. His dad followed and lived there until he died in 1907. The Mays farmed just south of town around the area that is now Dal Porto and Carmen Lane. Frank fathered Frank Curtis May, Jr. (1891), Ida Kate (1893), Fred Lester (1894), Ralph Earl (1897), and Harry Austin (1900). The children were orphaned after his accidental death in 1900 and his wife's in 1904.

The children were raised by various relatives: Frank by his uncle, George May, who owned the May Ranch on the Nipomo Mesa near Santa Maria. Fred also lived with his uncle George and aunt Laura (Noyes) while going to Santa Maria Union High School. Ralph May lived for a while in Santa Maria and was one of the first local "motorcycle speed cops." For most of his life he was a truck driver and roustabout in the Taft oil fields. He married Della Mathews, and they had a son, George ("Georgie"), who later moved to Ventura, where he was a baker. Harry May grew up in Santa Maria and, except for Army service in both World War I and World War II, he spent most of his life working with his brother Fred in the service station business at the corner of South Broadway and Jones.

Frank graduated from SMUHS in 1911, served in the U.S. Navy in World War I, and married Winnie Dugan. They had two children, Frank Curtis III

("Curt") and Marilyn Jane. Curt earned a Ph.D. degree and became the head librarian for Redwood City. Marilyn graduated from college, married Marvin Gold, and lived in a Central Valley towns until her recent untimely death from cancer. Frank was a partner with his brother Fred in the May Bros. Seaside, Standard and Gilmore gas station, just outside the city limit at the corner of Broadway and Garey (now Stowell) Road, where the Vandenberg Inn is now located. In 1940 Frank joined the city police force, becoming a captain during World War II. He was president of the Pioneer Association in 1939. Winnic May was for many years a leader of the Campfire Girls program in the Santa Maria Valley.

Fred L. May graduated from SMUHS in 1914, was an Army first sergeant in World War I, and spent most of his life in the oil and service station business. Active in town affairs, he was Commander of American Legion Post 56, a city councilman, SMUHS Trustee for 11 years, president of the Pioneer Association (1952), Rotary Club, and local American Red Cross. He married Elizabeth ("Beth") Oakley in 1917. She taught school at Mill St., Bonita, and Orcutt elementary schools until her retirement. She served 34 years on the City Library Board, and was president of the Pioneer Association in 1967. Their children, Fred Oakley, James Asa ("Jimmie"), and Elizabeth ("Wiff"), graduated from SMUHS and moved away after college and World War II. Fred Oakley May married Joyce Steinwert; they had two children, David and Peter, who live in the Seattle area with their families. Fred O. was a salesman and manager. He served on the Mercer Island City Council and in the Washington State Legislature before retiring. Joyce died in 2001.

"Wiff" May married Robert Lyman ("Rocky") Mason in 1943 and produced five children: James,

Janet, Barbara, Paul and Beth. Rocky, a petroleum engineer, moved with his family to many distant oil fields in the western U.S., Alaska and Iran. Wiff and Rocky are retired in Albuquerque, where most of their children and grandchildren live. They travel to Santa Maria Pioneer Picnics whenever they can.

Jim May returned to Santa Maria in 1977 with his wife, Jacqueline Argonne, and their children, after retiring from 34 years as a diplomat and consul in the U.S. State Department Foreign Service. He served in Paris, Israel, all the Arab countries of Africa and the Middle East, Vietnam, Mogadishu, Zambia, and Washington, D.C. Back home, he served on the City Council and Planning Commission for many years, was Pioneer Association President in 1992, and led the campaign to find and get control of the site for a permanent Pioneer Park and create the Pioneer Park Foundation. He sold real estate and authored a Santa Maria Valley illustrated history book.

Jim and Jacquie's children are Dr. Alice Barky (Los Angeles); Lt. Col. Jack A. May (U.S. Army); and, in Santa Maria, Anthony ("Tony") May (two children), and Fred L. May II (married Michelle Mathiesen, children: Morgan, Madison, and David). Jim's older children are Marianne Rankin (son, William James Cameron ["Will"] Rankin) of Washington, D.C.; and Stephen Michael May, musician and college computer instructor in Phoenix (married Tekla Petersen).

Carolyn Jane Conrad McCall
and Donald Randolph McCall

Carolyn Conrad McCall was president of the Santa Maria Valley Pioneer Association from 2000 to 2002, and served as vice president for the previous three years. She was the 72nd president to serve since 1924.

Carolyn's parents were Joseph Glenn Conrad, Sr., and Flora Johnson Conrad, who were both born and raised in Missouri. After they were married on March 15, 1916, they moved to Idaho to live and farm. In 1928, they made their move to Orcutt, California, bringing with them their two children, ten-year-old Opal and nine-year-old J.G., Jr. A few years later, the family moved into Santa Maria, where they owned and operated the Gateway Grocery Store and Service Station on North Broadway.

On December 15, 1936, Carolyn was born at the Airport Hospital in Santa Maria (located on what is now Hancock College property). Carolyn attended local schools, graduated from Santa Maria Union High School in 1954, and attended Hancock College. In 1953, while still in school, she went to work for KCOY Radio, becoming the youngest radio program/traffic director in the country. She continued to work in radio, doing on-air programs and commercials, until 1959.

On August 11, 1957, Carolyn married Donald Randolph McCall at the Santa Maria First Christian

Carolyn and Donald McCall with children Scott, Julie and Kirk

Church. Donald had moved to Santa Maria in 1936 at the age of six. He was born in Iowa on November 28, 1930, the son of Clinton Theodore McCall and Sarah Long McCall. He graduated from Santa Maria Union High School in 1949 and served in the U.S. Navy from 1949 to 1953; during the Korean conflict, he was aboard the *U.S.S. Higbee*. Don graduated from Hancock College in 1955 and moved to Los Angeles to further his education. He worked for Pacific Telephone / AT&T in Santa Maria from 1957 until his retirement in 1994.

Carolyn and Donald raised three children: Kirk Randolph McCall, born July 1, 1959; Scott Conrad McCall, born October 25, 1962; and Julie Carol McCall, born September 28, 1964. During the children's growing-up years, the parents were active in all the children's school activities and PTA work, as well as being active members of the First Christian Church. They were always involved in their community. Carolyn went to work for the Santa Maria Public Library in 1974 and retired in 1997.

After retirement, Carolyn and Don have enjoyed volunteer work with the Santa Maria Valley Chamber of Commerce and the Elks' Lodge, as well as indulging their love of working with the Pioneers. Travel and grandchildren round out their love of life together.

Carl N. McCoy Family

by Pauline McCoy Domingos, 1990

Carl McCoy, his wife Mae, and four children, Meade, Frank, Pauline and J.P., together with their huge German shepherd, Barry, arrived in the Santa Maria Valley in the winter of 1929. A house was rented from Union Sugar Company in Betteravia for $25.00 a month, and Carl, Meade, and Frank went to work "pulling ice" at Puritan Ice Co. in Guadalupe. J.P. enrolled in Betteravia Elementary School, and, after graduating, joined Pauline in riding the high school bus to Santa Maria Union High School, where they both graduated—Pauline in 1931½ and J.P. in 1933.

Meade and Frank, and eventually J.P., worked in the vegetable packing business, in the fields and in the sheds, for several years, while Dad (Carl) worked on the hay bailer for Draper Brothers, and then as foreman for Union Sugar Co. until his retirement in 1956. Mae and Pauline were quite active in the Methodist Church in Santa Maria: Mae participated in women's groups, where she gave readings and sang, and Pauline sang in the choir.

Meade married Katherine Fronaberger, and they had two children: Jimmy, who worked for a local radio station, and Janice, an official with Bank of America, now married to Tommy Trefts. Janice and Tommy have three children: Michael, Susan, and Tamara, and are the grandparents of five. Tamara is in her sixth year in the U.S. Navy. Jimmy died in 1965 of a congenital heart defect. Both Meade and Katherine are deceased.

Frank, who retired from Union Sugar Co. in 1973, died in April, 1987. He married Benita Powell, and they raised three daughters and one son. They have twelve grandchildren and three great-grandchildren. Donald, the son, is a highway patrolman in the Sacramento area, while Beverley (Settlemyre) lives in Lompoc, and Frances (Berrigan) took a leave from the Highway Patrol in San Luis Obispo and now lives in Bakersfield. Mary (Dooley) is a real estate salesperson in the Tehachapi area.

While living in Betteravia, Pauline was playing tennis one day when Bert Domingos drove by. He remarked to his friend that that was the girl he was going to marry. After meeting her, and courting her for ten years, this finally came true, and they are now retired and living in Santa Maria. Bert drove truck for many years, having worked for Bradley Trucking, Ralph Hughes, Whitey Stong, and others. Then he went to work for Union Sugar Co., where he retired in 1978. Pauline worked for General Telephone Co. for almost 35 years, first as an operator, then as a supervisor. She retired in 1977.

Pauline and Bert are the proud parents of three sons. Robert (Bobby) is a bilingual teacher in Hollister. He is married to Violette, and they have two children: Marie (Sasha), who was born on Pauline's birthday in 1976, and Clay, born two years later. Carl, the second son, owns and operates Carl's Muffler Shop in Santa Maria and is married to the former Georgeanne Guggia. He is an avid fisherman as well as a hunter. They have two sons: Tony, who is attending Cal Poly, San Luis Obispo, and Paul, who is a student at St. Joseph's High School in Santa Maria. Gary, the youngest son of Pauline and Bert, works for Kevex Corp. in Scotts Valley and resides in the beautiful Santa Cruz Mountains. He and Mandy have two dogs, Turkey and Pita.

Joy, the youngest child of Pauline and Bert, died of cancer at the age of seventeen in 1965.

Cal and Rosalie (Hartnell) McDonald

Cal McDonald came to Santa Maria in 1939, and married Rosalie Hartnell in 1941. He served in the U.S. Navy during World War II, and upon his discharge in 1946, went to work for the Santa Maria Valley Railroad, where he worked for 38 years before retiring in 1984 as Superintendent of Shops.

ANCESTORS OF ROSALIE HARTNELL

Rosalie's paternal ancestors arrived in California with father Junípero Serra in 1769 with the first expedition. Her great-great-great grandfather was a soldier in the army coming to California with the expedition of 1769. He was Raimundo Carrillo. Rosalie's great-great-great-grandfather Francisco Lugo was a soldier, also; he came to California with his wife and family about 1774, living first in Los Angeles, and then Santa Barbara. Lugo's daughter, Tomasa, was married to Raimundo Carrillo in 1781 at Mission San Carlos.

Their only daughter, María Antonia Carrillo, was married to Rosalie's great-great-grandfather José Antonio de la Guerra in 1804 at Mission Santa Barbara. José de la Guerra was commandant of the Presidio of Santa Barbara. Their eldest daughter, María Teresa de la Guerra, was married to Rosalie's great-grandfather, W.E.P. Hartnell, at Mission Santa Barbara in 1825.

W.E.P. Hartnell was the founder of California's first college at Monterey. In 1839-1840, he was vistador general of the California Missions. He was official interpreter and translator in the drawing up of the Constitution of the State of California in 1847-1850.

Their son, José G. Hartnell, was born in Monterey in 1834, and was married to María Ignacio Watson in Monterey. These were Rosalie's grandparents.

Rosalie's father, William A. Hartnell, was born to them in 1877 in Monterey. The family later moved to the family Land Grant of Todos Santos San Antonio, between Orcutt and Los Alamos. William Hartnell married Rosalie's mother, Alice M. Muñoz, in San Luis Obispo in 1910, and they made their home in the Santa Maria Valley, where all eleven of their children were born. Alice Muñoz was born in Nipomo in 1887.

Rosalie's maternal ancestors included Corporal Manuel Boronda, who arrived in California from Mexico in 1789. He was a teacher in San Francisco and Monterey from 1790 to 1818. He married Gertrudis Higuera, who was born in Monterey in 1776. Their son, Rosalie's great-great-grandfather, José Canute Boronda, was born in San Francisco in 1792. He was married to Francisca Castro, who was born in Monterey about 1797.

Their daughter, María Concepción Boronda, was born in 1820 in Monterey. She married Rosalie's great-grandfather, José María Muñoz, who was born in San Francisco in 1817. He was the first Sheriff of San Luis Obispo County and became San Luis Obispo County Judge in 1857.

Their son, Joseph G. Muñoz, Rosalie's grandfather, was born in San Luis Obispo in 1857. He married Mary Carmen Hames, who was born in Corralitos, California, in 1864. Her father—Rosalie's great-grandfather—was Benjamin Hames, a native of New York who came to California with his wife and family in 1852 by way of Valparaiso, Chile. He was a millwright, and built several flour mills in South America. He settled in Corralitos, California, in Santa Cruz County, and built the first flour mills in California.

Rosalie's grandparents, Joseph and Mary Muñoz, were married in San Luis Obispo, and lived there and then in Nipomo, where most of their children were born. In the 1920's they settled in the Santa Ynez Valley.

Rosalie Hartnell McDonald was born in Santa Maria in 1925. She and Cal have one daughter, Kathleen. Rosalie's father lived in the Orcutt area since 1890.

James and Veronica McDonald

We cane to Santa Maria in October, 1954. I was transferred here by the Union Oil Company as personnel supervisor at the Santa Maria Refinery on the Nipomo Mesa. I left Unocal in 1959 and joined Lockheed Missiles and Space Company, working there for 28 years until my retirement.

My wife, Ronnie, was employed by First Interstate Bank as an escrow officer, retiring in 1988.

Our three children, Sandra, Nan and Scott, all graduated from Santa Maria High School. Sandra and Scott graduated from Fresno State, and Nan graduated from San Diego State.

I served 14 years on the Elementary School Board and 13 years on the Allan Hancock College Board.

We are associate members of the Pioneer Association.

Irving N. McGuire

Irving McGuire was a man of excellent habits, and possessed a fine moral character. He was a member of the Methodist Church, and one of the oldest Masons in the Hesperian Lodge.

He was born in Jackson County, Missouri, in 1832. His father, with his family, moved to Buchanan County in 1838. There Irving received his education. They came to California in 1849, driving a team of oxen all the way, and settled in Vacaville, where they built the first house in town.

Mr. McGuire began raising cattle and horses, continuing until 1853, when he moved his stock to Sonoma County, buying 480 acres of land. He followed the stock business for twenty years. In 1873 he came to San Luis Obispo County, and engaged in raising sheep until his herd numbered 3500.

However, the dry season of 1877 produced some hard losses, so he closed out the business, and in 1880 moved into San Luis Obispo, where he took up the mercantile life. In 1883 he moved down to Santa Maria, where he engaged in the drug business until 1887. He later purchased an interest in the *Santa Maria Times*.

In 1884 Mr. McGuire married Miss Sarah Condit, who died in 1887, leaving six children—three sons and three daughters.

During his residence in San Luis Obispo, Mr. McGuire was elected to the Board of Supervisors. He was also elected Justice of the Peace at Oso Flaco, and elected again in Santa Maria.

He died in 1910 at the age of 78.

—*Glenn Roemer*

McHenry

by June McHenry Brumana, 1991

I was born June 15, 1929, in Santa Maria, California, the youngest of the four daughters of Martin Spencer McHenry and Florence Edna Bowers. My father was born in 1872 in Modesto, California, and died in Santa Maria in March 1944; my mother died in Idaho in 1986.

Martin was the eighth child born to William Spencer McHenry and Amanda Melvina Hamby. William was born in April, 1832, in Kentucky, and died in December, 1904, in Santa Maria. Amanda was born in 1839 in Kentucky, and died in Santa Maria in July 1909.

Martin worked at Wells Fargo as a messenger, and on the railroad. At the time of Martin's death, he was given an honorary membership in the Santa Maria Valley Pioneers. He was also a member of the Moose Lodge.

The McHenrys first arrived in Santa Maria Valley about 1875, living in Garey, Santa Maria, and the McHenry Ranch, located in the Tepusquet Hills.

My grandfather, William McHenry, came to California with his brother, James, in 1864. They are supposed to have driven a herd of cattle to California.

My grandmother, Amanda, was fourteen when her family traveled from Missouri in a covered wagon in 1854. My grandparents married in San Joaquin County in 1859.

They moved to Garey in 1877, when my father, "Dick" Martin Spencer, was born.

My daughter, Kayedeane, is married to a retired Air Force master sergeant. They have one daughter, Michelle.

My oldest son, Dennis, is married to Rita, and they have two daughters, Sofia and Brianna. He presently is the gaffer on the TV sitcom *The Wonder Years.*

My youngest son, Victor, is married to Sheila, and has three sons, Chris, Terry and Wilson. He presently is director of photography on the TV program *Gabriel's Fire.*

My youngest child, Susan, is married to John Wendel, who owns a machine shop. They have three sons, Robert and the twins, Arin and Nathan. Susan is attending college and holds a 3.5 average. She is working towards a liberal arts degree.

Donald Melby

I arrived in Santa Maria with Arnold and Jennie in 1922. We moved to Lompoc in 1923, and then back to Santa Maria in 1936. I attended elementary school through the eighth grade in Lompoc, and went to Santa Maria High School for four years. I graduated from Santa Maria Junior College in 1943.

I enlisted in the Air Corps in 1942, and was in active duty from March 1943 to August 1945. I served as a pilot, 2nd Lieutenant, with the 437th Troop Carrier Group, with service in England and France.

I married Joyce Jensen on February 10, 1946.

We have three children: Maureen, Margaret Ann, and Mark. I was associated with Melby's Jewelers from 1945 until my retirement in 1987. I was president of Melby's Jewelers for the last sixteen of those years.

Our present address (1995) is 419 East Camino Colegio. We have lived there for 39 years. We have seven grandchildren and 6¾ great-grandchildren.

Elaine Martin Miller

1991

My mother, Erminia "Ninnie" Lotti, ran away from home when she was eighteen, because the families of both my mother and my father opposed their coming marriage. My aunt, Maria Seidle, told me this story. My mother never told me the story because she was afraid I'd do the same thing!

Only her sister, Carrie, Mr. and Mrs. Ernest Taylor (friends of the family), and my cousin, Rosie Dutra Fernandez (who was eight years old) knew that she was running away—and my father, of course. Mr. Taylor took her to catch the train for San Francisco. (My mother's aunt took a long time to forgive him for this.)

Cousin Rosie said she found out about it when she caught my father, the bridegroom-to-be, stuffing rags in the telephone bell at his mother's house so the phone would not ring. She did not tell on him. My mother's aunt, Dinda Antognazzi, her legal guardian, tried to call the ranch when they missed her, but of course there was no answer, so they drove out to tell my grandmother that Ninnie was missing. (They lived at 420 South Pine Street—now 430—in Santa Maria.)

My father was in the bunk house, so my mother had gone alone.

Dinda became frightened, and recruited the Martins and others to look for my mother.

My father helped search, pretending he knew nothing.

In the meantime, a friend saw my mother on the train and asked where she was going. "To San Francisco," she replied, "to business college."

The friend called my aunt, and my aunt called the San Francisco Police, and the police met the train. They took my mother to the police department to see Chief O'Brien (father of actor Pat O'Brien). He determined that since she was eighteen years of age, he could not force her to return home, so he notified her aunt of his findings.

Chief O'Brien got my mother a room at the Y.W.C.A. and helped her get work at the Emporium, selling laces and trims. She had had experience at her cousin Flora's store, The City of Paris, on South Broadway in Santa Maria.

Shortly thereafter, when the harvest was in, my father followed Ninnie to San Francisco and they were married on October 12, 1918.

When my parents returned to Santa Maria, they lived on the ranch with Grandmother Martinez. My aunt Dinda didn't speak to them until I was born two years later.

My mother, Erminia Lotti (Martin), came to Santa Maria when she was 12; my father, Edward Martin, came here as an infant in 1896; my grandmother, Maria Luis, came in about 1896, having lived in San Luis Obispo County from about 1877. My grandfather, Francisco Martínez, came in about 1896, and also lived in San Luis Obispo from 1875. My other grandmother, Mary Antonia Hartnell, lived on the Hartnell Ranch near Orcutt most of her life, moving to Saratoga when she married in 1899.

Virginia Erickson Minks

In 1931, I moved to the Santa Maria Valley from Long Beach with my father, George Erickson, mother Esther, brother Dale, and sister Gloria. We lived on Section 8 ranch located five miles east of Orcutt. The ranch was sold and developed about 1972, and is now known as Lake Marie.

The home, guest house and barn still remain on the property by the Lake Marie clubhouse and the lake, which has been enlarged. As children, we swam in the lake, and also had a kayak to row around in. Our main crop was beans, but we also raised wheat, oats, and corn. We had riding horses and a herd of Texas longhorns. We also had mules and work horses. I used to raise white rats to take to Orcutt School. I learned to ride horses and shoot a 410 shotgun in target practice.

I attended Orcutt School until 1936, when we moved to Norwalk, California. My best friend was Pauline Lownes, now Mrs. Al Novo. She spent many nights at our ranch; we were together constantly. We have remained friends all through the years; in 1979, my husband, Newt, and I went to Hawaii with Al and Pauline. We always make it up to Santa Maria from Bellflower for Pioneer functions.

While in grammar school, Pauline and I took dancing from Gertrude France in Santa Maria, and danced in many programs together.

I've never forgotten Santa Maria Valley and my friends there. It was a wonderful place to live. During the Depression, we lived on what the ranch produced.

* * * * *

■ *Postscript:* Virginia passed away from cancer in 1988 in Bellflower. She is missed so much by the Novo family. Gloria, her sister, is the only one left; she lives in Louisiana.

Robert and Eva Mollica

The Mollicas have had family in the Santa Maria Valley over 100 years; their pioneer ancestor was Manuel Gracia, Sr. Robert came in 1940, Eva in 1936; they have three children, Terry, Darrell and Anthony.

Mortensen and Johnson

Peter and Karen Mortensen came to Santa Maria in 1933 on their honeymoon and stayed. They were both immigrants from Denmark, living in Denver, Colorado, before moving to Santa Maria. There were many other Danish people in this area at that time, most of them working in agriculture.

There were about 75 dairies in the Santa Maria Valley then. Peter started in the dairy business as a partner with Carl Jensen, Karen's cousin, in 1936 at the dairy located on the Arnold Donati Ranch at Blosser and West Main Street. In 1939, they moved to West Alvin Street with the dairy to the Louis Donati Ranch. When the partnership was dissolved in 1945, Peter moved his half of the cows to Betteravia on the Milo Ferini Ranch. Carl moved to Los Alamos.

Peter and Karen had three children: Anna Lisa, Agnes, and John. Agnes married Everett Johnson in 1954, and in 1956 Everett went to work for Peter at the dairy. Agnes and Everett had three children: Pamela, Alan, and Blaine. In 1957, Peter purchased 175 acres of land east of town from "Slim" Adam. There was an old abandoned dairy on the property, and one house. In 1958, Everett and Agnes and their family moved to the new dairy site on East Betteravia Road. The old milk barn was rebuilt, and new corrals were constructed, and in 1960 the 150 cows were moved from Betteravia to their new home.

In 1970 Mortensen & Johnson formed a partnership, and in 1979 Mortensen sold his half of the partnership to Johnson. Everett and Agnes expanded the dairy business to 500 cows. Their two sons, Alan and Blaine, worked on the dairy after attending Cal Poly in San Luis Obispo. Their daughter, Pamela, became a registered nurse. She married Gordon Rowland in 1982; they live in Nipomo, and she works at Marian Medical Center.

In 1986, Everett and Agnes sold the milk cows in the Dairy Termination Program, and today they raise beef cattle and farm the land for feed. At present there are only five dairies left in the Santa Maria Valley. The high cost of feeds and shipping has been detrimental to the industry in this area, especially since the Knudsen Creamery closed down.

Karen Mortensen died in 1983. Peter and John both live in Hancock Park. Anna Lisa married Richard Luis; they lived in Santa Maria and were co-owners with Richard's brother, Jerry, of Iversen Motors. Richard has passed away.

"I have many wonderful memories of growing up in Santa Maria, helping my father on the dairy farm," says Agnes. "We had horses instead of tractors then that pulled the wagons and plows to feed the cattle and work the land. My mother raised chickens to sell eggs for extra money during the hard times of the Depression. It was a small town then, and you knew almost everyone.

"Everett's parents moved here from Blanding, Utah, in 1934. Everett and I went to school together. Everett's father, Hyrum Johnson, worked as a carpenter and later with Union Oil Company. He helped build the Mormon Church on Miller Street, which is now The Salvation Army."

Clement Muscio

If his success is measured by his progress financially, as well as by his standing in the community where the scenes of his labors have been staged, Clement Muscio stands well towards the top round of the ladder. He started with nothing but a willing spirit, a strong constitution, and an aptitude to do whatever came to his hand, and to do it well. His career should be an object lesson to those who have been less fortunate and who have often despaired of getting ahead. The opportunities are here, and conditions equally as good, for the pioneering has already been done.

A native of Switzerland, Clement Muscio was born in canton Ticino on August 10, 1870, a son of Eustachio and Caterina (Giumini) Muscio, small farmers in Ticino, though the father was handy with tools of all kinds. He died at the age of seventy-eight years in 1910. The mother, now eighty-one, lives on the old home place in Someo. They had five boys and one girl: Seraphino, of Casmalia; Joseph, of Gonzales; Clement; Calimorio, who died in 1892; Victoria, Mrs. A. Franscioni of Gonzales; and Michele, who lives in far-off Ticino.

When a lad of seven years, Clement began working out for wages, and they were very small, but from that age he has been self-supporting and has made his own way in the world. The first pair of shoes he ever put on was bought with money he earned. Being ambitious, he could see no way that he could accomplish his aims in life by remaining in his native land, and he looked to the United States for a future. Accordingly, when he was sixteen, he borrowed money for his passage, and leaving home, sailed from Havre on September 1, 1886, on the steamer *Normandie*, his destination being San Francisco.

After his arrival in the east, he at once came to this state and reached Cayucos in October. He was unfamiliar with our language and customs, and took a job on a dairy ranch at twenty dollars per month. For ten years he worked for wages, saving his money, and later, from 1896 to 1911, engaged in the liquor business at Casmalia, and from July, 1898, to October, 1902, he served as postmaster there.

He bought his ranch of twenty-five hundred acres, part of the Arellanes ranch on the Punta de Laguna, incorporated the Soladino Land Company, was made vice-president and still holds that office. This company subdivided part of the holdings, four hundred acres of which was sold to Edward Doheny of Los Angeles, and five hundred twenty-five acres leased for oil development, the balance being farmed by the company. Of the balance retained by Mr. Muscio, he sold to the Doheny Pacific Petroleum Company in 1916 four hundred acres at a handsome figure. He still owns three hundred sixty-four acres, upon which are located the farm buildings, and which is being successfully operated as a bean ranch by its owner, in addition to his interest in the land company.

Mr. Muscio was married when he was twenty-two, in 1892, to Miss Matilda Righetti, who, like himself, was a native of Ticino—a friend of his youth. They have five children: Mabel; Nellie, who married C. Bassetti and lives on the home ranch; and Julius, Elvira, and Wesley. Mr. Muscio erected a fine residence on his ranch, has good barns and outbuildings, and is ranching on a large scale.

In 1911 Mr. Muscio took his wife and family for an extended visit back to his old home in Switzerland, but was glad to get back to California. Mr. Muscio is liberal and enjoys thoroughly the good things of life. He has a wide circle of friends and by all who know him he is counted one of the successful business men of the county. He is a Republican in politics, though he has never sought office.

Ole Nelson

A valued resident of Santa Maria Valley since 1876, Ole Nelson is one of the few pioneers who have been spared to witness the growth of the country and to recount the experiences of the early days, when game abounded in this section and cattle roamed at will. Few trees could be seen except on the sides of the mountains on either side of the valley. He remembers when Central City, as the thriving town of Santa Maria was first known, was but a settlement at the four corners where Main Street and Broadway intersect, with a few straggling houses scattered here and there.

He bought three hundred twenty-six acres from the Dana Brothers in 1885. The ranch is located three miles north of Santa Maria, where Nipomo Creek flows into the Santa Maria River.

Ole was educated in public schools, and was confirmed in the Lutheran Church when he was fourteen. He had read about America. He sailed from Copenhagen in 1873. He worked on a farm in Connecticut the first summer, and then two years in copper mines in Michigan.

He saved his money and headed for the West Coast, first visiting Washington, Oregon and British Columbia. He settled in San Francisco for one year, and in 1876 took a steamer to Avila Beach, where he got on a horse stage to Guadalupe, where he was hired to work on a ranch. Later he bought land and raised grain. He acquired a small dairy of twelve cows, raised beans, and kept 1000 white Leghorn chickens.

He married Margaret Christensen in 1883 in San Luis Obispo County. Mr. Nelson was a member of Lodge #613, I.O.O.F., and in politics was a Democrat.

Stephen Niverth and Rachel Bradley Niverth

Rachel was the first child of Charles and Elizabeth Bradley, born on June 9, 1871, soon after their arrival in Santa Maria. Rachel became an accomplished rider, and, with her brother, Bill, lived in a cabin where they took care of stock, so that the acreage could be homesteaded for their father.

On October 9, 1890, Rachel married Stephen Barney Niverth in a double wedding ceremony with her sister, Elizabeth, at the Bradley home southeast of Santa Maria.

Stephen Niverth was born in Polinka, Bohemia, on August 2, 1866. He immigrated to the Topeka, Kansas, area with his family, and then worked his way west to Santa Maria, where he learned the blacksmith trade from John Long, whose shop was located on the first block of East Main Street. John Long later became his brother-in-law when Stephen married Rachel Bradley, because Long was married to Annie Bradley.

The couple's first home was on the corner of Chapel and Church Streets in Santa Maria, where their first daughter, Alice, was born. Later they moved out to Garey, California, where Stephen established his own blacksmith shop. Three more daughters were born there: Barbara, in 1896; Mary Ellen, in 1899; and Louise Fredericka in 1902.

Stephen Niverth died on September 14, 1933, and his wife, Rachel, on April 13, 1951. They were survived by their four daughters, Alice Hinds, Barbara Goodchild Sumner, Mary Ellen Bello, and Louise Goodchild Bowles.

William B. Nolan
Margaret Barr Nolan 1917-1990

My wife, Margaret Barr Nolan, was born in Santa Maria and spent her entire life here. Pioneer ancestors of Margaret were the Barr and Grisham families.

I, Bill Nolan, was born in Nashville, Tennessee, on June 21, 1916. I attended public schools and received Bachelor of Science and Doctor of Jurisprudence degrees from Vanderbilt University in Nashville. My maternal ancestors came to North Carolina from England in the 1700's, and one of them served in the North Carolina militia during the Revolutionary War. After the war, they traveled over the Great Smoky Mountains in oxcarts into the territory that later became the state of Tennessee. My maternal grandfather, Dr. Henry Whitfield, practiced medicine for 52 years, and served as Brigadier General in the Confederate Army during the Civil War. My other ancestors were farmers but did not own slaves.

My paternal ancestors were born in Ireland, and came to the United States about 1840, during the Potato Famine in Ireland. My grandfather, James Nicolas Nolan, served as an officer in the Union Army during the Civil War, and remained in Tennessee after the war, ultimately being elected as comptroller of the state of Tennessee. In 1870 he built a residence in Waverly, Tennessee, which was my boyhood home. I sold this property after my parents died, and it is now operated by a local couple as a bed-and-breakfast inn, and is listed as an Historic Site of Tennessee, and also in the National Register of Historic Places, as is the Minerva Club house in Santa Maria.

After law school, I practiced law in my hometown until January, 1942, when I was appointed a Special Agent of the Federal Bureau of Investigation, and thereafter served in the offices at Washington, D.C.; Seattle, Washington; and Los Angeles, California, until August 1944, when I was assigned to the Santa Maria Resident Agency as the sole agent in a sole agency bounded on the south by Gaviota, on the north by Monterey County, on the east by Kern County, and on the west by the Pacific Ocean.

In December, 1944, I met Margaret Barr at a dance in the old Santa Maria Club, where I was living at the time, and we were married in July of 1945 at the Old Mission in Santa Barbara. Our two children, Nancy and Bill, grew up in Santa Maria and graduated from local grammar schools and Santa Maria High School.

I remained in the F.B.I. in Santa Maria until 1969, when I retired from the Bureau and thereafter worked for 15 years in an administrative capacity for Martin Marietta Aerospace at Vandenberg Air Force Base. My wife Margaret passed away in April 1990 of cancer, and is buried in the Santa Maria Cemetery, as I will be, as I now consider myself a Californian, and more specifically, a Santa Marian. My parents and all of my relatives are buried in Tennessee in the Nolan family cemetery.

I am now serving as a Director of the Santa Maria Valley Historical Society, and am very happy to be a member of the Santa Maria Valley Pioneer Association.

My Family from Portugal

by Peggie Novo, 1962
Santa Maria High School

My report is about my grandparents, and their life and family. I gathered all the information up to the 1940's from my grandmother, Irmalinda S. Novo; the rest I got from my mother. My grandfather, Angelo S. Novo, died in 1953. He was born on the Santa Maria Island in the Azores, Portugal. His father was a blacksmith. His parents had five sons and three daughters. All the sons followed in their dad's footsteps and became blacksmiths.

My grandmother, Irmalinda Soares, was born on the Flores Island, which is also in the Azores. She was born on February 15, 1887, in the town of Lomba. Her father was a brick building contractor; he was born on Santa Maria Island and married Catherine Texeira of Flores Island.

Being a blacksmith, a trade he had learned from his father, my grandfather, Angelo, left home and went to the Flores Island to work. There he met my grandmother and fell in love.

In 1901 Grandpa came to America. He came as a paying stowaway on a small sailing ship. There were thirty passengers aboard. He could see his mother from the porthole, hanging clothes in their back yard. It was the last time he ever saw her.

He arrived in New Bedford, Massachusetts, on April 25, 1901. It had taken 31 days to sail from the old country. He took a train to Nevada, where he worked as a blacksmith in the Adelaide Mines. He lived there and saved to bring Irmalinda to America. In 1904 he sent her the money for the voyage. Traveling on the ship *Patria,* she arrived in America on April 25, 1904. The boat docked in New Bedford, Massachusetts, after five days at sea. From there, she traveled by train to Gillcounter, Nevada, arriving on

May 8, 1904. She and Angelo were married on May 12, 1904, in Winnemucca, Nevada. Irmalinda was sixteen years old.

Their first home was a tent in the Adelaide mining camp, which was a big let-down from living in a fine home in Portugal. But despite the inconvenience, they were happy. Their firstborn, Josephine, was the first child born in the camp. She was born with a mid-wife in attendance on April 22, 1905. It was a festive occasion, and the wine flowed freely in celebration.

In succession and in the same tent, two more children were born. On September 3, 1907, Angelo was born, and named after his father. The following year, on October 3, 1908, Adelaide was born. They thought the name of Adelaide was pretty (the name of the mining camp) so Adelaide she was christened. After living in the mining town for eight years, the Novos picked up stakes and moved to Cherry Creek, White Pine County, Nevada. While living there, their fourth child was born. Betty Novo was born on October 7, 1911.

In 1912 they moved to Santa Maria, California, to their first real home on Cypress Street. In Santa Maria, Grandpa Angela was joined by two of his brothers, Frank and Morris, and together they founded the Novo Bros. Blacksmith Shop. They specialized in farm implements. In the years to come, Grandpa Angelo became the sole owner, buying his two brothers out as they went into other businesses. In 1917 Angelo and Irmalinda had prospered enough to buy their own home at 507 West Chapel Street. It was in this home that my father, Albert Novo, was born on August 9, 1921.

My grandfather donated $500 toward the building of the Municipal Plunge on South Broadway. For five years the family had the privilege of free swimming at any time. My father, Albert, being a small boy, took full advantage of that—and some days went in three times!

At a later date, Grandpa also donated $500 toward the building of Our Lady of Perpetual Help Hospital. My two brothers, Wayne and Carl, and I were all born there. My grandfather passed away in 1953 at the same hospital.

Carl was born in 1953, right after Grandpa's death.

All the Novo children attended local schools, all graduating from Santa Maria High School, with the exception of Angelo, who quit school to work, against his parents' wishes.

It was while going to Santa Maria High School that my father, Albert, met my mother, Pauline Frances Lownes. (She is of Irish, French, and English extraction, with a little Indian.) They both graduated and worked in the Santa Maria Valley. They often tell of all the fun they had in and around the Santa Maria Valley.

December 7, 1941, was a date my parents—and everyone else—will never forget. The Japanese bombed Pearl Harbor in Hawaii. War was declared, and my father joined the U.S. Navy.

On July 4, 1942, while my father was stationed at the Alameda Navy Air Base, my mother journeyed to San Francisco on the Greyhound bus and met Dad, who had borrowed a Model A Ford to go to Reno, Nevada, where they were married in the courthouse by a justice of the peace.

During the war, while my dad was serving in the South Pacific, I was born, on April 7, 1945. After the war, Daddy came home to us in Orcutt (we lived in the house my mother was born in). The first time he saw me I was seven months old.

On August 26, 1946, my brother, Wayne Stanley Novo, was born. We were still living in Orcutt. Seven years later my little brother was born in the same hospital. Carl Lewis Novo was born on December 4, 1953.

I am attending high school; my brothers are both attending Orcutt grammar schools.

At the time of this story, Angelo and Irmalinda Novo's family consists of five children, eight grandchildren, and eleven great-grandchildren.

■ *Postscript, 1992:* Needless to say, our family has grown and grown. We have a family reunion every year with approximately 70 people present.

Betty Novo married Earnest Brooks from Lompoc. They founded the Brooks Institute of Photography in downtown Santa Barbara. Later they bought a mansion up in the Montecito hills, and moved the school there. It quickly grew into an international school, with students from all over the world. Mr. Brooks died, and Betty still lives in Ventura. Their son, Ernie Jr., is now manager of the school.

Albert S. Novo

Albert S. Novo was born on August 9, 1921, to Irmalinda and Angelo Novo at their home, 507 West Chapel Street in Santa Maria.

Albert was the youngest of five children, following Adelaide, Angelo, Josephine and Betty.

They all attended Santa Maria grammar schools and Santa Maria High School. All of them graduated. Albert was an accomplished trumpet player in high school band and orchestra; he later played in the Navy band and dance band. He graduated from high school in 1940, and it was after the Japanese attack on Pearl Harbor that he enlisted in the U.S. Navy.

While stationed at Alameda Air Base, he married school chum and girlfriend Pauline Lownes on July 4, 1942. Pauline traveled by bus to San Francisco, met Al, and they went to Reno, Nevada, in a borrowed Model A Ford. They lived in San Francisco until he was sent to metalsmith school in Norman, Oklahoma. Then he returned to Treasure Island, following which he was sent overseas to the South Pacific area for 18 months. He came home for nine months, during which time he was stationed at Goleta Air Base, and then went back to the South Pacific until the war's end. While he was gone this time, their daughter, Peggie Annette Novo, was born on April 7, 1945. She was seven months old when Al was discharged and arrived home at San Pedro.

Al worked for a while for his father in the family business, Novo Bros. Blacksmith Shop, on West Main Street. His metalwork schooling in the Navy was geared to help him in the shop. Soon, finding out there was no future there, he quit and took up truck driving, in which trade he also did a lot of welding and shop work. His brother took over the business, and later sold it. Another old Santa Maria landmark gone!

While working for Bud Richards in 1948, Albert took a truck with a plain tank, and built the first vacuum truck in the Santa Maria Valley. He had to construct a lot of the parts because they could not be bought. Forty years later, he saw this truck again—it was still working!

A son, Wayne Stanley Novo, was born on August 26, 1946.

The third child, Carl Lewis Novo, was born on December 4, 1953.

Albert worked for Engel and Gray for many years, retiring in 1986.

This year, on July 4, 1992, Albert and Pauline will celebrate their 50th anniversary. They are happy in retirement; Albert, an Elk since 1942, has become very active, cutting wood on the Elks' wood crew and serving as a Greeter for three years. He helps rebuild the rodeo grounds and helps Bill Hadsell pouring cement and doing other projects around the Club. He also works on a barbecue crew. For the last 14 years, Al has been busy helping with Pioneer functions, hauling tables, doing cleanup, helping behind the barbecue pits, in charge of the bread crew and everything from soup to nuts.

Albert and Pauline still cut a rug on the dance floor and like to help with the grandchildren.

■ *Postscript, 1999:* Al and Pauline retired from the Pioneer Board of Directors after spending much time helping to build our Pioneer Park at the corner of West Foster Road and South Blosser Road. They had spent twenty years working for the Pioneers.

■ *Postscript, 2001:* Albert and Pauline were honored at the Pioneer Picnic, and the Pavilion Stage was dedicated in their name. There were 1000 persons present on that occasion.

Oakley Family History

The Oakley family, of Scotch-Irish descent, immigrated to North Carolina some years before the Revolutionary War. Cary Calvin ("Cal") Oakley, born in Franklin County, Tennessee, on June 15, 1829, rode his horse to California with a Forty-Niner Gold Rush wagon train. He didn't find gold, but he became a teamster of supplies to the gold fields—dangerous but well paid work.

Cal married Elizabeth Whaley in May, 1855, at Knights Landing. They raised horses around Sacramento, and in 1869 came by covered wagon (with six kids and a herd of horses and cattle) to the Santa Maria Valley, where they homesteaded and raised horses on 160 acres southeast of town, now bounded by Main Street, Depot, Blosser and the railroad tracks. Their home was later the site of Gamble's brick yard. Cal fathered 12 children and was a strong leader and supporter of schools. Cary Calvin Oakley School and the adjacent city park were named in his honor.

Four of his children died young. The other eight married locally and produced 35 grandchildren. In 1880 Cal sold the homestead and bought 2,283 acres of land on Alamo Creek for one dollar per acre. Cal and his wife both died in April, 1890, in the flu epidemic, and his sons, William C. ("Will") and James Asa ("Ace"), took over the ranch.

Will Oakley moved back to Santa Maria in 1904 so his children could attend school there. His children were Isabel Oakley DuBois, Elizabeth Oakley May, Marion Oakley McNeil, Helen Oakley Alexander, Lois Oakley Fraser, Harrison ("Harry") Rice Oakley, and Paul Mahlon Oakley. Their children are William ("Bill"), John ("Jack") and Andrew ("Andy") DuBois; Fred O., James Asa ("Jimmie") and Elizabeth ("Wiff") May; Bruce, Bertha Belle, Margaret and Robert ("Rob") Alexander; Willard ("Sonny") and Keith ("KO") McNeil; John Kimberly ("Kim") Fraser; Marjorie Oakley; and David Allen and Marion Oakley.

Will Oakley was a schoolteacher, rancher, blacksmith and butcher, and operated a threshing machine and combined harvester throughout the valley. Active in public affairs, he was elected City Councilman, second Mayor of Santa Maria, County Supervisor, and State Assemblyman. He and Ace Oakley hosted the first barbecue picnic for Valley Pioneers.

Will Oakley was a founding member of the Pioneer Association and its third president. His son-in-law, Fred L. May, and his daughter, Elizabeth Oakley May, were later presidents of the Association and involved in town politics and activities. The yearly Pioneer Picnics were occasions for the gathering of the clan and were attended by many members of the W.C. Oakley family, as well as many other descendants of Cary Calvin Oakley from near and far.

At this time (2002), Oakley descendants still living in the Santa Maria area include Jim May and his sons: Anthony J. ("Tony") May (children: Anthony J.and Lisa), and Fred L. May II, (married to Michelle Mathiesen, have children: Morgan, Madison and David); Bertha Belle Alexander Nicely (husband Quillie died 1995). They had 4 children: Aquila Jean, Virginia, Patricia, Donald, and many grandchildren. Margaret Alexander Clevenger (husband Stanley died 1985): Their children: Lois married Don Whitney, and they had three children, Kristen, Robin and Jonathan; Janette ("Jan") married Bob Shriner and they had children Tara and Eric. Robert Malcolm ("Rob") Alexander (Lompoc resident), continuing the Alexander Bros. Water Well Drilling & Pump business, married Elouise Parlier, and their four children are Robert M. Jr., twins Richard and Michael, and Pamela. Robert married Trudy Letson, and their sons are Robert M. ("Bobby") Alexander III and Brian. Carol Dunn Fraser (husband John Kimberly Fraser, Deputy Sheriff, died 1999) had three sons: Michael, Allan Scott, and Patrick. Allan married Nancy Goldstein and they produced twins, Stephen Allan and Thomas Christopher Fraser. Patrick married Kristen Broome and they had Derek, Danielle, and Madison.

David Oakley and his son William ("Will") Calvin Oakley, who married Lisa Adair Juckniess (their children are Alyssa Paige and Brandon Hall Oakley), reside in southern San Luis Obispo County. Other Oakley descendants live in many places in California and the west.

The Openshaw Family

by Ann and Jay Openshaw

The Poulton and Openshaw families lived in Oakley, Idaho. Jennie Lee Poulton married Alan Openshaw in Twin Falls, Idaho, on June 12, 1911. Grandpa Poulton raised sheep, and had one of the largest herds in the area. Grandpa Poulton and Alan Openshaw migrated to the Orcutt oil fields after World War I.

In 1922, they sent for Jennie and the six children, including two sets of twins—can you imagine the trip? With children ranging in age from 9 years (Reuel) to 9 months old (Jay and Joyce), they came on a train from Idaho to Casmalia. They were met by Mr. Tognetti and Dad, and driven to Orcutt. Fred Penter took the clan up to Orcutt Hill. Their neighbors included the Billingtons, the Knudsens, and the Penters. We had a great childhood, romping around those hills, sliding down slopes, and being loved by our extended families. "Friday night beans" with cinnamon rolls was a treat at the McGinley house.

Dad and Mr. Poulton worked the oil fields while Mom worked as a cook at the boarding house. Aunts and uncles lived with us at various times.

Dad (Alan) was killed in March of 1928, and Reuel, being the oldest at 16, was put to work. As my brothers grew older, they joined the company, while continuing their education. We all attended Orcutt Grammar School, and Reuel drove the bus. Missing the school bus meant a long walk home.

Joyce and I were spoiled by all the older kids, and we had lots of role models. I started tap dancing at an early age, and haven't stopped dancing yet. I remember dancing for pennies in a hat, and giving it to Mom to help feed the family.

After we all graduated from Santa Maria High School, World War II came along and disrupted our lives for a few years. Reuel continued to work for Union Oil, and became a foreman. He passed away this year, 1994. Si ("Myron") founded G and O Productions, and died in 1977. Bryan, his twin, became one of our early modernist artists, and died in 1978. Dale was killed in an auto accident in 1936.

Joyce married Steve Harding, and lives in Graeagle, California. I married Theo Openshaw, and we have two sons, Neal and Dale. After my divorce, I married Ann Wimbley in 1982, and between us we have six children, eleven grandchildren, and three great-grandchildren.

Currently we are involved in the Santa Maria Valley Pioneer Association.

This year I will be the president. We are also involved in the Santa Maria High School Alumni Association, and recently marched with graduates from as early as 1914 at the one hundredth graduation centennial celebration. We also work for the Food Bank as volunteers.

Filippo Pertusi

by Erlinda Pertusi Ontiveros, 1987

My father, Filippo Pertusi, was born in Masogno, Switzerland, on January 10, 1865. He was the second of six children, and the oldest son. He was educated in public schools, and brought up in the Catholic faith. He was a shoemaker, and learned the trade of mason and bricklayer.

When he was 25 years old, he decided to come to America. Ten days after arriving in San Francisco, he went to Santa Cruz Island, off the coast of Santa Barbara County. He worked for $20.00 a month plus board and room. He helped build a chapel. The four corners were built of large stones, and the rest in bricks.

In 1986, I flew to the ranch and saw the chapel. He was there only four months. He left there and came to Laguna Ranch, near Los Alamos. He remained there a short time, making butter and cheese. From there, he went to work for Joe Muscio on the Tognazzini Ranch in Foxen Canyon, also making butter and cheese. While there, he sent for his bride, Domitilla Milani, from Russo, Switzerland, in 1892. They were married at the ranch, and had five children.

Bernard James was born October 12, 1893, in Foxen Canyon. He finished, and spent his life as a farmer. He died on August 13, 1975, as the result of a tractor accident.

Angelina Linda was born on December 12, 1894, in Foxen Canyon. She graduated from Suey Grammar School, with teacher Ida Davis Devine, in 1910, and from Santa Maria High School in 1914 with a class of fourteen students. She attended the Los Angeles State Teachers School for two years and received her teaching certificate from Santa Barbara County. She taught for thirty years in rural schools of the Santa Maria Valley. She was brought up in the Catholic faith, and taught Catechism for fifty years. She retired in 1951 and lives on ten acres of the original Rancho Tepusquet Grant. She married Francisco Porfirio Ontiveros in 1929 at the Santa Barbara Mission, and they celebrated their fiftieth wedding anniversary in 1979. Porfy, as he was called, died of cancer on June 3, 1985.

Erma Michelina was born in Long Canyon near Sisquoc on May 15, 1896. She graduated from Garey Grammar School. She attended Santa Maria High School one year. She married Alonzo Carranza in 1918 at a Catholic church in Santa Cruz. They had four children. They lived at the old Miguel Carranza homestead east of Sisquoc. She was a homemaker, and a member of the Home Department of the Farm Bureau. When her husband died in 1941, she took over the office work at the Sisquoc gravel pit owned by Frank Gates. Southern Pacific Milling Co. bought out Frank Gates, and she continued to work for them until her retirement in 1954. She died November 28, 1956, of a heart condition.

George Andrew was born in January, 1898, near the Ideal Oil Field between the Palmer lease and Dominion Road. He graduated from Suey Grammar School, and helped on the farm until he married Esperanza Carranza, daughter of Miguel Carranza and Dana Ontiveros, in October, 1923. George worked in the oil fields. He built a home on Blosser Road. He died January 31, 1966, of a heart condition.

In the course of ten years, my father and his family moved from Valerio Tognazzini's ranch to four different places, and finally in 1901 to Joe Muscio's ranch near Suey School, ten miles southeast of Santa Maria on Dominion Road.

Emma Pertusi was born in 1899 and died in 1901 from inflammation of the bowels from eating green apricots.

In 1907, our family moved about one mile south of Suey School, and leased 300 acres from John Houk.

With the help of his wife and children, my father started in the poultry business, and in general farming. He hatched his own chickens in four incubators, and had four brooders and separate yards for the chickens of various ages on a space of twenty acres.

At one time he had 1,800 laying White Leghorns, and gathered more or less 1,000 eggs a day. The eggs were crated in boxes of 30 dozen each. They were sold through an egg association. We used a pickup-like buggy to take the eggs to Santa Maria. They were sold for as little as 24 cents a dozen.

My father's amusement was playing Pedro, a card came. He also played Boccie, an outdoor game with large wooden balls, now called lawn bowling. He died at home in October, 1937, from low blood pressure by taking my mother's high blood pressure pills. What was his motive? No one knows!

My mother died in July, 1938, at a friend's house in San Luis Obispo from quick pneumonia. All the family are buried in he Santa Maria Cemetery.

■ *Postscript:* Erlinda marched in the Centennial Alumni Celebration at Santa Maria High School in 1994, representing the class of 1914. Other marchers represented classes from 1914 to 1993—it was lots of fun. There was big participation from alumni.

Robert W. Rivers

In 1880, my grandfather, William Rivers, emigrated from England to Silver City, New Mexico, to manage a ranch owned by another Englishman. My father, Arthur Joseph Rivers, was born in Silver City in 1884. A few years later the family moved to California, where my father finished his education. He met Flora Lowdermilk in Phoenix, where she was secretary to the Territorial Governor. They were married in 1911.

In 1914, A.J. Rivers began his banking career at the Union Bank in Santa Barbara. In 1917, at the suggestion of L.P. Scaroni, he took a position with the Bank of Santa Maria. At that time Flora was pregnant with me, so she waited until my birth on November 28, 1917, before joining my father in Santa Maria.

My brother, A.J., Jr., sisters Virginia and Dorothy and I attended schools in Santa Maria from elementary through high school. I graduated in 1935½ and worked several jobs before joining the U.S. Army Air Corps in 1939.

After wartime service I attended Cal Poly in San Luis Obispo. Elinor LaFranchi and I were married in 1946. After finishing college in 1949, I went into business for myself and retired in 1983.

Bob Rivers' Capture in World War II

Adapted from the Santa Maria Times, *1989*

During World War II, when many young men were trying to avoid the draft, one young fellow with a passion for flying, 21-year-old Bob Rivers, thought he might as well sign up. His induction into the Army Air Corps came a year before the draft was re-established in 1940.

When Japan fired 23 rounds at the Gaviota Refinery in 1942, Bob was 9000 miles away, honing his flying skills in bombing missions based in England, flying the British-made Spitfire plane over enemy targets on the Continent.

When his company was called to aid the North African campaign, his final mission ended in capture and a 28-month ordeal as a prisoner of war in Germany.

"When I crash landed my Spitfire in Tunisia," says Bob, "I didn't know where I was or if I was behind enemy lines. About a hundred yards from me I saw a soldier approaching, and when I could finally make out the swastika on his helmet, I remember getting

Robert W. Rivers looked confident as he received his commission as a reserve second lieutenant in the U.S. Army Air Corps early in World War II.

169

'Old Man Rivers'

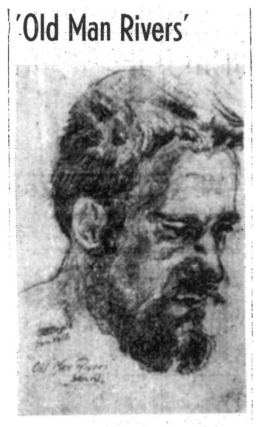

Lieut. Robert Rivers, son of Mrs. Flora A. Rivers, Santa Maria city clerk, a prisoner of the Germans—a sketch by a fellow prisoner showing the beard the youthful Santa Marian has grown since being captured

LIEUT. RIVERS GROWS BEARD IN PRISON OCT 16,'43

This clipping from the Santa Maria Times *of October 16, 1943, showed Santa Marians a glimpse of Bob Rivers during his time as a prisoner of the Germans during World War II.*

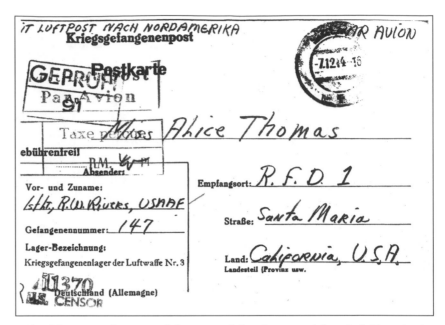

Alice Thomas Anderson saved this postcard that she received from Bob Rivers in the POW camp. See the obverse on the next page.

that kind of empty feeling in my stomach."

If baseball is a game of inches, then it might be said that war is game of miles. Nine more of them and Rivers would have been home free.

But that wasn't to be the case. The young Santa Maria High graduate, who just a couple of years before was facing adulthood without a clear idea of what he wanted to do with his life, found himself conducting dangerous espionage missions and learning new survival skills necessary for such a hostile environment.

"My mother was allowed to send a cigarette parcel every two months, but soon I started asking for cigars, because I discovered they were better to trade with," said Bob.

Rivers' bartering skills made life somewhat bearable.

"I wanted to get that cup of hot chocolate with real chocolate and real milk every day," he said.

Rivers was picked to pass messages regarding train movements, enemy installations and any other pertinent information. Letters written in code to his mother in Santa Maria were passed on to government officials. Likewise, his mother was the conduit for official messages back to camp.

A smuggled radio was the prisoners' sole source of information on the war's progress that did not come from Nazi sources. As German defeat seemed more and more imminent, the prisoners feared Nazi leaders might kill them all.

"We had plans that we were going to go down fighting," said Rivers. The inmates were hoping to overcome their captors with rocks, wire cutters and their sheer numerical superiority.

"I remember I wasn't getting any mail and I thought my mother had died," he said. "And then after about three weeks I don't know how but I just got over it."

Liberation finally came in May of 1945, and Rivers arrived home a few months later. He went on to operate a successful ranch and cattle operation, the fruits of which he enjoys in his Old Orcutt retirement. While the cattle business may have its stresses, with fortunes made and lost, the two years Rivers spent as guest of the Third Reich kind of put things in perspective for his later life. "No matter what happens, even if I lost everything and had to start over, it still couldn't be worse than what I went through," he said.

Kriegsgefangenenlager   Datum: *Sept. 30, 1944*

Dear Alice— How are you'n all the Thomases? I haven't had a word concerning you for ages. Are you or any sisters married yet? And is Eddie still rating No. 1? Gosh what a lot of questions I'd like to ask but not enough space. Can you imagine a guy like me cooped up for two years? Guess there'll be a lot of wolves in our bunch when we're home again but not me. I've slowed down too much. Was gonna say "too old" but 'tain't appropriate. Say hello to any of the kids you may see + how about an epistle or two? Regards to you all. —as ever
Bob

Bob's postcard message to Alice Thomas seems optimistic and philosophical.

RIVERS TYPE
(THE ONE AND ONLY)

Fellow prisoner of war Barney McClure included this cartoon of Bob "Shorty" Rivers in a collection of caricatures he drew during their detention in the German prison camp. "Shorty was the camp character," he remembers.

Fifty years later, Bob reflected on his wartime experiences for an interviewer from the Santa Maria Times. *In the foreground is a model of the Spitfire plane that he flew in the war.*

The Life of Joseph Roemer

by Jessie Roemer Loughridge

Joseph's parents (given names unknown) left Austria-Hungary in about 1835 and sailed for the new world and New York City. While they were in quarantine in the harbor, Joseph Roemer was born, which made him a registered American citizen. Sadly, while his father was on the dock seeking provisions, he was killed in a street riot. Consequently it was necessary for his wife and infant son to sail back to Europe. (There is a narrows on the western side of New York Harbor called Roemer Strait, which may or may not bear allusion to this incident.) It is not known whether there were children older than Joseph, or whether his mother remarried.

Joseph learned the blacksmith's trade in Austria under his uncle, and he prided himself that he knew the trade by eleven years of age. He had no memory of his mother or his family. By the advice of his uncle, he returned to New York. In 1853 he journeyed to St. Joseph, Missouri, and from there traveled across the plains in a covered wagon train. En route there were skirmishes with Indians, and Mr. Roemer lost a finger as a result of one of these raids. He lived in Portland, Oregon; San Francisco, Mayfield, Riverside, Santa Ynez, and Santa Maria. It is conjectured that he came to Santa Maria on two different occasions in an attempt to establish a business (one perhaps in 1892).

Mr. Roemer's first place of business was on the corner of Chapel Street and Broadway, where he had bought out the firm of Mark & Grover. In an effort to patent his pipe tong wrench, Mr. Roemer sent two men to Washington, D.C., for that purpose, and later went there himself, only to find that his idea had been stolen from him, and was already patented under the name Roemer Pipe Tong Wrench. In this venture, he lost more than $10,000, and also his blacksmith shop property on Chapel Street.

He then moved his business back a block to the corner of Mill and Broadway. Here, through the years, his business increased to include not only a blacksmith shop, but a woodworking shop (a header-wagon a day); an iron and steel construction shop; an oil-well repair and machine shop (lays costing $1,000); and agencies for various famous-make wagons (Studebaker), and surreys with fringe; farm implements (John Deere); automobiles (Chalmers, Winton and Maxwell); bus bodies (Greyhound): and commodities. This was all swept away in a $100,000 fire on January 13, 1921. A modern building was then constructed, but Mr. Roemer had retired, and the business property became diversified under the management of his two sons, Frank and Alfred Roemer.

As places of residence, Mr. Roemer built an eleven-room reinforced concrete house on the opposite corner from his business on Broadway in 1903, and a concrete farm house in 1917 on his property on the river on the old Barton place. A previous concrete storehouse had been built on Chapel Street to test the original formula for pouring the concrete, an idea which Mr. Roemer had always hoped to patent. The Broadway house was demolished in 1936 after Mr. Roemer's death to make way for a modern service station, but Mr. Roemer had spent many years there among his berry arbors and flowers.

Mr. Roemer was a tall, statuesque man, possessed of innate dignity; he wore dark clothes and a broad-brimmed black hat. He had a mustache and goatee, and was an imposing figure wherever he appeared. Though a man of few words, he had a ready wit, and was gentlemanly and kind to all, lending a helping hand wherever needed, but stern and forthright where justice and integrity were concerned. He was thirty years older than his wife, Elenore Roemer. He passed away May 27, 1929, at his home, having attained the age of 94.

The descendants of Mr. and Mrs. Roemer are:

Son, Frank Lloyd Roemer; granddaughters, Jo Ann Roemer and Ruth Roemer Forrest; great-grandchildren, Patricia Marie Forrest, Michael Roemer Forrest, and Casey Terrace Roemer.

Son, Alfred Renault Roemer; grandson, Glenn

Arthur Roemer; and great-grandsons, Vard Alfred Roemer and Robert Renault Roemer.

Daughter, Jessie Renault Roemer Loughridge; granddaughter, Lorraine Loughridge Williams; grandson, Renault Frank Loughridge (deceased).

—Submitted by Glenn A. Roemer, graduate of Santa Maria High School, 1928.

■ *Postscript:* In 1995, Al and Pauline Novo attended Glenn Roemer's 85th birthday celebration at the Elks Club in Santa Maria. Over 400 attended this dinner dance given by his family.

Ida Irene Walker Rojas

by her daughter, Ione Novo

Ida was the second child of six who blessed the lives of the Pioneer family of Robert O. Walker and Mary Irene Walker. Robert was born in Castroville, and came to Guadalupe, California, in 1872. Mary came out from Conneautt, Ohio, with her family, and they settled in the Santa Maria Valley in the late 1800's. Santa Maria was then named Central City, where Ida Irene was born. She was delivered by a midwife, and lived her 99½ years of life here until her death on August 29, 1991.

The Walker family moved to the small community of Orcutt. Robert became constable, and Mary was Postmistress for many years. The discovery of oil on the Orcutt Hill made Orcutt a boom town. By that time, Robert had a small meat market and grocery store—and an ice cream parlor—all run by family members.

Ida Irene married Clarence Evans in 1908 at the age of 16. He had come to work in the oil fields. They lived in a tent house on Orcutt Hill with many others. When she became pregnant, they moved into town. A baby girl was born: Pheoby Ione Evans.

Sadly, the marriage broke up, and in 1916 Irene took her baby and moved in with her parents.

Orcutt was growing, and business was good. A two-story building, The Orcutt Mercantile, was built. It was a general store with a few apartments and a dance hall upstairs. Ida Irene was hired as a bookkeeper and was employed there for eighteen years.

Later, another two-story general merchandise store was built, with a dance floor upstairs. Called the Co-op, it was very popular. Dances were held every Saturday night.

The Walker family were great outdoorsmen. Every summer, they would load up the old touring car and go camping, traveling on gravel roads and sleeping on the ground. Their favorite spot was Lake Tahoe, where Indians sat along the road weaving baskets and blankets for sale.

Irene and Ione became very close, going to dances and doing things together like two good friends, until Irene married. She married Joseph William Rojas, called Bill. They dated for twelve years because Irene didn't want to marry until Ione graduated from high school. They were married until his death in 1963.

Ione's real father had gone to Australia to work in the oil business, where he helped bring in the first gas well in Perth. He remarried, and lived in Australia until his death.

Ione met Angelo Novo at a school dance. They were married during her senior year. She went on to school, and graduated in 1930 from Santa Maria Union High School. They had a daughter by the name of Carole Jean Novo. She was the light of their lives. She spent many hours and special times with her grandmother.

Carole also graduated from Santa Maria High School, and soon married her classmate, Bill Harrison. They had four children, all close to Grandma Irene. Their names are Vickie, Sheri, Billy and Michael.

Irene was a great lady, always with a smile on her face. When she passed away in 1991, she left a great void in all of our lives. We all have our cherished memories that will keep her dear to us all the days of our lives.

Ancestors of Robert J. Rowe

Only Robert's maternal ancestors are from the Santa Maria Valley. Aprise Santa Clara (later St. Clair) immigrated from Portugal in the early 1880's. Shortly after his arrival, he married his wife, Maria, who had also immigrated from Portugal to the Santa Maria Valley. They had five children, the youngest of whom was Christophoro. In adulthood he became Christopher (Christy) St. Clair.

Lars Jensen and Maria Jensen (not blood relatives) immigrated to the U.S. from Denmark, settling in our Santa Maria Valley in the early 1880's. They married and had eight children, one of whom was Minosa Jensen, known as Minnie.

Christy St. Clair and Minnie Jensen married in the Santa Maria Valley and had four children: Ellen, Josephine, James, and Catherine.

Ellen St. Clair was born in 1916. She married Robert V. Rowe of northern California in 1939. They had one child, Robert J. Rowe, born in 1941 at Our Lady of Perpetual Help Hospital in Santa Maria. Robert V. Rowe died in Santa Maria a few years later. Ellen St. Clair Rowe still lives in Santa Maria.

Josephine St. Clair married William Siliznoff. They had three children: John, Ronald and Suzanne. Josephine and William are both deceased. John is single, and lives in the family home in Santa Maria. Ronald lives with his wife, Lupe, on the outskirts of Santa Maria. Suzanne married John Higuera, and they live with their four children near Santa Margarita. James died in 1977. He had no children, and was living with Ronald and Lupe.

Catherine St. Clair is single and lives in Santa Maria.

Robert Rowe was born in Santa Maria and lived in our valley until he was five years old. He moved to Santa Barbara, where he was raised. After high school, Robert served twenty years in the U.S. Navy, the first fourteen years in aviation electronics and the last six years as a criminal investigator. After retiring from the Navy, he obtained a B.A. degree in psychology from San Diego State University, and an M.A. degree and a Ph.D. degree from Wayne State University in Detroit, Michigan. He is a neuropsychologist in private practice in Livonia, Michigan, and hopes to return to the Santa Maria Valley when he retires.

The Sheehy Family:
Santa Maria's Strawberry Pioneers

The Sheehy families of Santa Maria and Nipomo can trace their ancestors back to County Cork in the southwest of Ireland. They are all descendants of John Sheehy and Mary Donovan, who were both born in 1790. With restrictive policies that did not allow the Irish to own their own land, and the Potato Famine of the 1840's beginning to take its toll, the first Sheehys began to immigrate to America in 1846.

Timothy Sheehy came to America in 1846. His son, Patrick Henry, lived in Watsonville, California, and eventually married Isabel ("Belle") Adam. Belle's father was William Laird Adam, the well known Santa Maria Valley pioneer who came from Scotland and settled in Santa Maria in 1869. Little is known as to how Belle and Patrick (P.H.) met and eventually married, but it is more than likely they met while Belle was in school in the Bay Area. In Mary C. ("Lade") Adam's diary of 1908 there is mention of Mary's trips to Watsonville to visit her sister and P.H.

Belle and P.H.'s sons, Kenneth and Rod, often took the train to visit relatives in Santa Maria. During their first trip to Santa Maria, the boys were instructed to throw their bags out of the train as it came to a stop in Santa Maria. When the train reached the top of the Cuesta Grade, it slowed almost to a stop before descending. The boys assumed they were in Santa Maria, did as they were instructed—and never saw their bags again!

One of Timothy's other sons, Jeremiah, eventually moved to Nipomo and is the ancestor to the many Sheehys in the Nipomo area.

Strawberry Fields Forever

While World War II raged, Kenneth and Rod, still living in Watsonville, began to talk with Ned Driscoll, founder of Driscoll Strawberry Associates. They all felt there would be a demand for fresh berries after the war ended. Ned wanted them to move to Southern California in order to expand the growing season that was limited to Watsonville at the time. At first they were to move to Gardena and grow there, but Ken and Rod felt it was too far from Watsonville, so they decided on Santa Maria, where they already had family and friends. So it was that in 1944 Ken and Rod, along with their wives Byra and June, moved to Santa Maria and began their first test plots of strawberries on Whitney Road (now Donovan Road). Prior to this, there hadn't been any berries grown commercially in Santa Maria, so no one was sure what varieties would do well. Their first farm in Santa Maria was called the Gardena Ranch. It is interesting to imagine what the Sheehy family would be doing today had they bought land in Gardena instead of Santa Maria.

When the Sheehys moved to Santa Maria during the war, Ken and Byra's son Bob was fighting in Europe with Patton's Tank Corps while his brother Terrance was serving in the Pacific. Bob and Terry both received letters from their parents telling them to return to Santa Maria instead of Watsonville.

The Sheehys were instrumental in bringing back Japanese Americans to help grow for them—an unpopular move at the time. Housing was provided for them, first in tents and later in pre-fab structures. Over 90 houses were built altogether. The workers were consuming so much rice that Ken bought an entire rail car full of rice and parked it in Guadalupe. Several weeks later agents from the Bureau of Alcohol, Tobacco and Firearms paid Ken a visit—they thought he was making sake with all that rice! Many Japanese families, including the Furakawas, the Kagawas, and the Matsumotos went on to form their own berry companies.

Ken died in 1953, followed by Rod in 1956. Bob and Terry continued farming together and eventually formed their own separate companies in 1985. Bob Sheehy passed away in 1993. His children, Rob, Patrick, and Bonnie, all live in Santa Maria. Patrick continues to grow strawberries for Driscoll's. Terry's son, Brian, also grows strawberries in Santa Maria. His oldest daughter, Clair, lives in Grover Beach. His other daughter, Mary Ellen, is married to Dr. Eric Kirk.

THE SIMAS FAMILY
OF SANTA MARIA VALLEY

Manuel Machado Simas and Anna Concepcion Simas were born and raised in the village of Lajes do Pico. They were married in 1877 at the Chapel of Sao Pedro on the island of Pico, Azores Islands. Manuel was the son of Manuel and Maria Simas, and Anna was the daughter of Mr. and Mrs. Frank Soares de Rosa. Manuel migrated to Oceano, California, in 1883, and Anna followed with two small children in 1885.

Shortly after Anna arrived, they moved to Oso Flaco in the Santa Maria Valley, where they raised most of their sixteen children. Six of the children died at an early age. The survivors were Manuel M. Simas, Jr.; Alfred M. Simas; Joseph M. Simas; Anna Simas Brebes; Angelica Simas Reis; Antone Simas; John J. Simas; Peter M. Simas; Maria M. Simas Reis; Lawrence M. Simas; and Violinda Simas Silva. Manuel and Anna spent most of their lives raising their children and farming in Oso Flaco. They spent a few years on a ranch he purchased in Toro Creek, Cayucos, California. His last ranch was purchased in the Tepusquet area on the banks of the Santa Maria River next to Rancho Sisquoc. Manuel retired and later died on October 20, 1920; Anna died on August 17, 1945.

Manuel Jr. never married. He worked on the ranches for his father and then later for his brothers on various ranches until his retirement. Manuel enjoyed working with wood and making many items with his beautiful hand carving.

Alfred M. married Louise Silva and they had five children: Clarence, Alfred Jr., Edward, Joseph, and Annie Scolary-Cardoza. Alfred Jr. died as a young boy. After the loss of Louise, Alfred married Helen Avila and they had seven children: Arthur, Johnny, Helen Possom, Ralph, Mary Bonner, Rosaline Pardo, and Evelyn Covert. Johnny died in infancy. Alfred devoted most of his life to farming and doing carpentry work.

Joe Simas married Leanora DeRosa and they had seven boys: Melvin, Elmer, Isadore, Leland, Arthur, Vernon, and Gerald. Joe spent his younger life farming with his father and brothers; later, he farmed on his own at Fugler's Point at the eastern end of the Santa Maria Valley. He devoted most of his life as owner and operator of the Ideal Motel, one of the first motels in the Santa Maria Valley.

Anna Simas married Manuel Brebes and they had ten children: Freddie, Adlena Ormonde, Manuel, Josie Machado, Frank, Ida Reviea-Mello, Henry, Johnny, Eva Bersticker, and Evelyn Boutcher. Anna and Manuel lived most of their lives and raised their family in Morro Bay, California. The Brebes family was well known for their involvement in the fishing industry in that area.

Angelica Simas married Louis M. Reis and they had five children: Louis Jr., Aileen Pipkin-Wilson-Crum, Dorothy Roza-Pierrera, Leonell, and William. Louis and his boys operated a dairy farm near Lodi, California, where Angie and Louis raised their family and spent most of their lives.

Antone Simas married Olga Ramonetti. They had a son, Clarence, but also raised as their own one of his sister Anna's grandchildren, Loretta Machado Reade. Tony worked on the ranches with his father and brothers, and later went to work for Allan Hancock on the Rosemary Farm and the Rosemary La Brea Ranch of Santa Maria Valley.

John J. Simas married Geneva A. Flood. They had four children: Edward, Wilfred, Dolores Killgore, and Johnny. Edward died as a young boy. John worked with his father and brothers on the ranches; he was later the owner and operator of the Sunset Dairy on Simas Rd. (which was named in his honor) near

Guadalupe, on the Arthur Tognazzini Ranch. John's son and later partner, Wilfred L. Simas, continued operating the Sunset Dairy after his retirement.

Peter M. Simas married Daisy Dutcher, but they had no children. After Daisy's death, Peter married Hettie ("Butch") Simas. The Simas family was honored to welcome her daughter, Belva Souza, to the family. Peter devoted most of his life to working as an auto mechanic and operating his auto garage in Morro Bay, California.

Maria M. Simas married John M. Reis and they had four children: John, Edward, Joe, and Frank. Mary and John lived at several different locations, as John worked as a ranch hand and ranch foreman for ranches in the Santa Maria Valley area until retiring.

Lawrence M. Simas married Evangeline Flood and they had three children: Barbara Sweeney, Thelma Sumner, and Stephen. Lawrence worked on various ranches in his early years and devoted most of his life to raising his family by working as a carpenter for building contractors in the Santa Maria Valley. He enjoyed making miniature play furniture for children of the Simas family and friends.

Violinda Simas married William P. Silva and they had six children: Aurora Bright, Arthur, Lawrence, Lorraine Berger, Alice Villa, and little Betty, who died in infancy. Lena and Bill devoted most of their lives to raising their family in the Santa Maria Valley. Lena was only 35 years old when she died in an auto accident at the intersection of Stowell and Rosemary Road.

The Simases have always been a very talented musical family. John J. Simas started and led the Simas Orchestra with his brother, Lawrence Simas, and later his nephew, Clarence Simas. They played for dances from Los Alamos to Cayucos, with one of their favorite spots being the dance hall in Sisquoc. Over the years they played for dances at the Pioneer Park on the raised dance floor among the oak trees east of Santa Maria on Highway 166. Private parties and Portuguese folk dances like "The Chamarita" were a fun time for the whole family. John's oldest son, Wilfred L. Simas, also had an orchestra, called the Blue Notes, which played for dances in the Santa Maria Valley area. Several members of the Simas family are also known for their musical gifts and beautiful singing voices.

Some of the businesses owned and operated in the Santa Maria Valley area by members of the Simas family have included the Ideal Motel, by the Joe M. Simas family; the Sunset Dairy, by the John J. Simas family; Edward and Ida Simas Farming, by the Silva and Edward Simas family; Simas Sporting Goods, by the Leland ("Butch") Simas family; the Bradley Lounge, by the Melvin Simas family; Avila Plumbing, by the Avila and Arthur Simas family; Simas Smart Shoes, by the Gerald ("Ike") Simas family; Simas Ranch & Farming, by the Johnny M. Simas family; Simas Electric, by the Robert E. Simas family; the Valley Farmer Restaurant, by Vernon, Gerald, Robert L., Tim, and families; Kirk & Simas, by the Alex Simas family; Jocko's Restaurant, by the Fred and Sandy Simas Knotts family; and Simas Trucking, by the Mark Simas family, to name a few. Many members of the Simas family are well known for their employment at various businesses, and some of the younger generations are becoming involved in various ventures.

Several of the Simases have been well known for their ability to cook and prepare Santa Maria style barbecue and all the trimmings for large crowds. Gerald ("Ike") Simas is one such person, and has shown his ability and generosity at past Pioneer days and many other functions in the Santa Maria Valley.

Steven Agustus Slater, Sr. and Erla Kelley Slater

by their granddaughter, Pauline Novo

Steven Agustus Slater, Sr.
Born March 28, 1876, Chicora, Butler County,
Pennsylvania
Died April 1, 1961, Santa Maria, California

Erla Kelley Slater
Born April 11, 1878, Chicora, Pennsylvania
Died June 12, 1932

Steven Slater came to the Santa Maria Valley in the early 1900's to work in the oil fields on Orcutt Hill. In 1909 he sent for his family in West Virginia. They arrived by train. Never having seen the ocean before, they were spellbound by Pismo Beach. Steve met his wife and six children in Orcutt; they arrived on the old narrow gauge train. He loaded them and all their belongings into two horse-drawn buggies, and they moved into the tent city on Newlove Hill. The children attended the schoolhouse that still stands.

The Slaters lived in Santa Maria and Arroyo Grande before settling into their own home in Nipomo. The house stood about a quarter mile north of Jocko's until it was torn down in 1998. The Slaters raised twelve children in that house. They had a big orchard, and flowers everywhere. It will never be the same.

The children all attended Nipomo and Arroyo Grande schools.

Steve became Constable of the Nipomo area, and served his community for a long time. He was always being called on the old crank phone. At that time there were very few homes on the Mesa—only a few ranches. The pea-picker camps were there, though, and there were murders, fights, and all kinds of trouble.

Jocko's bar was the busiest thing in Nipomo. I went to Nipomo Grammar School in the first grade. After school, Papa would let me dance for pennies in Jocko's for all his friends. I would buy candy with the money. One day I got greedy and kept the money,

and Grandma found out. Needless to say, that was the end of my dancing career at Jocko's.

My grandmother died at an early age; Steve and Frances were the only two still at home. She was buried in the Santa Maria Cemetery next to her two daughters that preceded her in death, Madeline and Eva. Later, Papa was buried by Erla.

STEVEN AND ERLA SLATER'S CHILDREN

1. Hazel Slater, born July 1, 1899, in Brink, West Virginia. She died in April 1982. She married Carl Lownes in 1919. In 1920 Pauline Lownes was born. Three months later, Carl was killed in an auto accident south of Los Alamos. Hazel later married Al Gardner, and they had two sons, Bob and Bill Gardner. They still live in old Orcutt, as of 1993, leaving only for their stints in the Navy (Bob) and the National Guard (Bill).

2. Dorothy Slater, born 1901 in Mannington, West Virginia. She married Dell Lownes in 1918. She died in 1980 and is buried at Los Osos. They had two daughters, Doris and Betty.

3. Eva Slater, who died as a child on Orcutt Hill when she fell into a sump hole. It was a terrible tragedy.

4. Phillip Slater, born 1904 in Mannington, West Virginia. He married Florence Helling, and they lived their life in Coalinga, California. They had one son, Jack, who still lives there in the family home.

5. Clair Slater, born February, 1906, in Mannington, West Virginia. He married Blanche Theriot, and they lived in Ventura and had one

daughter, Dana. Clair died in 1989.

6. John Slater, born 1907 in Mannington, West Virginia. He died in San Diego in 1968. John was a Navy man. On his retirement, he, his wife Mitzie, and their five children manned the Point Loma Lighthouse at San Diego.

7. Daisy Slater, born 1909 in Sisquoc, Santa Maria Valley. She married Lewis Hebard, and they had one son, Donald Hebard. Lewis died at an early age. Daisy raised her son in Santa Paula. She married Arthur Leighton in 1946 and they had one son, Lee Leighton. As of 1993, she lives alone in Huntington Beach in a nice condo complex.

8. Madeline Slater, born 1911 in Santa Maria. She died young.

9. Erla Slater, born 1912, lived in the Santa Maria Valley most of her married life. She married Russell Cook and they had two daughters. Russell died in 1990, and Erla went to live with her granddaughter, Julie, in Santa Maria. She died July 29, 1995, in her home.

10. Kathleen, born 1913 in Arroyo Grande, died 1970. She married Everett Brickey, and they had five boys and two girls. They lived on a ranch by Los Alamos for many years. Everett was quite prominent, serving on the school board, the fair board, and working with 4H.

11. Frances Slater, born 1917 at Graciosa oil lease, Santa Maria Valley. She served in the Navy during World War II. As of 1993, she lives in Cambria.

12. Steve Slater, Jr., born 1919 at Graciosa oil lease. He married Dottie Laten and they have three children, all raised in Arroyo Grande. Steve served in the Army during World War II. They have lived for years in Grover Beach.

* * * * *

John Slater, the progenitor of the Slater family in Butler County, Pennsylvania, enlisted at the age of eighteen in Count de Rochambeau's Army, and came to America to fight in the Revolutionary War.

He was a native of Alsace, which then belonged to France.

He arrived with the fleet off Rhode Island in 1780 and served under Lafayette for four years, including the Battle of White Plains, as a cavalry man until the war ended. He was discharged in 1783 in the state of Delaware.

He was present at the surrender of Cornwallis, and the framing of the Constitution of the United States, and was one of the few men who witnessed the signing of that now famous document.

After the war he stayed in America . . . and that is how the Slater family got started in America many generations ago.

Marie Myers Sluchak

1993

The Myers family moved to Santa Maria in the fall of 1929. We lived at 913 Haslam Drive. My parents were True and Edna Myers; both are now deceased. I married Dr. John M. Sluchak. I lost him in 1980 after a marriage of 38 years. We have two children, twins, Jan Edward Sluchak and Robin Marie Sluchak. We have one grandson.

At present I am a park supervisor at Tahoe Cedars Park in Lake Tahoe. I am very involved in the Federated Women's Club of Lake Tahoe as president of the executive board.

My brother, Edward Myers, lives in Arroyo Grande, so I do come home to the Santa Maria area often.

Barbara A. Snyder (Victorino)

Born at Sisters' Hospital, 1948

Manuel J. Victorino was my paternal grandfather. He was born in 1901 in the Edna Valley area. He married Angelina Gomes of San Luis Obispo. In 1923 their first son, my father, was born. They moved to the Guadalupe area in the mid-1920's. Manuel worked for the Ferini-Ardantz Ranch as a foreman for 43 years. He retired in 1976, and passed away in 1980.

Isaac Sherrell was my maternal grandfather. He moved to the Guadalupe area from Arkansas. Evalee Sherrell was one of Isaac and Verna Sherrell's six children. Isaac passed away in 1951. Verna Sherrell, my grandmother, continued to live and work in Guadalupe until the 1960's. Then she moved to Santa Maria, and lived here until her passing in 1983.

My father, Erwin M. Victorino, was born in 1923 in the Edna Valley. The family moved to the Guadalupe area in the mid-1920's. He moved to Santa Maria in 1952. He was involved in trucking until his passing in 1971.

My mother, Evalee Sherrell Victorino Mitchell, was born in Arkansas in 1927. She moved to the Guadalupe area in 1938-39, and in 1952 moved to Santa Maria, where she still resides.

As for me, Barbara Victorino Snyder, I was born on November 24, 1948, in Santa Maria, and lived in Guadalupe until 1952, when we moved to Santa Maria. I attended Santa Maria schools, graduating from Santa Maria Union High School in 1966. I graduated from Hancock Junior College in 1968, and then graduated from Cal Poly, San Luis Obispo, in 1970. I obtained teaching credentials from Cal Poly in 1971, and have been employed as a teacher since 1971 with the Santa Maria Elementary School District. I currently hold the position of Independent Study Teacher with the Elementary School District.

Rowene Kortner Spears

Mrs. Peter Peterson came to America from Denmark in 1884. After four years she divorced, and married Christian Kortner, and lived in Tepusquet with her four children, Olga, Laura, Christian (Chris), and Henry. Henry lived here, but died in his early thirties. Chris lived in Santa Maria until his death in 1979; he had four children. His daughter, Rowene Kortner Spears, lives in Santa Maria. She has two daughters; the older one, Barbara, lives here. Rowene married Jack Spears in 1938, and has lived here all her life. Jack died in 1978.

Her father, Chris, who was born in Tepusquet, worked at the country club as greens superintendent until his retirement. The family all lived at the Country Club.

Rowene has served the Native Daughters twice as president, and is very active. She is also active in the Santa Maria High School Alumni Association. She was a Camp Fire leader and is a lifetime member of the Parent Teacher Association. She is now active in the Marian Medical Center Auxiliary.

Her other daughter, Carol Lovell, lives in Bakashi, Oklahoma.

Morris J. Stephan

Morris was six years old when he was brought to Santa Maria in 1912 by his father, Paul B. Stephan, and his mother, Ida M. Stephan, with his eight-year-old sister, Frances. His parents had traded their home in Los Angeles for sixty acres of bare land four miles south of Santa Maria. His father built a small shed on the property—"the ranch." He and his family lived there on a dirt floor while his father built a small four-room house on the land. There was no gas, electricity, or water available, so water was hauled in a wooden barrel by horse and wagon from the Twitchell horse-trough about a mile north of Orcutt. When gas was available, they piped into it and enlarged the size of their home. They later added electricity. A soft water well was drilled; they also supplied neighbors with water.

Morris and his sister Frances attended Washington Grammar School, located on the northwest corner of Foster Road and Orcutt Road. They had one teacher for all eight grades; she was Frances Jessie Tilley, who drove a horse and buggy 4¼ miles to get to school. Later, May Grisham became their teacher, but she drove an automobile.

Morris later attended Santa Maria High School, a two-story wooden building. He and other students campaigned for passage of school bonds for a new high school. He played end on the first championship football team in 1923. He was student body president in 1924, the year he graduated. He went one year to Santa Maria Junior College and helped organize their first football team. He transferred to U.S.C. as a sophomore. He entered the intramural boxing tournament, and won the gold medal in his division. He received his B.A. degree, and attended U.S.C. Law School, graduating in 1930. He passed the state bar examination and became a lawyer, working with Preisker, Goble and Twitchell. In 1931 he married Lois C. Rice. Daughter Mary Joyce was born in 1933, and a son, Richard Paul, in 1935.

In 1939 they built their home at 920 South McClelland Street, one block east of Santa Maria High School. In 1942 he volunteered to serve in the U.S. Naval Air Force. He was Legal Officer—Legal Assistance and Civilian Personnel Officer. He also served on the Court Martial Board, attaining the rank of Lieutenant Commander. He was released in 1946 and returned to Santa Maria, where he resumed practicing law with the same firm, now Twitchell and Rice.

His daughter, Margaret Kay, is now a legal secretary in Palo Alto, California.

In 1950, Morris Stephan was elected Justice of the Peace in the Seventh Judicial District in Santa Maria, taking office in January, 1951. He was later Judge of the Justice Court in Santa Maria. The population in Santa Maria mushroomed; at the same time, court cases multiplied. In 1961, the Santa Maria Justice Court was enlarged and became Santa Maria Municipal Court. Stephan had to forego his law practice, since the new judicial job required him full time. He served as Judge until 1970, when he was appointed by the Governor of California to be Judge of the 2nd Department of Superior Court of Santa Barbara County in Santa Maria. He retired from this post in 1972 after being in judicial office for 22 years.

In 1975, he returned to the bench at the death of Judge Robert Trapp. He so served until the Governor appointed Judge Royce Lewellen, who is still serving.

Morris Stephan performed many weddings in the Santa Maria area. In December 1986, he and his wife Lois moved from Santa Maria to San Jose, California, so they could be nearer to their three children, now living and working in the Bay area.

He and his wife Lois were active in the First Christian Church.

Dale Stockton

Fulton, California, June, 1993

My name is Dale Stockton. I was born August 18, 1925, in Orcutt, California. My father's name was Lyman Stockton. He was a teacher at Pine Grove School between Orcutt and Santa Maria. My mother's name was Edithe. Dad died in 1927 when I was two years old. My mother later married Fred Strong, who worked for the county road department. During the 1930's, he drove the water truck for the annual Pioneer Picnic when it was held in Cuyama. I remember riding with him. If I recall right, there was a dance pavilion at the picnic grounds, and permanent barbecue pits. The Cuyama River was across the road.

I left Santa Maria in my junior year of high school (1942). I attended kindergarten at Miller Street School and went to El Camino Junior High School. My class graduated in 1943. I obtained my diploma later while in the U.S. Army.

Marie Sweet

Marie Sweet Dunlap should have been born in Orcutt. Her father, Walter Sweet, came to Orcutt around 1907. He married Mary Jamison in 1910. They lived on North Pacific Street, and had a barn and eight horses across the street, on the corner of Pacific and Park Street. Walter hauled equipment up into the oil fields above Orcutt by team and wagon. Later they sold all this, and moved to Newlove Hill. Walter Sweet's father became very ill two years after Walter and Mary were married, so they went to Oregon to care for him. Marie Sweet was born while they were up there. They returned to Orcutt when Walter's father was well enough, and brought him back with them.

Marie always felt that she should have been born in Orcutt. Her two brothers were born on the Newlove oil lease.

Minnie Silva Tonnelli

My father, Manuel P. Silva, immigrated to California in 1910 and lived in the San Luis Obispo-Morro Bay area for three years, working as a farm hand. In 1913, he moved to Santa Maria, and started farming for himself at the Calderon Ranch near Garey, and lived there until 1918, moving to Los Alamos for one year, and then back to the ranch at Dominion and Clark Roads. (At that time it belonged to Charlie Moore.) He farmed there until 1923, then moved back to Los Alamos to the Careaga Ranch, and farmed there for 33 years, retiring in 1956. At that time he and my mother moved to 527 East Orange Street in Santa Maria. He passed away in 1979. My mother and dad married July 30, 1908. My mother immigrated to the Santa Maria area in 1916 to be with my father. They are the parents of seven children; six are still living. Mother is still living, at the age of 93. Our family has always lived in this area for the past 72 years, making us real Pioneers.

I still live in the family home on East Orange Street, and have a son, Gerald John Tonnelli. I have two granddaughters, Jennifer and Christen Tonnelli.

The Joseph A. Thomas Family

Joe Thomas migrated to Santa Maria from the island of Pico in the Azores in 1906. He was one of the most aggressive farmers in the valley for many years, having learned his trade from his father on the island. In 1915 he married Augusta Carvalho at St. Mary's Catholic Church. Augusta had come from the Azore Island of Terceria in 1914. She was a seamstress by trade, but she worked alongside her husband on the farm.

They farmed in Tepusquet, Oxnard and Mesa Road, and the last farm where they lived and worked was on Stowell Road. Their main crops were beans and grains. They also grew hay and raised cattle, sheep, turkeys and hogs. Sugar beets were grown on the home ranch and were supplied to the government from 1941 until the end of World War II. Joe Thomas was also an avid horseman, and rode in many parades on his silver saddle.

Six children were born from the union of Joe and Augusta Thomas:

• Joseph Jr. was born in 1916. He married Helen Ryzner and had two children, Robert Joseph and Joanne. He died in 1969.

• Mary was born in 1917. She married Lawrence Mora at St Mary's Catholic Church. They had five children: Thomas, Marily, Barry, Larry, and Rebecca.

• Louise was born in 1920. She graduated from Santa Maria High School in 1939 and married Rex Turner. A homemaker, she had four children: Carol (who married Mike Neiggmann of Santa Maria), Barbara, Timothy, and Dayna.

• Alice was born in 1922. A homemaker and artist,

Augusta Carvalho Thomas (far right) with her daughters (from left) Esther, Bea, Alice, Louise and Mary

she graduated from Santa Maria High School in 1941 and married Ed Anderson at St. Mary's Catholic Church in 1944. Their three children are Victoria (now known as three-term Pioneer Association president Vicki Anderson Wilson), Teresa and Thomas. Alice died in 1998.

• Beatrice was born in 1924 and graduated from Santa Maria High School in 1943. She became a real estate agent, and in 1952 married Peter Vallozza, who had come to Santa Maria in 1948. They had two children, Patricia and Anthony.

• Esther was born in 1926. She married Eli Santos at St. Mary's Catholic Church and had two children, David and Dennis. She died in 1951.

Joe and Augusta Thomas lived in this valley from the time they entered the United States until their deaths, Joe in 1958 and Augusta in 1977. They are both buried in the Santa Maria Cemetery. Esther Thomas Santos, Alice Thomas Anderson, and Edward Anderson are also buried in the Santa Maria Cemetery.

Beverley Louise (Hendrickson) Waid

A newspaper article entitled "Fifty Years Ago," July 27, 1889, tells how Odel (Audel) went from the Santa Barbara Potrero with seventy head of fine beef cattle the previous week. The reporter stated: "He is not on speaking terms with an old bear that recently killed two head of cattle." It seems that two men were kept up a tree for half a night by a grizzly, while they were camping on the San Emidio.

The Castros' ranch thrived, with many horses of all kinds. Liliencrantz told another story of his experiences with the Castros. He met an Englishman who lived in the hills with an Indian wife. They had six boys who spoke only Spanish, and had never been to school. Liliencrantz was surprised to know that at this time in history such people as this pioneer still existed. Yet these crude men often visited the Castros. The Indian wife and Mother never left home.

Other neighbors of the Castros were the Libeus, who lived on Zaca Rancho, which joined the Sisquoc Rancho. My mother, Emma "Peggy" Bagdons Hendrickson, remembers visiting with the Libeus. The countryside is very mountainous and beautiful, with the ranch house near a lovely lake. It was always an exciting trip for everyone, as the road was very difficult.

Family customs were adhered to, with strict discipline by Vincente and Vincenta. They were strict as to the protocol and manners of their Spanish ancestry and Catholic faith.

Aptos Rancho was the birthplace of my grandmother, Aurora Castro. After her grandfather, Rafael Castro, sold much of Aptos to Claus Spreckles, the remainder of the rancho was inhabited by Vincente and his family. Claus and Vincente had many fiestas together and went hunting every afternoon.

As Vincente grew older, the damp air of his rancho began to bother him. He sold and moved near Santa Barbara or San Juan Capistrano. A brother-in-law of Claus Spreckles, Claus Mangels, bought the last of Aptos Rancho from Vincente in 1887. Before leaving, the Castros gave a banquet for 300 friends at the Spreckles Hotel.

Found in the Santa Barbara Courthouse, Book of Deeds 14, page 225, May 25, 1885, are the following records: "Francis Fugler sold to Vincente Castro, for $2,000 in gold coin, subdivision 11 of the agreed partition of Rancho Tepusquet in 1880." It contained 870 acres.

My great-grandparents: Vincente and Vincenta Pico Castro.

My grandparents: Aurora Castro Bagdons and August Bagdons.

My mother: Emma Clara "Peggy" Bagdons.

Peggy Bagdons married Clarence Leslie Hendrickson, January 22, 1923.

Lila M. Walton

I am the third child of James and Annie Nelson. James was the firstborn son of Ole and Margaret Nelson, who settled in Santa Maria on a ranch at the Coast Highway and the Santa Maria River in 1876. Annie was the fifth daughter born to Soren and Maria Paulson. Their ranch was located a mile and a half south of Nipomo on Thompson Road. It has since been sold and torn down. Mrs. Paulson became a widow after having eight children, and subsequently married Mr. Jenson, and had three more children. This family also settled there in the 1850's.

James and Annie made their home in Southern California, and had five children.

P.S.: We did have fun at your Pioneer Picnic!

Robert D. and Mary Wardell

I should have graduated from Santa Maria High School in 1933, but didn't. I worked for Tomooka Produce on East Church Street, and for Safeway on West Church, in 1935. I moved to Fillmore and married Mary Jensen of Santa Ynez, and later moved to San Luis Obispo to work at the A&P and The White House Store in 1940. In October, 1940, I joined the Navy, and stayed in the service until September, 1945. Then I worked in the Santa Maria Post Office for a year, and finally re-enlisted in March, 1948, and stayed active until my retirement in July, 1969. In all, I served 26 years, retiring as an E7 (C.P.O.). After my retirement, we lived in Chula Vista, California, until March, 1979, when we moved to our present home in Oak Harbor, Washington.

Many of us Pioneers have seen some of these changes in the Santa Maria area during this period 1800 to 2000

Layout by R.H. Tesene • Artwork by John R. Reynolds • Graphics by Richard Cole
Courtesy of Santa Maria Valley Chamber of Commerce & Visitor & Convention Bureau, 614 S. Broadway, Santa Maria

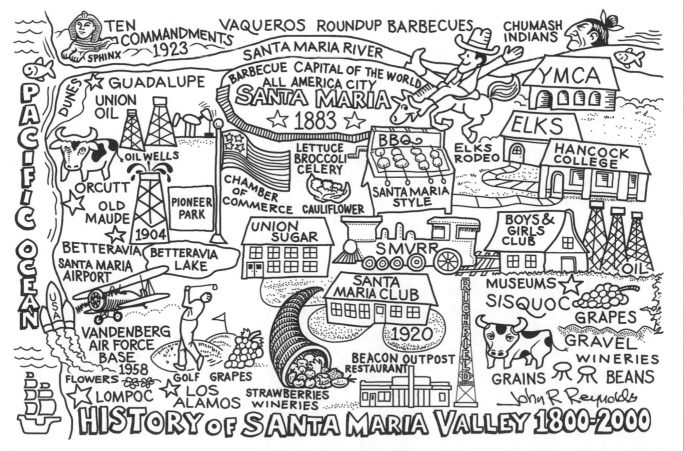

Thomas Weldon

Thomas Weldon was born in Eureka, Utah, a mining town and one-time site of major silver mining. Tom attended elementary and high school in that area, and then went off to college at the University of California at Berkeley. After graduating, he attended Boalt Law School there.

During the summers he often worked in the Santa Maria and Lompoc area, doing field work and working in the sugar plant.

After graduating from law school, he opened a practice in Lompoc. He was in a law partnership with his brother-in-law, Fred Shaeffer, for a few years. In 1930 he ran for the office of Santa Barbara County District Attorney. It was a very close race, and he came within a few hundred votes of winning.

Percy Heckendorf was the winner of that election. He and Tom Weldon became very good friends; Mr. Heckendorf appointed Tom as Deputy District Attorney in Santa Maria in the early 1930s. Tom Weldon served in that capacity for over 29 years until he retired from that position in 1959.

The Deputy District Attorney job was part-time, allowing Tom Weldon to practice law privately on his own time. From the 1930's until 1954, he practiced alone. Particularly skilled in trial work, he often was associated in cases by other attorneys to conduct the litigation part of disputes.

As Deputy District Attorney, he was one of the first called upon to conduct felony trials for the County. He handled several murder cases and other serious felonies in Santa Maria and Santa Barbara. In criminal trials he was noted for being thorough, well prepared, and an excellent cross-examiner. He had a very good success rate on his trials.

In 1954 Tom's son, Richard, joined him in his law practice. They practiced together until Tom became a Municipal Court Judge in 1964. He died in 1969. Richard is still in practice as an attorney in Santa Maria.

Tom was married to Olga Giacomini Weldon. They had two sons, Richard and Thomas Weldon, Jr.

Thomas, Jr., was Redevelopment Director of the City of Santa Maria when the Town Center Mall was planned, developed and built. He was instrumental in the development of several other malls throughout the western United States. He later became president of Harris Construction Company, which built several large stores in the Santa Maria area. Thomas Weldon, Sr., was an Exalted Ruler of.the Santa Maria Elks Lodge in 1933/34. He was an excellent speaker and master of ceremonies.

Olga Giacomini Weldon was born in Guadalupe, California, in 1903, the daughter of Paul Giacomini and Elizabeth Grisingher. Her father was a rancher in the valley for many years. He was also associated for a time in the flower seed business.

Olga Weldon attended Immaculate Heart College in Los Angeles and was married to Thomas Weldon in the mid-1920's.

Olga Weldon was active in the Minerva Club and the Marian Medical Auxiliary. She was an avid gardener, well known for her beautiful roses, camellias and begonias. Today she is 99 years of age, one of the oldest residents in the Santa Maria area. She has ten grandchildren and fifteen great-grandchildren.

Olga Weldon had two sisters: Irene Giacomini Johnson, who was married to Frank Johnson, the former principal of the Guadalupe Elementary School, and Lela Axline, who was married to Rea Axline. Mr. and Mrs. Axline were principal owners of Metco Manufacturing in New York.

Willett Family History

John A. and Vera C. Willett moved from Santa Barbara to the Casmite Oil Lease (2 miles from Casmalia, California) in 1931 with their four children: John A., Jr; Clark A.; Homer N.; and Phyllis L. The children attended the Casmalia Elementary School until 1934, when Homer, Clark and Phyllis transferred to Orcutt Elementary School. John graduated from the 8th grade (1/2 yr.) in Casmalia and rode the bus to high school until moving into Santa Maria. The family moved to West Cypress Street in Santa Maria in 1938. John, Clark and Homer were already attending Santa Maria Union High School and Phyllis transferred to El Camino Junior High. She started Santa Maria High School in September, 1939. John graduated from Santa Maria High with the Class of '39½. Homer was to have graduated with the Class of '41, but he received his diploma earlier in order to enter the armed services. In 1940 the family moved to a home on Tunnell Street in Santa Maria.

In January, 1941, Mr. Willett, Sr., was called back to active duty with the U.S. Navy and Homer enlisted in the U.S. Army Air Force the same month. In May of that year, John was called to active service with the U.S. Navy (transferring to the U.S. Naval Air Force), after he had completed a year at Hancock College of Aeronautics. That same year Vera Willett went to work in the Quartermaster Laundry Office at Camp Cooke. Upon graduation from Santa Maria High School in 1942, Clark enlisted in the U.S. Navy Seabees. During her summer breaks in 1942 and 1943, Phyllis also worked for the laundry at Camp Cooke. Vera and Phyllis then moved to an apartment on what was called Airport Road, but now called College Avenue.

Phyllis graduated from Santa Maria High School in 1943 and attended Santa Maria Junior College for one year before enrolling in Sawyer's Business College in Los Angeles for six months. She then returned to Santa Maria to work as secretary to the Post Exchange Officer at Camp Cooke.

After spending the time during World War II overseas at various places, all of the Willett men were discharged from service in 1945, with the exception of John. He remained with the U.S. Navy until his discharge in 1971 as Lt. Commander. After his discharge in 1945, Homer returned to school in Santa Barbara, but was called back to active duty in 1950, where he remained until his discharge in 1980 as a Lt. Colonel. After his discharge in 1945, Clark (having married Barbara Fagerborg, Class of '44, in 1944), returned to live in Orcutt.

In 1945, Vera and Phyllis moved to Dallas, Texas, but returned to the Los Angeles area in 1946 and 1948 respectively. After a divorce in 1946, John Willett, Sr., moved to Santa Barbara, where he remarried and had a second daughter, Carol, in 1953.

John, Jr., met his wife, Donna, while attending a Naval School in Chicago. They have a daughter, Cheryl, and a son, John Alden, III. Donna passed away in 1989, but John is still living in Chula Vista at the present time. He is the proud grandparent of five granddaughters.

Clark and Barbara have four children: Robert, Nancy, Rex and James. They have resided in Arroyo Grande for a number of years and are the proud grandparents of six grandsons and four granddaughters and two great grandsons.

Homer met his wife, Shirley, while attending school in Santa Barbara. They have two boys, Glynn (Chip) and Stephen, and are now dividing their time between their homes in Lady Lake, Florida, and Sinclair, Maine. They enjoy time with their four grandsons and one granddaughter.

Phyllis met and married Neal Hovland while living in Los Angeles. They have a daughter, Susan, and a son, Peter, and one granddaughter. Neal passed away in 1988, and in 1992 Phyllis married Reid Searle and is living in Sun City, Roseville, California.

John Willett, Sr., passed away in 1966. Vera Willett married Leonard Baines in 1955 and at the age of 97½ is still in pretty good health and residing in Chula Vista, California, in a Residential Care Home at this writing.

—September 12, 1998

The Williams Brothers

Lawson B. Williams, the late Edward Williams, and Merrell Williams were the co-founders of Williams Brothers Markets. They began with a small store on East Church Street in Santa Maria in 1950 that eventually grew into a 19-store chain supermarket dynasty in the Central Coast area.

Lawson was responsible for getting Williams Bros. involved in the Santa Barbara County and Mid-State Fairs. It was his idea to support the local youth through the purchase of their farm animals.

The Williams Brothers eventually sold their entire market chain to Vons Markets in 1988. As part of an exchange, they purchased an office building in the Santa Maria Financial Center at 2236 South Broadway, known as Tri W Enterprises, which they still occupy.

Above, left to right: Lawson B. Williams, Edward L. Williams, and Merrell M. Williams were photographed for the Santa Maria Times *in 1967.*

Lawson Williams (left) got the Williams Bros. Markets involved in supporting local youth by purchasing their livestock at the county fairs in Santa Barbara and San Luis Obispo Counties.

David and Dorothy Wood

by their daughter, Dorothy Wood Benford, 1985

David and Dorothy Wood moved to Santa Maria in 1923. My father was employed by the Golden State Creamery. He was transferred to San Luis Obispo in 1925, just long enough for me to be born there. We returned to Guadalupe in 1927, moving to Santa Maria in 1930. We lived on the Dante Acquistapace ranch for a year, and then moved into the home which my mother designed at 604 East Cypress Street. My husband and I now live in the house.

My father worked for many creameries in the valley, including Guernsey Dairy, of which he was co-owner, and Knudsen Creamery, until the late 1930's. In 1942 he went to work for Union Sugar, retiring in 1969. My mother died in 1982. She was employed for many years by the Building Trades Council of Santa Barbara County as an office manager in Santa Maria. Before that, she had worked at the American Bakery, Braggs Cafe, and at J.C. Penney Co. During World War II, she and I were both part of the emergency crew work force at the Union Sugar Co., often working twelve-hour shifts.

Among my childhood memories of living here is going with my father as he helped to lay the floor in the St. Peter's Episcopal Church. Both of my parents were active members.

Sometimes as I look around Santa Maria, I feel that most of my past history has been erased from view. I attended Main Street School—now gone! My husband and I, when we were first married, lived in the duplex on Lincoln Street where the new Santa Maria Inn parking terrace now sits. Later we moved to Betteravia, and now that whole town is gone!

We were away for many years, but even with many landmarks now missing, it is good to be home.

Lawrence and Blanche Wylie

I was born in my grandfather's house on Lincoln Street about two blocks north of the Santa Maria Inn. My mother, Doris Pullizos, and my father both attended Santa Maria High School. They were living on an oil lease by Casmalia.

Before I was a year old, my father was transferred to Ventura. I grew up in Ventura, but visited Santa Maria often, especially my aunt, Ida Wylie Jones. From 1951 to 1962, my wife, two sons and I lived in Santa Maria. My two sons were born in San Luis Obispo, where I attended Cal Poly.

I left Santa Maria in 1962 for the same reason I did not go back to Ventura after I was discharged from the Navy: too much development! And now it has started in Bishop—but we live ten miles out from town. I'm getting old and get to stay home.

—*Sincerely, Lawrence A. Wylie*

The Young Family

Oil in Orcutt, California, and a drought and crop failure in Nebraska brought Floyd Clarendon and Mary Belle (Anderson) Young to the Santa Maria Valley.

In 1905, they put their five children, their pony and mule team on the train and headed west from Wilsonville, Nebraska. Mary and her four daughters rode in the coach car while Floyd and his young son, Bert, rode in the box car with the animals, in order to care for them. The family settled on the Glines Ranch in Orcutt and the children attended the old Pine Grove School, riding there on their pony, Sanko. Floyd Young transported the oil in wooden barrels from the oil fields to the refinery with his wagon and mule team. They lived on the Glines Ranch until their children were grown. At that time, they moved to town and lived in a house on Orange Street; Floyd became an insurance agent They were active in the Methodist Church and later in the Presbyterian Church. Mary Belle died in 1945; Floyd died in 1959, and both are buried in the Santa Maria Cemetery.

The oldest daughter, Edith, married Harry S. Nelson, whom she had grown up with in Nebraska, and they built a house and opened a garage at the corner of Miller and El Camino Streets. They had one son, Arthur Wayne Nelson, who was employed in the Santa Barbara County Welfare Department and served as the department's Director from 1966-1981. He retired to teach Social Welfare and Sociology at Westmont College in Santa Barbara. He lives in Santa Barbara with his wife, Martha, the former Martha A. Patterson of Pacific Palisades, California. They have a grown daughter, Catherine, and a grandson, Cory.

The Youngs' second child was Ruth. She married Horace Chaffin of Santa Maria. (The Chaffins were a pioneer family, also.) Their two daughters are Georgina Utley, who lives in Santa Maria, and Jean Langley of Clinton, Connecticut. Both have several children and grandchildren. Georgina's daughter, Susan Meireles, is a resident of Orcutt, and her son, Floyd, lives in Lompoc. All of the other family members live elsewhere. Ruth and Horace owned and operated a variety store in Guadalupe for many years. Ruth was 99 years old on May 24, 1995, and lives in Santa Maria. She has many memories of the early days of Santa Maria, her family and their activities.

Edna married Mark Whitney. The Whitney family owned a ranch on Whitney Road, now Donovan Road. Mark's father died when Mark was a little boy, so he went to work at an early age. He was the superintendent of the Santa Maria Cemetery for many years. Edna and Mark built a home on the corner of Vine and El Camino Streets. They had three daughters: Mary Ellen, Edna Mae and Shirley.

Mary Ellen met and married an Air Force pilot, Arthur K. Schultz, who was stationed in Santa Maria during World War II. They became the parents of a son and two daughters. Mary Ellen was a talented writer and a renowned nature photographer. Art and Mary Ellen lived in many places in the world, but they returned to make Santa Maria their home in about 1985. On February 6th of this year (1995), Mary Ellen lost a long and valiant battle with cancer.

Edna Mae married a soldier from Camp Cook, Harry Powell. The Powells had three children, a daughter and two sons. Later, the family moved to Sacramento, California. Harry has since passed away, but Edna Mae continues to live near her children, grandchildren and great-grandchildren in Sacramento.

The youngest, Shirley, married Alvin Van Stone of the pioneer family and they moved to Santa Rosa, where Al works on the newspaper. They have a daughter and three sons and two grandsons.

Bert Lewis Young, the only son, lived and worked

in Santa Maria until his death. He married Doris E. Glenn of the pioneer family. Their daughter, Grace, married Alan Kyle of Santa Maria (also from a pioneer family), and they have two daughters, Jeani and Julie. They have been very active in the community. Grace has been active with Campfire Girls, the Methodist Church, and teaching ballet. She is an active member of the Minerva Club and has served as their president for two terms. Julie Kyle married Scott Marks, and after living in Santa Maria all of her life, has recently moved to Georgia.

Jeani married Larry Evans, whose family has lived in the valley for several generations. Jeani and Larry have two children, Diana and Kyle. They live in Orcutt, and Jeani works with her father, Alan, in the family business, Kyle Roofing.

Lucretia was Floyd and Mary's youngest child. She grew up in Santa Maria and married Howard Wines. He was a schoolteacher, coach and principal. After their marriage, they moved to the San Joaquin Valley. They had two sons, Floyd and Robert. After Howard's death, Lucretia married John Slaugh, and they had a daughter, Marianna. She now resides in Clearlake, California.

Audrey Walsh Zastrow

We came to the Santa Maria Valley in the spring of 1938. My father, William J. Walsh, was transferred to Santa Maria to oversee and build an oil pipeline five miles north of Casmalia, which is now Vandenberg Air Force Base.

Our location was known as Port Petrol. My mother, Virginia H. Walsh, was a homemaker. I left the area after graduating from Santa Maria High School in 1940 to attend Southwestern University in Los Angeles. My parents left for security reasons when World War II broke out, closing the port.

I am married to Bill J. Zastrow, a building contractor, and live in Redlands, California. We have two children. Our daughter, Audree Jeannie Zastrow Anderson, is married to an investigator with the Los Angeles Police Force. His name is Donald, and they live in Chino, California, where she raises champion miniature goats and Schnauzers. Our son, Steven, is married and works in construction with his father.

My parents had three plastic plants in Anaheim, which they sold when they retired in 1975. My mother is living in Anaheim and is well. My father passed away in 1978.

■ *Postscript:* Audrey died in 1995.

GENERAL INFORMATION
about the Pioneer Park Association and Pioneer Park Foundation

*This concrete monument for mounting 5"x9" bronze family or memorial plaques is almost full.
An addition to the monument will be made in 2002.*

When the Pioneers in the Santa Maria Valley held their first Pioneer Picnic in 1925, their decision was to name their organization the "Pioneer Association." At that time, money was hard to come by, so in order to join the Pioneer Association, an individual only paid a one-time fee of ten dollars with no annual dues in the future. This policy remains to the present day, and there are no plans to change it. Later, an accommodation was made for Pioneers who have lived in the area for thirty or more years; they could become an Associate Member by paying a one-time fee of twenty dollars without any further dues. This policy will also continue.

Thus, you may become a member of a very active Pioneer Association that has no annual dues but does have its own Pioneer Park on West Foster Road in Santa Maria. The Pioneer Park Foundation was approved by the necessary governmental agencies in 1995 as a vehicle to receive tax-free contributions and as a means to coordinate and simplify management, planning and construction of Pioneer Park.

Pioneer Park is located on a thirteen-acre parcel of land owned by the Santa Maria Airport District and leased to the City of Santa Maria for the purpose of establishing Pioneer Park. The arrangement is that the Santa Maria Valley Pioneer Park facilities would be built and maintained by the Pioneer Park Association and would be administered by the Santa Maria Recreation and Parks Department.

The Pioneer Park Association and the Pioneer Park Foundation have built and paid for most of the park facilities to date, but other facilities will be added in the future.

Since Pioneer Association members are not required to pay annual dues, we invite you to consider making a donation in other ways, as described below, so that the Association will be able to complete and maintain the facilities in Pioneer Park in the future.

1. Buy a 5"x7" bronze plaque for your family or as a remembrance of a departed friend or relative for $300 each. Call Al and Pauline Novo at 937-5957.

2. Make a cash donation to the Pioneer Park Foundation.

3. Buy one or more copies of this book, *The Story of the Pioneer Picnics.*

Note: These types of donations are all tax-deductible if the payment is made to the Pioneer Park Foundation.

A Get-Well Card

Tese — 3/14/02
We are having our Pioneer's board meeting this morning and sending you our good wishes to be well soon. *Carolyn Conrad McCall*

Clarence Donati
Good Luck

Best wishes for a speedy recovery *Roberta Benford*

Ernie Girod

Jim Gamble
Thank You
Keep up the *Good Work*

Earl Jennings

Jean Hulsey

Hope you are well and enjoying your writing. *JoAnn Kaufmann (Enos)*

Looking forward to your book. Hope you feel better soon. *Jo Silveira*

HOPE YOU'RE FEELING BETTER — GLORIA HEIDE

Roger Selhon
S.M. Lions Club

Bob Rivers

Hurry & get well — Love *Al & Pauline Novo*

See you soon *Ike Simas*

Dear Mr. Tesene,
Hope you are getting better with each day —
Vicki Anderson Ahlcon

So sorry to hear you're not well, We both hope you have a quick recovery soon. *Les & Susan Seal*

Hi Sweetie,
Take care and Be healthy
Love *Annie Openshaw*

Santa Maria Valley Pioneer Assn.

A FINAL WORD FROM R.H. TESENE, AUTHOR

It's members like this that have made the Santa Maria Valley Pioneers Association the wonderful organization that it is.

I appreciated receiving this card signed by the present dignitaries. This encouraged me to complete the book this month so that it can be prepared for publication, reviewed and printed, in order to be available for all members and their friends to enjoy at the next annual Pioneer Picnic in Pioneer Park on West Foster Road. It will be a beautiful hard-cover book.

R.H. TESENE, *author*
March, 2002

INDEX